Ancona to the Midwest:
A Culinary Journey

A story of survival for an Italian family and their accomplishments through music, food and love

Paul Cortellini

ISBN: 0615898858
ISBN 13: 978-061589885-8

Library of Congress Control Number: 2013918873
LCCN Imprint Name: Cortellini Publishing, Chicago, IL

I dedicate this book to the memory of my mother.

Acknowledgments

I want to thank my beautiful wife of forty-one years who provided me guidance in creating this book and who tolerated my many trial runs in testing the recipes. Truth be told, she is probably the better cook between the two of us.

I would also like to thank Robert T. Thopy, my editor, for helping me self-publish this book; my numerous cousins, including Italo and Etta DiSanto, Anna Maria Mosci and Paolo Rismondo, Maurizio and Anna Grazia Mosci, and others, for contributing to my recipe collection; and to my loyal blog followers, who have supported my blog and have encouraged me to press forward in the book's development.

Contents

Preface

Stories abound about Italian immigrants who made the challenging journey to America with great expectations of a new life after having survived a terrible war under the misguided ideology of Mussolini. Mine is one such story, involving two talented individuals from an industrial part of Italy who tell of their struggles and joys in raising three boys in a non-Italian community. I focus on the threads that held them together through difficult times and their dedication to classical music and traditional Italian cooking which helped them to succeed:

For many years I have contemplated a project to document the many recipes from our family's cooking history. This includes memorializing the life of my talented mother, Anna Maria, who provided cherished memories and a tradition founded on coming together to enjoy the making as well as the eating of simple but excellent Italian cooking. She was devoted to my father, Ferdinando, a virtuoso, and made great sacrifices to please him. Father's classical music talent and Mother's artistry in the kitchen, combined with their love of family and friends, made for a happy household when we were together.

The journey begins in Ancona, Italy, with a number of detours and bumps along the way to the Midwest of America, where it continues today. The recipes I will share with you are traditional Italian, with a slant toward the regional tastes of the Marche region, but with variations necessitated by the scarcity of true Italian ingredients. Many are my mother's, which I saved through the years, but also included are recipes collected from relatives, friends, and colleagues during my fifteen years of living and working in Europe.

I hope that you will enjoy both the stories and the recipes.

Paul J. Cortellini

Chapter 1

Ancona

My life's journey has not been a traditional one. I have been fortunate to experience different cultures and locales during both childhood and my adult years, but the one constant wherever I have called home has been good food and the joy associated with it. This is a story that begins during World War II in Ancona, Italy, and continues today in three Midwestern cities—Chicago, Indianapolis, and Detroit.

Anna Maria and Ferdinando Cortellini had three sons: Corrado, Douglas, and me. My older brother Corrado, my mother, and I were all born in Ancona. My father was born in Pescara and later moved to and was raised in Ancona. Ancona can be considered our place of origin.

Ancona is a port city of about one hundred thousand people on the Adriatic coast in the province of the Marche. Its origin dates back to Greek settlers from Syracuse who arrived in Ancona around 387 BC. The name comes from a slightly modified translation of the Greek word Aykwva, meaning "elbow." The harbor was originally protected only by a promontory on the north, shaped like an elbow. As a strategic port, Ancona's history is rich with stories of conquerors. Ancona became a part of the Kingdom of Italy when Christophe Léon Louis Juchault de Lamoricière surrendered there on September 29, 1860, eleven days after his defeat at Castelfidardo.

Ancona coat of arms

Historic map of Ancona

In 1944 the Italians surrendered to Allied Forces. The Germans considered this surrender a betrayal by the Italians who would no longer impede the Allied movement north. As a result the Germans diverted troops from the Russian front to support the Italian front.

On November 1, 1943, over three hundred Ancona citizens
die under colle dei Cappuccini in a bombardment

Ancona came under bombardment from the Allied Forces during the German occupation. After the fall of Mussolini, Ancona was occupied by the Germans, who encountered some local resistance. The city suffered about 180 aerial bombardments from October 1943 to July 1944 by Allied Forces. The first occurred on October 16, 1943, killing 165 and injuring 300. The port, shipyards, and a railway junction were of strategic importance to the opposing forces. November 1, 1943, was the date of one of the most tragic events in the history of the city. Beginning around 12:45 p.m. that day, about 24 Allied bombers dropped a substantial load of bombs over a thirty minute period. More than fifteen hundred people lost their lives, and an entire district became unrecognizable. Even the cathedral was hit. In addition, three hundred people died in a shelter under colle dei Cappuccini, the hills surrounding Ancona. After this painful day, most residents fled to the countryside, where they remained until midyear 1944. On July 18, 1944, following the battle of Ancona, General Andrea Władysław, and head of the Second Corps of the Polish Army, entered Ancona and freed it from the German occupation. On August 4, 1945, the administration of the city was passed to the Italian government.

During this period of turmoil in Ancona, Dad suspended his work with the Santa Cecilia Orchestra in Rome, where we were then living, to join the Italian navy. Corrado and Mom then left their home in Rome for Ancona to stay with Mom's sister Zia Marisa. Due to the advancement of the front line from the south to Ancona by mid-1943, Zio Memo, Zia Marisa's husband, brought Mom and Corrado and Gabriella, Zia Marisa's eldest daughter, to join the rest of Zia Marisa's family in a safer place: a farmer's house in the countryside north of Ancona, near Rimini. It was vintage time, and Gabriella remembered a bountiful harvest with beautiful grapes despite the war. Zia Marisa became restless and could no longer stand the countryside, and after several weeks, she returned to Ancona and civilization. Mom and Corrado remained in the countryside on the wishes of Nonno Peppino, Dad's father. Unfortunately, Zia Marisa and her family arrived in Ancona just in time to be subject to the bombings. After the Polish Army forced the German troops to move further north, Mom and Corrado were able to return to Ancona and live with Zia Marisa and her family. Dad returned to Ancona after duty in North Africa. I was born in Ancona in 1945 during an Allied bombing raid. Mom told me there was no electricity or running water at the time of my birth. Later that year, we all returned to Rome, where Dad resumed playing for the Santa Cecilia Orchestra, and stayed until 1947.

Chapter 2
Ferdinando and Anna Maria

My father, Ferdinando, was born in Pescara in the province of Abruzzi on May 27, 1916. He grew up in a modest Italian household, the son of a tailor, Giuseppe Cortellini. Giuseppe fought in World War I and was wounded, losing an eye. Unable to continue in his chosen profession, he obtained a position with the Italian railroad upon his return to Pescara. His first wife (Dad's mother), Maria Giancola, died at an early age of a heart attack, and Giuseppe then married Emma Ferio. Dad had a sister named Clelia and a half-brother named Italo. Prior to World War II, Giuseppe (Dad called him "Nonno Peppino") refused to join the fascist party. For this he was punished by his state-owned employer and transferred to Ancona to perform lesser administrative tasks. In addition to his work with the railroad, he resumed his work as a tailor from his home. He loved the arts and encouraged Dad to develop his musical talents.

Nonna Maria Giancola,
Zia Clelia,and Ferdinando

Nonno Peppino
in Later Years

Nonno Peppino enrolled Dad in the Conservatory of Pesaro (near Ancona), where he learned to play and graduated with flying colors as professor of viola and violin. Dad had a passion for playing the viola and, not having the means to purchase one of his own, stole his first viola, or so the story was told. He commuted back and forth to Pesaro from Ancona to complete his lessons and performed at the Theater of the Port of Ancona. He also performed at seasonal occasions such as the Feast of San Ciriaco, the patron saint of Ancona. I am told that he was applauded fervently at all of his perform-ances.

In 1939 Dad married my mother, Anna Maria Dominelli, one of three children of Nonno Gino Dominelli and Nonna Lea Liberti. I'm not quite certain of Nonno Gino's trade or profession, but Nonna Lea was a well-known dressmaker in the community and ran a shop that employed about twenty seamstresses, including Mom. The lessons Mom learned in that shop kept food on the table and clothes on our backs in later years.

Nonna Lea and Nonno Gino

Mom was madly in love with Dad and accepted whatever life he provided her, despite the long periods of separation, and his occasional indiscretions as revealed in later chapters. They were a beau-tiful couple, much loved by family and friends.

Anna Maria and Ferdinando

Dad served in the Italian military in Ethiopia. During the African campaign, the British maintained a blockade of the Libyan seaport of Tobruk. When Italian ships departed from this port, they were stopped by British forces. It was during one of these encounters that Dad's ship was torpedoed, requiring him to swim for his life. I was told that Dad was in the water, wounded, for fourteen hours before being rescued. He suffered hypothermia and exhaustion, which may have been the beginning of his ailments in later years.

Ferdinando in Ethiopia

In 1942, after his discharge from the military, Dad accepted a position in Torino with the Augusteo Orchestra, which was affiliated with the Academia di Santa Cecilia in Rome, a renowned symphony orchestra. It was this job that eventually took the family to Rome to reside.

Offer Letter from Academia di Santa Cecilia in Rome

Life was difficult in Rome during the war years. What little food was available was rationed. Mom liked to tell the story about Corrado's pet chickens, which were kept in a rooftop pen at the apartment in Rome. One day Mom served chicken cacciatore (recipe to follow) for dinner. When Corrado discovered that some of his pets were missing, he refused to eat chicken for the longest time.

After a while, Dad remained in Rome while Mom returned to Ancona with Corrado to have family support as she was then expecting my birth. The Nazi occupation made travel between Rome and Ancona difficult and risky, forcing Mom and Dad to spend considerable time apart. I was born during this period. Mom told stories about how frightened she was during the aerial bombardments of Ancona and the heartache she suffered from the loss of friends and loved ones. I was born at my mother's home at Via Marrata 27, Ancona, Italy, on January 10, 1945—during, according to Mom, an Allied bombing raid on Nazi positions that knocked out lights and water.

In the aftermath of the war, work was scarce for a musician. In 1947 Dad, wanting to pursue his profession, accepted a position as first viola with the Dominican Republic Symphony Orchestra. After depositing Mom, Corrado, and me at Nonno Peppino's house in Ancona, he left with several colleagues on a journey to the Americas to pursue their musical ambitions.

With his colleagues and in concert in the Dominican Republic

Dad spent the next two years with the Dominican Republic Symphony Orchestra and also performed on Dominican radio. He later extended his visa to January 1952 and also applied for entry into Puerto Rico. Having turned down a four-year offer to teach in the Escuela Libre de Música in Puerto Rico, he spent the next two years performing concerts in Puerto Rico. With his visa nearing expiration and a desire to find a position in the United States, he accepted an invitation from Nonno Peppino's brother, Antonio Cortellini, to travel to New York City and stay with Antonio and other relatives to make contacts in the United States. Soon Dad received an offer of the first chair viola position with the Indianapolis Symphony Orchestra.

Chapter 3

The Three of Us

After Dad's departure, we depended on family in Ancona, living part of the time at Nonno Peppino's but mostly at Nonna Lea's home which was very near. We also spent time in Torino with Dad's sister, Clelia. Dad occasionally sent money from the Dominican Republic, but it was never enough. As was common with that generation of Italians, our extended family pooled its resources. The somewhat nomadic lifestyle kept the ties between us very close.

Corrado, Mom and me

We spent most of the time at Nonna Lea's home. She had more room for us than did Nonno Peppino, even though Mom's sister Zia Marisa, her husband Memo, and their five children were also living under Nonna Lea's roof. Nonno Peppino acted as guardian over Corrado and me. Mom continued learning from him the art of tailoring while Emma worked her magic in the kitchen. Since Emma was considerably younger than Nonno Peppino, she preferred that we call her Zia Emma rather than Nonna Emma. Zia Emma was a major influence on Mom's culinary abilities. Nonno Peppino and Zia Emma had only one child, Italo Cortellini. As Italo was just a few years older than Corrado, he was like a brother to us.

Nonno Peppino, Zia Emma   Italo, Corrado and me

Zia Marisa and Zio Memo's five children are Gabriella (the eldest), Maurizio, Claudio, Anna Maria, and later Massimo. Finding a place to sleep was always a challenge. Our cousins became more like brothers and sisters, which explains our close ties today. I am the same age as Anna Maria, and during this period, she was my closest playmate. I was told stories of the two of us playing in bomb craters in the grounds across from the house at Via Maratta. I was considered the comedian of the family. On one occasion I made a lady friend of the family laugh so hard that she wet her pants, to which I proudly announced to everyone, "La signiora a fatto la piscia a dosso." I'll let you do the translation.

Zia Marisa   Maurizio, Nonno Gino,
Gabriela, Anna Maria,
Massimo and Claudio

Zia Clelia's home in Torino was also a busy, fun place for a four-year-old boy. Zia Clelia and her husband Zio Ireneo had five children, three girls and two boys. These cousins were Corrado's and my best friends, and to this day we remain close. I will elaborate more on this in later chapters. My cousin Anna, one of Zia Clelia's daughters, died tragically at the age of three during our stay in Torino. She was receiving an injection, and the needle broke. She was rushed to a hospital to remove the needle, but during the administration of anesthesia, she suffocated. This was a traumatic experience for all. Zia Clelia never quite recovered from it.

We enjoyed Torino, but Mom, Corrado, and I looked forward to summers in Ancona.

TORINO DAYS

Zia Clelia

Angela, Vittoria, and Italo

Corrado and me

Zio Ireneo, Zia Clelia,
and Mom

Anna DiSanto
died at age three

Corrado (second row, fifth from the left)
at school in Torino, first grade

It was during this period of Dad's absence that Mom perfected her sewing talents while working as an understudy for Nonna Lea and being guided by Nonno Peppino. She also began to learn the art of traditional Italian cooking. Unlike today's generation of Italian teenagers, her generation learned to cook in the traditional Italian way. Zia Marisa was an extraordinary cook. She began each day by planning and then shopping for the ingredients needed. The day's primary meal included pasta, of course. An early task each day was the preparation of the sugo for the pasta, followed by a daybreak visit to the local market for the fresh ingredients. Such trips usually included a stop at the church for a prayer along the way. I observed this tradition again twenty years later, when Roz and I visited with family during our honeymoon. In the interim it seemed that not much had changed in the preparation of traditional daily Italian meals. Etched in my memory are those morning aromas, which I never seem quite able to replicate to this day despite regular efforts. Mom brought the lessons she learned from Zia Marisa and Zia Emma to America, and they became her standard repertoire of Italian cooking. Mom earned great renown among Dad's social and professional circles. I suspect that lots of Mom's recipes memorialized in this cookbook had their origin in this period of our family's life. I only remember a few of the recipes that specifically stand out in my mind as being from this period. One such recipe is Polenta con Sugo di Pomodoro. It was no doubt born of the necessity to feed a number of young children quickly while also making it fun for them to eat. I offer this as my first recipe. The keys to its success are its simplicity and the joy it brings to a family dinner. A soft polenta is spread on a cutting board, and then covered with a simple tomato sauce. Each child is then armed with a spoon and given an assigned territory on the serving board from which to eat the polenta.

Polenta con Sugo di Pomodoro (Polenta with Tomato Sauce)
Category: Paste (Pastas)
Origin: Mamma Cortellini
Serves 4

The Sauce:

This is a recipe for a simple tomato sauce Mom made for whatever occasion needed a sweet sauce for topping. She also made it to be added to dried pasta like rigatoni as a quick meal. It can be used to top polenta or as a pizza topping. When in season, fresh ripe tomatoes can be used instead of canned tomatoes. To add spice to the sauce, depending on what you are topping, add flakes of chili peppers, oregano (pizza flavor), or marjoram.

Ingredients:
½ stick unsalted butter
1 small yellow onion
1 can of Italian plum tomatoes (I use a box of Pomi tomatoes), chopped to small pieces or crushed
Kosher salt and pepper to taste
If you want to spice it up, add some chili pepper flakes, oregano, or marjoram
16-oz. box of dried pasta like penne or rigatoni (I use De Cecco), if to be used as a pasta sauce

Preparation:

1. Finely chop the onion.
2. In a saucepan, add the butter and sauté the onion until soft and golden.
3. Add the tomatoes and spices.
4. Let simmer for about an hour.
5. Use it as a topping or as a sauce for the pasta.

The Polenta:

Polenta is a dish that I remember having when living with my grandparents in Ancona, where there was a need to feed a lot of people in a quick, efficient manner. It was served for either lunch or dinner in a creamy consistency, spread over a large cutting board placed in the center of the table. After spreading the tomato sauce over the polenta, each child was given a spoon and a territory on the cutting board to consume his or her portion until finished. The quicker eaters were often confronted for attempts to trespass into another child's territory. It can be a raucous atmosphere, so parents are forewarned to be on their guard.

Basic Polenta

Ingredients:

6 cups water
2 tsp. salt
1¾ cups yellow cornmeal or polenta
3 Tbsp. unsalted butter
Kosher salt
Simple Tomato Sauce (See Tomato Sauce with Butter and Onions)

Preparation:
1. In a heavy saucepan, bring the water to a boil and add salt.
2. Gradually add the cornmeal stirring continuously.
3. Reduce the heat and continue stirring until the polenta thickens, about fifteen minutes.
4. Don't let the polenta become too thick; it should have a creamy consistency when poured onto the cutting board.
5. Add the salt and butter and remove from heat.
6. Spread the polenta on a large wooden cutting board.
7. Cover it with the tomato sauce.
8. Provide everyone with a spoon, and let the eating begin.

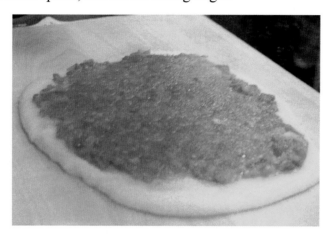

Another recipe I remember that Zia Emma prepared (and that she made for us when we visited her twenty years later) was Calamari Ripieni, or stuffed squid. The quality of this recipe is totally dependent on the freshness and size of the calamari.

Calamari Ripieni con Piselli (Stuffed Calamari in Pea Sauce)
Category: Pesci (Fish)
Origin: Zia Emma
Serves 6–8

This may not be exactly how Zia Emma prepared it, but it is close. She was a fantastic cook, but unfortunately I don't have many of her recipes.

Ingredients:
12 calamari, cleaned, with tentacles retained for the stuffing
2 cloves of garlic, finely minced
Bunch of Italian parsley, finely chopped
2 cups bread crumbs (preferably homemade)
Kosher salt and ground pepper to taste
¼ cup extra-virgin olive oil
Small glass of dry white wine
2 Tbsp. tomato, chopped (Italian plum tomatoes)
16 oz. frozen or canned peas

Preparation:
1. Clean the calamari, removing the head, beak, and the membrane in the body so that what remains is the body shell, which can be used to contain the stuffing.
2. Chop the tentacles to be used as part of the stuffing.
3. In a mixing bowl, combine the tentacles, garlic, parsley, bread crumbs, salt, and

pepper, adding some of the olive oil to moisten the stuffing mixture.

4. Stuff the calamari, using a toothpick to close the opening; do not overfill as the contents will expand during cooking.

5. Place stuffed calamari a frying pan with the remaining olive oil, cover, and cook on low heat until pink in color (about fifteen minutes).

6. Add the wine and cook for another ten minutes.

7. Add the tomatoes and continue cooking for a total cooking time of forty-five minutes.

8. Add the peas and continue to cook until the peas are done. If you use fresh peas, consider adding them in step seven for longer cooking time.

In November 1951 Mom, Corrado, and I, accompanied by Nonno Peppino and Italo, set off for Naples, where Mom, Corrado, and I boarded the cruise ship Saturnia for our voyage to New York City. I cannot imagine the courage that it must have taken for Mom to leave the comfort and safety of her parents and siblings to embark on a voyage to a new country, unable to speak its language, entrusting her life and the lives of her two children to a man she had not seen for five years but loved unconditionally.

Chapter 4

Ferdinando in Latin America (1947–1951)

U nable to find meaningful work in his profession in Italy, Dad and a number of his colleagues had learned of an opportunity to perform in the Dominican Republic. During this period, the Dominican Republic suffered under the brutal dictatorship of Rafael Trujillo (called El Jefe, or "the chief"). With the support of the United States, General Trujillo seized control in 1930 and ruled until his assassination in 1961. Trujillo amassed a huge fortune at the expense of his people while repressing all opposition. A movement of young Dominicans tried unsuccessfully on June 14, 1949 to overthrow the dictatorship. His rule ended in 1961 when wealthy Dominicans, unhappy with the dictator, had him killed.

Trujillo wished to expand the culture in the Dominican Republic by introducing classical music. A program was created to bring musicians in need of work from Italy. A trip to the Dominican Republic guaranteed them work, food, and shelter in return for their performing in the Dominican Symphony Orchestra. One of these Italian musicians was my father, Ferdinando Cortellini.

Ferdinando and colleague in the Dominican Republic

On March 4, 1947, Dad sent a letter to Mom from Ciudad Trujillo (now Santo Domingo), describing his experiences on the airplane trip to the Dominican Republic. Santo Domingo was known as Ciudad Trujillo from 1930 until the dictator's assassination in 1961. His route took him to Lisbon, the Azores, Newfoundland, New York City, and finally Ciudad Trujillo.

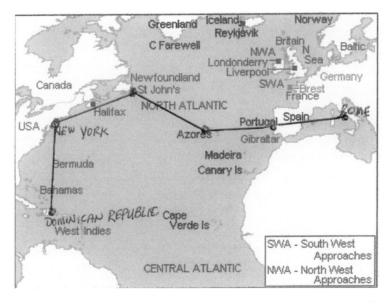

He wrote about being apprehensive as he watched the Roman landscape disappear. Although concerned, he believed that the sacrifice he was making would prove worthwhile for himself and his family.

Foul weather at Lisbon caused a two-day delay, requiring the musicians to sleep at the airport on cots. The refueling stop at the Azores was also delayed by bad weather. To help the airplane to gain lift in the inclement weather, the airline made the decision to lighten the load. Dad and his colleagues (nine in all) were left behind and told to take the next flight. They were provided rooms at the Santa Maria hotel and treated very well, he wrote. At the hotel he and his colleagues performed for their hosts. Dad said they were most appreciative. At midafternoon the next day, in overcast conditions, their plane lifted off with assurances that the weather would improve. After a half hour of turbulence, they broke through the clouds into the sunlight. Dad described the ocean crossing as difficult, with continuing bad weather. They headed to Newfoundland in darkness to refuel. Dad wrote about the airplane bouncing up and down so severely that they had to be strapped into their seats and were handed small brown bags in case they got sick. The landing at Newfoundland was like a nightmare, he said, as they faced a snowstorm with high winds. Once on the ground, the nine musicians headed to the bar.

After only one hour on the ground, they departed, as the weather was worsening. Upon reaching an altitude above the storm, Dad described a sea of lights that seemed like paradise as they flew over Boston and approached La Guardia.

To enter the United States at New York, the musicians had to pass through customs inspections and be examined by a physician. This took four hours. They had reservations on the 4:00 p.m. flight to Ciudad Trujillo the next day, so they contacted the consulate of the Dominican Republic, which secured a hotel room in the city for them. They were too tired to visit the skyscrapers of New York and, considering that the next day's flight would take twelve hours, they decided to sleep instead. At noon the next day, they all decided to complain to the airline that they were too exhausted to make the all-night flight to the Dominican Republic. The airline insisted that they had a confirmed reservation on the 4:00 p.m. flight that could not be changed. They pleaded their case to the president of the air-line, who gave them a twenty-four hour extension.

This extension allowed Dad to contact his relatives in New York. At 6:00 p.m. he set off to search for his uncle, Antonio (who later helped Dad gain entry into the United States). The hotel owner spoke fluent Italian, so with him in tow, Dad tried to find Antonio's home. Dad's misspelling of Antonio's address created difficulties, but the hotel owner and Dad finally found the house on Garfield Avenue. Antonio and his children, Dad's cousins, were totally surprised. Dad had not seen some of his cousins since his childhood in Pescara. Living on different floors in the same building were his uncle Antonio (Nonno Peppino's brother), his wife Zia Leonia, and cousins Ornella, Filomena, Erina, and Eneo. They immediately forced Dad to check out of his hotel and stay with them, and the festivities began. The next day Eneo invited all of his colleagues to his home for dinner. This solidified Dad's connection with his New York relatives.

That evening, Eneo accompanied Dad to the airport for the departure of the flight to Ciudad Trujillo. The plane left at 8:00 p.m. and flew through the night to the Dominican Republic. In Ciudad Trujillo Dad was greeted by the general director of the Dominican Republic Radio. Dad wrote that his first impressions were favorable and that when he and his colleagues first played, it was a jaw-dropping performance. He wrote that music in the Dominican Republic was appreciated but was in a primitive stage, and there was a lack of understanding of classical music. An extensive educational push was needed, but Dad was not optimistic that this could be accomplished. Dad said that the basic essentials needed for living were inexpensive, but imported goods were quite costly. Airmail was also expensive, but he continued to correspond.

The Dominican populace did not share their dictator's desire to develop interest in classical music, so the program eventually failed. Dad had to supplement his income by playing in a "merengue" band, which was not to his liking. In 1949 he accepted a position in an exchange program between the Dominican Republic and Puerto Rico, which gained him access to the US territory. Having turned down a four-year offer to teach in the Escuela Libre de Música in Puerto Rico, he spent the next two years performing concerts in Puerto Rico. At the end this two years of engagements, and with his visa issued by the Italian consulate in the Dominican Republic expiring in January 1952, he was running out of time to either return to the Dominican Republic to renew his visa or try to enter the United States by securing an appointment and a sponsor. He chose the latter. So in late 1951, he accepted an invitation from Nonno Peppino's brother, Antonio Cortellini, who had emigrated from Pescara at an early age and then lived in the Bronx borough of New York City. In Dad's search for a sponsor, he auditioned for the vacant first chair position in the Indianapolis Symphony Orchestra with its conductor, Fabian Savitsky. Dad finished first in the competition for this position. He needed to qualify with the musician trade union's requirement of six month's delay for due diligence, which allowed him time to bring his family to the United States. The cause of this delay was not known to me but probably was needed to perform a background check on Dad and complete the necessary visas and sponsorships for his entry into the United States.

My father, a passionate person, was lonely in the Dominican Republic. He found solace in the company of a beautiful Dominican woman named Mercedes. It was during this relationship that my half-sister Maria Rita was born.

Mercedes

Maria Rita

After Dad's departure from the Dominican Republic, Mercedes eventually married and had four sons from this marriage. The family moved to New York in 1957; and after their first winter in a non-tropical climate, they moved to California, where they lived until 1965. They then moved to Miami, where Maria Rita now lives. I only recently connected with her through LinkedIn. I have never met Maria Rita but have seen many images of her in photos Dad left. Mercedes now resides in the Dominican Republic and has just recently celebrated her eightieth birthday.

Mom never spoke to us about Dad's actions during his period away from us. I suspect that his decision to leave Latin America was driven by his desire to find meaningful work in the United States and the fear of being repatriated to Italy at the expiry of his visa to San Domingo. Dad's actions also created friction between him and his father Nonno Peppino who was providing for his family back in Italy which added pressure on Dad to right the situation.

Cortellini family in New York

Nonno Peppino's brother Antonio

Tony Cortellini's family in the Bronx   Dad in New York City

So with great uncle Antonio Cortellini's help in October 1951 the Cortellini trio from Ancona was reunited in New York City with Ferdinando to begin a new chapter of an interrupted life together.

Chapter 5

The Voyage

On September 22, 1951, Mom, Corrado, and I boarded the cruise ship Saturnia for a voyage that changed our lives forever. It had to have been a difficult day for my grandparents, not knowing if they would see their daughter again. For Corrado and me, it was an adventure, but regrettably, we never saw our grandparents after that day. I still have the booklet given to me by Mom's sister, Zia Marisa, entitled "Miracles of Jesus"; and inside the front cover, my aunt wrote in Italian: "To Paoletto from Zia Marisa and little cousins with much affection and hoping that our gift will remain in your little heart." Indeed, it remains.

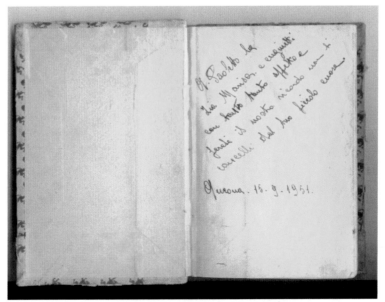

Departing gift from Zia Marisa

The Saturnia had an interesting history. It was built for the Cosulich Line by Cantiere Navale

Triestino in Monfalcone, Italy, and first set afloat in 1927. Following a merger, the ship was transferred to the Italian Line in early 1935. She saw duty as a transport in 1935 for the Italian military, moving troops to and from East Africa. She was chartered to the International Red Cross for evacuation voyages from East Africa in 1942. On September 8, 1943, she steamed into a port controlled by Allied forces following the Italian capitulation. The US military then converted her to a hospital ship, the US Army hospital ship Francis Y. Slanger. She was returned to the Italian Line in late 1946, and her original name was restored. She returned to transatlantic sailing until 1965, when she was withdrawn from service. On October 7, 1965, she arrived at La Spezia, Italy, to be scrapped after a thirty-nine-year run.

La Saturnia as the Frances Y. Slanger hospital ship

The Saturnia and her sister ship, the Vulcania, were two of four Italian Line ships to survive World War II. Many of the Saturnia's more beautiful furnishing were removed and never restored after the war. The number of passengers that the ship could carry was never increased to her prewar capacity of 2,100. After she was refurbished for passenger use, she had a capacity of 1,300. Her new Sulzer diesel engines and twin screw layout could generate a top speed of twenty-one knots. The Saturnia displaced about 23,970 tons. The ship cruised on the North and South Atlantic runs and was conservatively decorated, in contrast to the French Art Deco style that was so popular at that time.

Saturnia posters

On departing from Naples, the commotion at the seaport instilled excitement and fear in me. We traveled tourist class, so the accommodations were modest. The ship's manifest lists Mom as age thirty-one, Corrado eight, and me six; it shows our destination as 1651 Garfield Street, Bronx 60, New York. The manifest states our arrival date in New York as October 3, 1951, meaning that our voyage lasted twelve days with stops in Palermo, Gibraltar, and Halifax.

Saturnia manifest of inbound passengers (aliens)

Calm seas made the voyage across the Mediterranean pleasant. At Gibraltar the crew began to line the ship's edge with rope railings, which foretold the rough ride to come. The North Atlantic in early fall was angry. Mom suffered seasickness and spent most of the twelve days seated on potato sacks stored in the fulcrum of the ship (as this was the point of the ship with the least up-and-down motion). She was not alone. With Mom not feeling well, Corrado and I were on our own to explore the ship's amenities, including movies, snacks, and other pleasantries. The rough seas did not affect us as much as they affected Mom.

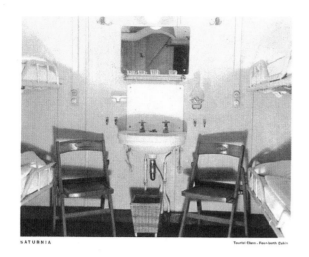

Tourist-class cabin

Tourist-class dining roo

Tourist-class lounge

We arrived at the Port of New York early in the morning. We were on the lookout for the Statute of Liberty. A heavy fog prevented us from seeing her until, suddenly, she appeared before us. It was like a scene from a movie about immigrants landing at Ellis Island. I don't remember much of my days as a six-year-old, but that day is etched in my memory. When we docked, Mom was able to pick out Dad waving among the crowd gathered on the pier. This is my earliest memory of my father. It took what seemed like forever to clear customs and immunization control. When we were finally allowed to exit the ship, Dad and his cousin Eneo were waiting. Mom rushed forward to Dad's embrace. And so began our lives in America.

Statue of Liberty emerging from the fog

Chapter 6

Our Stay in New York

Dad had arranged for us to stay in the Bronx with his cousin Eneo, Eneo's wife Marie, and their son Edmund at 1651 Garfield Street, the same address that Dad originally could not find on his layover in New York on his way to the Dominican Republic. This address was in the heart of the Bronx.

Eneo, Marie, and Edmund

Over time, and especially after Dad's death in 1962, I lost track of Eneo and his family. Recently I was able to make contact with Edmund through the Internet in an effort to reestablish a relationship. Through him I am hoping to contact Antonio and Leona Cortellini's descendants, who I believe all live on the East Coast.

Our initial exposure to life in America suggested that life here would be easy—everyone in the Bronx spoke Italian. In 1951, the Bronx was a haven for Italian immigrants and perhaps the birthplace of Italian American cuisine. Today the Bronx is no longer recognizable to most of the immigrants who called it home during the early postwar years. Uncle Antonio eventually moved to New Jersey, and the house at 1651 Garfield Street has since lost its Italian charm.

Uncle Antonio's home in the Bronx

Dad and Mom with Uncle Antonio and Aunt Leona in the Bronx, and Dad's first car, which was a 1947 Oldsmobile, Series 66 Special Coupe

Today, 1651 Garfield Street looks like this

During our short time in New York we were introduced to two of the novelties of American life. At Uncle Antonio's house we discovered television and Italian American cuisine at the same time. The first television was an RCA console model.

RCA console television

I remember the television commercial for Italian spaghetti by Chef Boyardee:

http://www.youtube.com/watch?v=Vx9KzBx4nNc&feature=related.

Chef Boyardee—that jovial, mustachioed Italian chef—was a real person. Ettore "Hector" Boiardi founded the company with his brothers in 1928, after the family immigrated to America from Italy. The Boiardi family settled in Cleveland, where they opened an Italian restaurant. The restaurant was successful, and customers wanted to learn how to make Italian dishes at home. So the Boiardis started sending people home with pasta, sauce, and cheese and instructions on how to cook and assemble the dishes. This was the seed of an idea that eventually turned into his Chef Boyardee Company. That company played a major role in introducing Italian food to America, and it also changed the way American supermarket shelves were stocked. At the time Chef Boyardee Company started in 1928, it was the largest importer of Parmesan cheese from Italy. The brand name "Chef Boyardee" was spelled so that the American consumer could pronounce the name properly. In 1946, the company was sold to American Home Products. Products under this brand were distributed for use by US armed forces. American Home Products turned its food division into International Home Foods in 1996. Four years later, International Home Foods was purchased by ConAgra Foods, which continues to produce under the Chef Boyardee brand canned pasta with labels bearing Hector Boiardi's likeness.

The Chef Boyardee canned spaghetti story and the sale of the company to a US conglomerate demonstrates the commercialization in the United States of specialty or ethnic foods. Going corporate marked the transition of "ethnic foods" into the marketplace and the culture of mainstream American life. Dishes like spaghetti were adopted, albeit modified or Americanized, and incorporated into everyday American cooking. The prevalence of spaghetti and meatballs on American menus exemplifies how Italian dishes have contributed to the evolution of twentieth-century American cuisine.

So this was our introduction to Italian American food. Mom, being the creative person she was, learned to make spaghetti and meatballs. Of course, once one tasted her recipe, no one could ever return to Chef Boyardee's product in a can.

Mom's recipe was a mainstay in our diet growing up, and today it is still one of my favorite pasta recipes to make. Mom's variations are subtle but important.

Spaghetti con Polpette di Carni (Spaghetti with Meatballs)
Category: Paste (Pastas)
Origin: Mamma Cortellini
Serves 6–8

We were introduced to spaghetti and meatballs by a Chef Boyardee television commercial. I have never seen this dish actually served in Italy. The first time that I saw it served was on television when we were living in the Bronx with our cousins back in 1952. When I saw them serving up the spaghetti on television, I yelled out to my cousins in a very distraught tone of voice that they were placing something inedible on the spaghetti, to which everyone within earshot got a big laugh, but my comment was probably closer to the truth than not.

I was almost seven years old, and we had just recently arrived on the Saturnia ocean liner from Naples. Back then the Bronx was an Italian neighborhood where everyone spoke Italian. In fact, we thought America was going to be an easy place to live because everyone spoke Italian. Did we ever get a rude awakening when we moved to Indianapolis.

To Roz's discomfort, whenever I prepare Mom's recipe for meatballs, I break into singing "Bella Notte." Nevertheless it is one of Roz's favorite Italian American dishes from the Bronx that everyone in my family makes. In fact, Roz has occasional cravings for it and forces me to make it. The key to this dish is the preparation of the meatballs, going light on the garlic, using plenty of parsley, and using just an accent of lemon. I also like to keep the sauce on the light side. I use chopped tomatoes instead of canned tomato sauce or passato. The lemon zest is what makes the recipe interesting.

http://www.youtube.com/?v=9gwZC5s2IU0&feature=related

Ingredients:
Meatballs:
1½–2 lb. of ground sirloin (not very lean)
Bunch of fresh flat leaf parsley, minced
2 good-sized cloves of garlic, minced
¼ cup whole milk
2 slices Italian bread, crust removed
6 Tbsp. (or more) either Parmigiano-Reggiano or Pecorino, or a mixture of both
1 tsp. grated nutmeg (optional)
Fresh ground pepper and salt to taste
Zest of 1 whole lemon, grated
Bread crumbs for covering the meatballs (preferably homemade, certainly without seasoning)

Sauce:
- Small to medium onion, finely chopped
- Bunch of fresh basil, chopped
- 1 box (26.5-oz.) of Pomi chopped tomatoes (alternatively, canned San Marzano plum tomatoes, chopped and peeled, can also be used)

- Kosher salt and freshly ground pepper
- Extra-virgin olive oil to fry the meatballs
- Parmigiano-Reggiano or Pecorino cheese

Preparation:
Meatballs:
1. Prepare the ingredients before beginning to integrate the meatballs:
    a. Use a mezzaluna to chop the parsley and garlic to a minced texture.
    b. Pour the milk into a shallow bowl and dunk the bread in the milk until saturated.
    c. Grate the cheese.
2. In a mixing bowl, add the ground beef and the prepared ingredients:
    a. Grate the nutmeg over the meat.
    b. Grate the lemon zest with a cheese grater.
3. Squeeze the milk from the bread and break up the bread into crumbs and add to the mixture.
4. Add the beaten egg and knead the mixture thoroughly by hand.
5. If the mixture is dry, add some olive oil.
6. Shape the mixture into small meatballs about one and a half inches in diameter, not too large.
7. Place the bread crumbs in a shallow dish and roll the meatballs in the bread crumbs.
8. Place the meatballs on waxed or parchment paper.
9. Heat the oil in a large, heavy casserole.
10. Brown the meatballs evenly on all sides. Turn them frequently to maintain their round shape.
11. After they are well-browned and almost to the point of sticking, add the chopped onion and sauté for five to six minutes and until the onion is soft.
12. Add the tomatoes and basil and simmer, with lid ajar, for at least an hour and until the oil rises to the surface of the sauce.
13. Add salt and pepper to taste.
14. After cooking, let the meatballs stand in the sauce. Meatballs can be reheated when pasta is ready to serve.
15. Combine with spaghetti, penne, or rigatoni.
16. Add grated Parmigiano-Reggiano or Pecorino, or a combination, at the table.

Mixing the meat

Preparing the meatballs

Serving the meatballs

In later chapters I will introduce you to more of Mom's American variations on Italian dishes. Our stay in New York was short-lived. Dad needed to get to Indianapolis to begin his appointment to the Indianapolis Symphony Orchestra. As luck would have it, however, our departure was temporarily delayed when the engine to Dad's newly acquired Oldsmobile required an overhaul. After an oil change, the mechanic did not properly reinstall the oil drain plug, and the engine seized.

We finally set off for Indianapolis and the beginning of our Americanization in the Midwest.

Chapter 7

Indianapolis

We arrived in Indianapolis in late 1951. Unlike the Bronx, everyone in Indianapolis spoke English. Ironically, our first location in Indianapolis was the "English Hotel," not to be confused with the famous English Hotel and Opera House, which was demolished in the early 1900s to be replaced by JC Penney on Monument Circle. While staying at the English Hotel, the first English language phrase that I spoke was "No speak English." We were somewhat of a novelty in Indianapolis, as one can imagine that not many Italian immigrants chose to make their initial home in Indianapolis. The local newspaper ran a short story, asking the public to help us find a place to live.

New Hoosiers Need Only House to Make Home

Finding a house to rent can be tough these days, but when you can't speak English on top of it, you've really got troubles. Ask Ferdinando Cortellini. He can tell you (if you can understand Italian).

This season's new first violist for the Indianapolis Symphony Orchestra brought his family to town this week and began to hunt a house—with an interpreter. Fortunately for the Cortellinis a colleague in the orchestra could talk their language and read the rental ads for them.

Renate Pacini, assistant concertmaster and assistant conductor, who studied in Rome and learned to speak Italian fluently, stepped in as interpreter when the family arrived at the English Hotel.

An interview with the Cortellinis, the family consisting of the musician's wife, Anna, and two sons Corrado, 8, and Paul, 6, had aspects of a UN session. Questions directed in English were translated into Spanish by Mr. and Mrs. Pacini, in deference to the latter's native tongue and Cortellini's recent years in Spanish countries. While the Pacinis related the answers in English, Cortellini translated the dialogue to his wife in Italian.

Cortellini spent four of the last five years in Santo Domingo and Puerto Rico, while his wife and boys remained in Ancona, Italy, awaiting the day that a contract with an American orchestra might be signed. That day came last April when the violist auditioned for Fabien Sevitzky in New York City and won the Indianapolis appointment.

A native of Pescara, Italy, Cortellini studied both violin and viola at the Conservatory of Pescara. He played with the Augusteo Orchestra, affiliated with the Academy of St. Cecelia, Rome. He left Italy in 1947, accepting a post with the Dominican Republic Symphony and performing over the radio for two seasons.

Cortellini then forsook a four-year renewal offer for a better proposal to teach in Puerto Rico at the Escualo Libre de Musica and to give concerts there. At the end of another two-year contract, he accepted invitations from New York relatives to visit them and make contacts in the United States.

Result: The Indianapolis appointment.

The family is seeking an apartment or house, furnished or unfurnished. They plan to make Indianapolis their home. If you have any leads, they ask you to call the symphony office, PLaza 9596.

Indianapolis newspaper article

Although inaccurate, no doubt due to translation problems, the call to assist us in finding a home worked. Mr. Larry Keenan offered us a home in the guest house behind his family residence, located at 5110½ Indianola Avenue. The guest house had three rooms and one bath. Given Dad's meager earnings as a classical musician, the small quarters were probably all he could afford. Despite the small size of the house, we took joy in being reunited as a family. Mom managed to make the home livable by using her sewing talent to make curtains and tablecloths. She and Dad soon began to entertain the symphony society, where Mom displayed her remarkable talents as a cook and hostess.

Entertaining at 5110½ Indianola
(close quarters)

The Keenans on my eighth birthday

The life of a classical musician in the Midwest turned out to be more difficult than Dad had anticipated. The Indianapolis Symphony season did not run the full year, and the wage scale was dismal.

Dad was forced to take on temporary work in the summer to make ends meet. His jobs included working as a janitor and house painter. Until recent decades, most symphony musicians did not have full-year positions, and many resorted to working another job—some teaching, some performing chamber music. Dad ultimately obtained a teaching position with the Jordan College of Music at Butler University. I blame Dad's economic struggles as his reason for not encouraging my brothers or me to pursue a musical career.

A Stanford University research paper titled "Symphony Musicians and Symphony Orchestras," Robert J. Flanagan reports that the mean wage for symphony orchestra musicians in 1952 was $15,917. This statistic includes wages paid by orchestras on the east and west coasts, which were at least 30 percent higher than wages paid by Midwest orchestras. The rate of growth for symphony orchestra musicians' wages over the following thirty years is shown in the following table published in the report:

Real Minimum Annual Salaries for Symphony Orchestra Musicians (Year 2000 dollars)

Decade Rates of Increase 1952 level	52–62	62–72	72–82	82–92
Mean	$15,917	71.9%	68.5%	14.2%	20.11%
Maximum	$32,226	56.0%	39.9%	28.0%	-11.0%
Minimum	$6,800	-23.1%	63.0%	136.4%	30.1%

"The rapid growth in the succeeding decades after 1952 is partially explained by the lengthening of the orchestral season. Lacking data on weeks worked, one cannot determine the respective contributions of increasing weeks and increasing weekly salaries in this development. During 1962–1972, a decade that includes the influence of the Ford Foundation grant program, the median real salary advanced more rapidly, but then it dropped about 20 percent per decade for the next twenty years. In short, the golden era of real annual salary advances for musicians in the top symphony orchestras was in the 1950s and 1960s"[1]

According to the Stanford research paper, symphony orchestras are also one of the last bastions of union representation in the United States. The working conditions of musicians in all but two of the top sixty orchestras are governed by collective bargaining agreements. Musicians today struggle to obtain the following objectives:

- representation by symphony musicians in negotiations with symphony management;
- the right to ratify proposed collective bargaining agreements;
- improved job security, including more transparent hiring (audition) and dismissal procedures;
- a guaranteed work year;
- health and hospitalization insurance; and
- a pension.

---

1   Note: data on symphony musicians' annual salaries between 1952 and 2002 are from the official ICSOM newspaper Senza Sordino of March 2001. The archives of this newspaper can be found at

http://www.icsom.org/senza/issues/senza392.pdf

Unfortunately, the increase in salaries brought on by talented musicians demanding higher compensation, along with the union's contribution to this increase (consider the $2.2 million Riccardo Muti is being paid today in Chicago), has created a financial struggle for most symphonies. Since 1980 the wages of symphony musicians has increased more rapidly than the wages of most workers. The sad reality is that classical music in general is in a crisis. Over the past thirty years, musicians have demanded higher and higher paychecks while ticket sales and recording revenues have continued to drop dramatically. There is no business in the world that can sustain a negative revenue model like this.

The Stanford study defines a successful business model as one having "financial balance," meaning that total revenue (including "Performance Revenue (PR)") is in excess of total expenses, and those not having this balance result in a "Performance Revenue Income Gap (PRIG)." The study states that the rapid wage increases were not correlated to the PRIG or overall financial balance in orchestras but rather depended on private and government contributions. The availability of public and private support creates an ambiguity about the true economic viability of the orchestra, which resulted in a large number of bankruptcies in the last 15 years. Bankruptcies included the Florida Symphony (1991), Birmingham (1993), Honolulu (1993), Hawaii (1993), Louisville (1996), Oakland (1994), Sacramento (1996), San Diego (1996), Tulsa (1998), Orlando (2002), San Jose (2002), and more recently the Philadelphia Orchestra on April 16, 2011, filed for Chapter 11 under the Federal Bankruptcy Act. Twenty-first century PR of the three largest orchestra covered only 59 percent of total expenses. More broadly, PR of the thirty-two largest orchestras declined from 52 percent to 45 percent between 1987 and 2000. Public and private support had to offset the decline.

Publications titled "Where We Stand: The Classical Music World Today" by Greg Sandow and the Internet publication titled "Musik Think Tank 3/27/2013" state that there are many ways to look at the causes of this financial decline. Orchestras are selling fewer tickets and raising less money; and the culture is changing—classical music keeps playing a smaller role in our culture. There are fewer classical radio stations, fewer newspaper critics, fewer classical recordings, and an aging audience— which, as it ages, also grows smaller. The following graph illustrates the decline in attendance between 1987 and 2003.

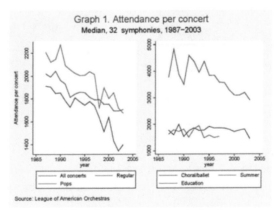

Attendance per concert chart

The major symphony orchestras in the United States are facing an increasingly dire financial situation, not just because a decrease in demand and decades of economic recessions but also because of systematic, short-sighted, and self-inflicted deficiencies in their business model. There is both conservative and radical change being discussed in the classical music world, which may or may not improve their situation.

Corrado and I entered the public school system at an elementary school near our house on Indianola Avenue. I entered the second semester of the second grade, while Corrado had to repeat the second half of the third grade. We had some very accommodating teachers who volunteered to tutor us in English after school. The tutoring, coupled with television, allowed us to quickly learn English.

Because of Mom's strong Catholic faith, the fourth grade found us enrolled at Christ the King elementary school on East Kessler Boulevard.

My fourth-grade class picture, with me in the foreground

Mom and Dad enchanted the Symphony society with Dad's musical performances, while Mom made her name through her dressmaking and her cooking.

Indianapolis newspaper articles

Mom's reputation as a great Italian cook originated with her own version of lasagna. This is a dish for which she is most fondly remembered. I call it her version because the ingredients used were uniquely hers. Having to improvise due to financial hardship and lack of authentic ingredients, she substituted Kraft American cheese with pimento and Kraft Swiss cheese instead of besciamella sauce. She alternated layers of American and Swiss cheese adding Parmigiano-Reggiano cheese to each layer. The most important element of the lasagna is, by far, the quality of the pasta, which Mom would roll out paper-thin by hand. I remember guests raving about the lasagna. She even took lasagna to one of Dad's favorite weekend diversions, the American picnic outing. I recall several trips with Dad's musician colleagues to Brown County State Park, with the highlight of the adults' day being Mom's lasagna.

Picnic at Brown County State Park; included in these pictures are Dad and Mom (carrying my younger brother, Douglas, born August 14, 1952), Gilbert Reese (first cello), Elizabeth Rosenblith (wife of Eric Rosenblith, concertmaster), the Nash family, and others

Left to right: Corrado, Dad, and me;
Elizabeth and Eric Rosenblith; and Doug

Below is the original recipe of Mamma's lasagna that everyone loved so much:

Mamma's Original Lasagna
Category: Paste (Pastas)
Origin: Mamma Cortellini
Serves 6–8

Sauce for the lasagna:
½ lb. ground sausage (she used Jimmy Dean)
1 lb. ground chuck
1 large onion, finely chopped
6 basil leaves or 1½ tsp. dried basil
3 Tbsp. extra-virgin olive oil
Kosher salt and freshly ground black pepper to taste
2 large (28-oz.) cans tomato sauce (she used Hunts)

Sauté the sausage and ground chuck in the olive oil in a saucepan until well browned, breaking up the larger chunks to a fine ground consistency. Add the onion and let cook until it becomes soft and translucent. Add the tomatoes, basil, salt, and pepper and let cook until the oil rises to the top (or at least one hour).

Making the pasta:

These days, you would probably use a pasta machine to roll out the pasta to a thickness one number less than that for ravioli, which on my machine would be number 6. However, Mom would roll out her pasta on a wood board using a rolling pin. The rule of thumb is one egg for every two people served and two-thirds cup of all-purpose flour for each egg used. So for serving six, you would use three eggs and two cups flour. Mom made a mound of flour on her wood board, poking a hole in the middle and forming the mound like a volcano. She broke the eggs into the hole and then beat the eggs while caving the inner walls of the mound into the eggs. Eventually the mixture formed a dough ball, which Mom kneaded for about five minutes. When the dough became pliable, she wrapped it in a damp towel and let it stand for twenty minutes. She then cut pieces from the dough ball and rolled the pasta to the appropriate thickness. She then cut it to size to form lasagna sheets and let it dry on top of a hand towel on a table in the dining room.

Combining the lasagna:

In a large pasta pan, Mom boiled water and dropped in enough sheets of pasta to form several layers of the dish. When pasta rose in the water, after about three minutes, she removed it from the water and laid it out on a cutting board. In a lasagna baking dish, she spread some of the sauce on the bottom of the dish. She then added a layer of pasta, then six slices of processed cheese. Using Kraft pimento American cheese and Kraft Swiss cheese, she alternated layers, one pimento and the next Swiss, and so on. She added sauce on top of the cheese, sprinkling some grated Parmigiano-Reggiano (probably domestic) over the sauce. She repeated cooking the pasta and forming the layers in the same fashion until the pile reached near the top of the baking dish, taking care not to overfill the dish, as pasta tends to expand when baking and could overflow. She sprinkled grated mozzarella on the top layer.

She baked the lasagna at 350° F for twenty to thirty minutes, until the cheeses began to bubble. She let it stand for fifteen minutes before serving.

Pasta Fresca (Fresh Pasta)
Category: Paste (Pastas)
Origin: Mamma Cortellini
Serves 8–10

Process:

Use the ratio of two-thirds cup of flour for each egg when making fresh pasta. For eight to ten servings, I use four eggs for ravioli, five eggs to make a large plate of lasagna, and three eggs for a dish of cannelloni.

- Using a Cuisinart mixer, put the flour and eggs in the mixer with one tablespoon water.
- Mix with flat blade for twenty seconds on low speed, Cuisinart mixer speed number two. Replace with dough hook and mix for another two minutes at the same speed.
- Remove dough and knead by hand for another minute or two until the dough is pliable but not sticky.
- Cover tightly with cling foil and let stand for twenty minutes.
- Cut small pieces from the dough ball, setting it aside and keeping it tightly covered while working with the pasta roller.
- The pieces to roll out should not be too large; otherwise, the pasta sheets will be too large to handle.
- Using the Cuisinart pasta attachment to the mixer, roll out the pasta sheets from the

small pieces of dough.

- Work the pasta in position #1 of the attachment until pliable. You may need to dredge the pasta through more flour if too moist.
- Once pliable, run the pasta through positions #2 through either #6 or #7 of the attachment until the pasta sheets are very thin but thick enough for the pasta intended.
- Cut the pasta for the intended purpose and let partially dry. Do not let the pasta dry too much as it may break.
- Place the unused cuttings back with the dough ball to be reworked with the next piece unless the dough is becoming too dry.
- Cook the pasta until it rises to the top of the boiling water.

Ragu alla Bolognese (Bolognese Sauce)
Category: Paste (Pastas)
Origin: Traditional Bologna
Serves 6–8

There are numerous variations of Ragu Bolognese. My mother made a much simpler version, which she called meat sauce (see Mamma's Ragu recipe). The key is slow cooking and letting the liquids reduce during the cooking process. Cooking time is well over two hours. This sauce is excellent for preparing fresh Tagliatelle con Ragu and is the sauce I use for my Lasagna Bolognese. It is complimented with generous helpings of Parmigiano-Reggiano. It can be frozen and served when needed.

Ingredients:
2½ Tbsp. unsalted butter
1 Tbsp. plus extra-virgin olive oil (from Lucca or Puglia)
Trita (see preparation below) of 1 large yellow onion, 1 large carrot, and 2 stalks of celery
1½ lb. ground beef. Use a more favorable choice, such as sirloin or chuck, with a higher fat content
6 oz. mild Italian pancetta, chopped finely, or ½ lb. of sweet ground pork (no fennel)
Kosher salt and freshly ground black pepper to taste
2½ cups of milk
Freshly grated nutmeg (from the nut, not the can)

1¼ cups dry white wine
2¼ cups chicken stock (homemade is preferable)
2½ cups canned diced or chopped Italian plum tomatoes (I use a 26.4-oz. box of Pomi chopped tomatoes or an equivalent good-quality brand)
A small bunch of fresh basil, chopped

Preparation:
1. A "trita" is the combination of three standard ingredients (onion, celery and carrot) finely chopped and used in the process of making Italian tomato sauces. I use a mezzaluna to chop the trita as opposed to using a food processor.
2. Put the oil and butter in a large, heavy-bottomed saucepan and heat until the butter melts.
3. Add the pancetta and fry over medium heat until it begins to become crisp.
4. Remove the pancetta from the pan and set aside; alternatively, skip the pancetta and add the ground pork to the ground beef.
5. Add the tritata to the oil and fry until the vegetables soften (about ten minutes).
6. Return the pancetta to the sauce and add the ground beef, breaking up the meat with a wooden spoon to eliminate any large pieces.
7. Add salt and freshly ground pepper and continue cooking until the meat is thoroughly cooked, being careful not to burn the meat or to let it get too brown.
8. Add the milk slowly and let simmer over medium-low heat until juices are clear.
9. Add the nutmeg to taste and cook until the milk evaporates (about thirty minutes; the liquids should be clear).
10. Add the wine and let simmer until liquids are reduced by half.
11. Add the chicken stock and simmer again until liquids have reduced in half (about fifteen minutes).
12. Add the chopped tomatoes and basil and continue to cook for at least another hour and until the oil rises to the top of the sauce.
13. Add salt and pepper to taste.

Lasagna Bolognese (Lasagna with Bolognese Sauce)
Category: Paste (Pastas)
Origin: Traditional Bologna
Serves 6–8

See: Ragu Bolognese recipe for the sauce
See: fresh pasta Recipe (for the pasta, use #6 thickness)

This dish is labor-intensive, but it is well worth the effort. The trick is to make plenty and freeze what you don't serve. It keeps well in the freezer, and with a son like Nic around, it won't last long. There are variations using ricotta, mozzarella, and other substitutes for the besciamella. I have even seen meatballs and hard-boiled eggs inserted in the lasagna. However, for me, the traditional version using besciamella sauce is far superior. By the way, Mom used Kraft American cheese with pimento and Swiss, which always brought praise.

Besciamella sauce is the sauce that is mixed with the ragu as topping for the lasagna layers. My preference is to have thinner pasta with more layers (five to six layers per dish)

Ingredients:
7 Tbsp. unsalted butter
6 Tbsp. all-purpose flour
3½ cups whole milk, heated just until steaming
Pinch of freshly grated nutmeg
½ tsp. kosher salt
Freshly ground black pepper

Preparation of the besciamella:
1. In a heavy medium saucepan, melt the butter over medium-low heat.
2. Add the flour slowly, stirring continuously for two to three minutes—do not let it burn.
3. While stirring, add two tablespoons of the hot milk.
4. Continue to slowly pour half of the remaining hot milk into the saucepan while continuing to stir.
5. Cook until the sauce thickens, stirring with a wooden spoon, making sure that the bottom and sides do not stick. If lumps form, stir quickly with a whisk. Cook for approximately fifteen minutes.
6. Season with salt and pepper, remove from heat, and let stand thirty minutes before applying to the lasagna.

Preparation of the Lasagna:
1. Prepare the pasta per the Pasta Fresca recipe, using four eggs. Roll out the pasta sheets to a #6 thickness.
2. Cut the pasta sheets into 5x5-in. squares and let dry (does not need to be fully dried before cooking).
3. In a large pasta pot, boil salted water and drop four or five squares of dried pasta at a time; cook for three to four minutes, until pasta is al dente and pliable.
4. While water is heating, thoroughly butter the bottom and sides of a lasagna dish (13x5x2-in.). I use a glass dish.
5. Drain the pasta and let cool to the touch.
6. Ladle a scoop of the sauce on the bottom of the lasagna dish and spread the sauce thinly over the bottom.
7. Layer the cooked pasta over the sauce, fully covering the dish and minimizing overlap.
8. Ladle the sauce over the pasta, again thinly covering the pasta.
9. Dollops the besciamella over the sauce and, with a spoon, blend the besciamella into the sauce.
10. Sprinkle grated Parmigiano-Reggiano over the top of the layer.
11. Repeat steps 7 through 10 for each layer, making five to six layers.
12. On the top layer, completely cover the top with Parmigiano-Reggiano, add pepper,

spread some small dollops of butter over the top, and sprinkle with olive oil.

13. Bake at 350°F for forty-five minutes until the cheese begins to turn golden and the juices from the pasta bubble.

14. Remove from heat and let stand for fifteen minutes before serving.

Chapter 8

The Happy Years

The decade between 1952 and 1962 was the most gratifying period for the Cortellini family. Dad became recognized as a formidable, gifted violist in the Indianapolis Symphony Orchestra. As a full professor of music at Butler University, he performed on the side with Eric Rosenblith, Gilbert Reese, and Mildred Linn in the Jordan String Quartet. As a duet, Eric and Dad recorded a performance of Mozart's "Sinfonia Concertante in E Flat Major for Violin, Viola, and Orchestra." It is the only recording I have of Dad performing.

Eric and Dad in concert
Below are the YouTube videos of this recording:

https://www.youtube.com/watch?v=bkVSwXhE1C4

https://www.youtube.com/watch?v=f-LINHUoDmk

https://www.youtube.com/watch?v=iKG00DqSayI

He was also acclaimed for his performance of Handel's "Casadesus Concerto for Viola and Orchestra."

Indianapolis newspaper article and Dad rehersing

The Jordan String Quartet toured nearby universities and also performed free outdoor summer evening concerts at the beautiful J. I. Holcomb Gardens on the Butler campus. I remember attending these concerts and having to swat away an occasional mosquito.

Jordan String Quartet

Mom gained notoriety on two fronts: as an excellent dressmaker with the fashionable symphony society and with the musicians for her home cooking. Because Dad performed most Saturday evenings, my parents entertained mostly on Sunday evenings after the Sunday matinee performance. Mom would attend the Saturday night performance and cook on Sundays. Corrado and I would attend the Sunday matinee performances. Dad took us through the stage door entrance, and we would mingle with the younger female musicians until they were ready to go onstage. We would then scout out the best seats, and for matinees there were plenty. As American teenagers exposed to rock-n-roll and Elvis Presley, our ability to appreciate classical music was probably somewhat compromised. However, afternoons at the historic and beautiful Murat Temple Theater were magical. As the music played, my eyes roamed the great hall, and I dreamed. On October 18, 1963, the venue for the Indianapolis Symphony changed to the new Clowes Memorial Hall on the campus of Butler University. Dad never had the chance to play in this new hall. Today the Indianapolis Symphony Orchestra performs in the renovated Circle Theatre at Monument Circle.

Mingling with the artist and Izler Solomon, conductor with Dad

Murat Temple Theater

For Mom, Sundays were for cooking. Dad would normally invite friends to join us for Sunday dinner, and it was these dinners that gained Mom recognition as an excellent cook. Mom and Dad made numerous friends in the symphony social circle, and each was eager to get an invitation to a dinner party at the Cortellini home. I remember most fondly Eric Rosenblith, concertmaster, and Gilbert Reese, principal cellist. Eric, Gilbert, and Dad were considered the master performers for the Indianapolis Symphony during this period (akin to the Three Tenors), and their bond as friends and professional colleagues was well-known.

Indianapolis newspaper article on the trio

Eric Rosenblith was a violin virtuoso and a wonderful person. He was married to a beautiful British ballerina named Margaret. Eric and Dad complemented each other professionally. Eric was Austrian born, and, to avoid Nazi persecution, his father moved the family to Paris, where Eric, at the age of eleven, entered the Ecole Normal de Musique and studied under Jacques Thibald. He later went to London to study with master violinist/teacher Carl Flesch. In 1939, once again in the face of the impending Nazi invasions, he and his family fled their home in Paris and sailed for New York. In the United States, when war was declared, he enlisted in the US Army, serving as a clerk and a translator for German prisoners of war. He also performed for the troops. After the war Eric toured with the ballet orchestra of Saddler Wells, where he met and married ballerina Margaret Sear. In the years that followed, Eric served as concertmaster first for the San Antonio Symphony Orchestra and later the Indianapolis Symphony Orchestra, where he remained for thirteen years. It was during this period that we were fortunate to get to know Eric and Margaret.

Indianapolis newspaper articles on Dad and Eric

Eric suffered a tragic loss in 1956 when his car hit a patch of ice and he lost control. He was returning from a quartet performance at Ball State University in Muncie, Indiana. The accident claimed the lives of both Margaret and Eric's mother. In the years that followed, Eric rededicated his efforts to teaching and performing music. Sadly, Eric passed away at the age of ninety in December 2012 in Massachusetts after a long and productive career.

Margaret, Eric, and Eric's mother   Eric shortly before
his passing

Gilbert Reese was the third member of the performing trio. He was a tall, handsome blond from Long Beach, California. He loved Mom's cooking. The son of an accomplished pianist and music teacher, Mae Gilbert Reese, he grew up engulfed in music. Rather than follow his mother's footsteps, Gilbert took up the cello. Like his mother, he attended the l'Ecole Normale de Musique in Paris, where he earned his master's degree in music. He also studied under the legendary cellist Pablo Casals. When Gilbert was not traveling, he served as principal cellist for the Indianapolis Symphony Orchestra and taught music at Butler University with Eric and Dad. He performed in Indianapolis for eleven years, overlapping the same time as Eric and Dad. He raved about Mom's cooking. After returning to California and settling in Long Beach, he started his now-legendary "Concerts in the Home," which took place in a music studio on the top floor of his home. Three to four times a year, he would host concerts and prepare the food for his fifty to eighty guests. Surely some of the recipes prepared for these dinners were Mom's? Gilbert Reese died of pancreatic cancer in Long Beach on November 18, 2004.

Gilbert Reese performing

Another of my parents' friends during this period was Joe Bellissimo, first French horn for the symphony. Joe, of Italian descent, grew up in Harrisburg, Pennsylvania, and was married to a lovely Native American with long red hair named Joan. They had two children, Joe and Jim. Joan was strikingly beautiful. Mom and Dad were the godparents for their firstborn son, Joe. I remember picnics and Christmas feasts with the Bellissimo family. We were very close, and Mom treated Joan like the daughter she never had. They even stayed with Corrado and me when Mom, Dad, and my brother Douglas traveled to Italy for an extended holiday with family.

Baptism of Joe Bellissimo and picnics

Christmas with the Bellissimo family

Joe and Joan still live in Pennsylvania, and Joan is currently working with her son Joe in his medical practice. Joe, Sr., no longer plays the French horn; he is now eighty-five years of age and has retired.

Recent photos of Joe and Joan

There were numerous other friends with symphony connections with whom we socialized during this period. I have fond memories of Renato Pacini (Pach), assistant concertmaster; his wife Stella Pacini; and their son Richard, a classmate of mine at Scecina Memorial High School. They were our first contacts upon arriving in Indianapolis and assisted us in acclimating to our new life. Richard "Dick" Dennis, violinist with the symphony, played at the symphony between 1952 and 1959. Mom and Dad were godparents to their firstborn. Two of our closest non-musician friends were Irv and Bea Fink and their five children. Irv was—and still is, at the age of ninety-two—a practicing attorney in Indianapolis. I remember babysitting their daughter Elaine while Irv and Bea attended a symphony performance. I also painted their house one summer. What a hot job! No wonder I went into accounting.

Dick Dennis son's baptism

Dinner with the Finks

It was during this period that Mom gave birth to my younger brother, Douglas. Dad decided on the name as he wanted his baby to have a more English-sounding name. Douglas was born on August 14, 1952, approximately ten months after Mom and Dad reunited in New York.

Doug with his curls

Mom would not let anyone cut Doug's hair for the longest time; as a result, he began to look like a little girl (maybe a hidden desire?) with beautiful hair. One Saturday morning, unbeknownst to Mom, Dad took Doug to the local barbershop, where he quickly transformed him into a little boy. Mom cried her eyes out.

Doug after haircut

Doug was the baby of the family and as such attracted all the attention. He even made the newspaper with Eric.

4-2-1957

TINY VIRTUOSO—Hardly big enough to hold his half-size violin, Douglas Cortellini, con-
centrates as he listens to his teacher, Eric Rosenblith, concertmaster for the Indianapolis
Symphony. Douglas is the son of Mr. and Mrs. Ferdinando Cortellini, 3039 E. 38th. His
father plays first viola for the Symphony.

Indianapolis newspaper article of Douglas and Eric

When we moved from Indianola Avenue to Thirty-Eighth Street, Corrado and I first attended St. Andrews Catholic School. Later, however, Dad decided that the tuition burden was too much, so we attended Public School Number One, which was within walking distance of our home. We both had paper routes and grew up as typical American kids for that period in time. Our first dog was named Zisca. She was jet black, with a white stripe down her chest. She was part Doberman and part Dalmatian. She was fast and could easily jump the fence that enclosed our backyard.

Our dog Zisca

Corrado and I played in the woods behind our house and on construction sites in the neighborhood. We enjoyed those times immensely. Because our Italian accents made us seem different to the other children, Corrado and I formed a strong bond that lasts to this day. Corrado was incredibly strong, both physically and mentally; and because he was two years older, he was my protector. On East 38th Street, we lived next door to a couple of Italian descent named Giuseppe and Rosa Barbieri. They were in the construction business and seemed to be prospering. Their house, of Italian stucco design, was elaborate for the neighborhood, with fountains and figurines throughout the garden. Rosa's granddaughter was a very attractive young girl named Jean. Although older than Corrado, she enjoyed our company and our flirtations. She loved to have us sing to her in Italian. She must have known that we were both in love with her—or at least with her beauty. She eventually grew out of enjoying our company and flirtation, but not before Corrado and I spent many warm summer evenings on the front lawn, watching traffic on East 38th Street as we fantasized about being her amante.

Mom with Rosa next door   Jean with Corrado and me at Indiana Beach

Both Corrado and I played football at Public School Number One. After Corrado graduated, he enrolled at Shortridge High School. I finished elementary school the following year and started high school at Lawrence Central High School. However, Mom, a devout Roman Catholic, made us transfer to the Catholic Scecina Memorial High School after our parish priest threatened Mom with excommunication if we continued attending the public schools. Father Harold, the tyrannical parish priest, was notorious for telling his parishioners they were going to hell for this or for that. He would lock the doors when mass started, and those arriving late were sent away. He would halt mass and force those standing in the back, hoping for a quick getaway, to sit in the front rows where nobody wanted to sit. For Mom, the threat of excommunication was unacceptable, so Corrado and I changed schools after the fall semester was already underway. One effect of the transfer was that it was too late for either of us to join the football team. But for the unfortunate timing of the transfer preventing me from playing football, I would surely have eventually made it to the NFL!

In 1958 we purchased a home in a northeast suburb on Audubon Road. It was a modest new split-level home with three bedrooms, a walkout basement, and an attractive living room with a vaulted ceiling. Our move to the new house was reported in the Indianapolis Star. Dad's prominence in the symphony drew unexpected attention at times.

Indianapolis Newspaper Articles

Our home at Audubon Rd.

In her new house, Mom was better able to prepare and serve food for her guests. The house was always alive with the fragrance of good food, fine music, and laughter.

Making pasta for Christmas at the kitchen table

Entertaining for colleagues, friends, and family

Christmas at Audubon Road

Mom was especially busy cooking during the Christmas season. Holiday meals were meticulously prepared in strict Italian tradition. For Christmas Eve there had to be fish. For Christmas Day it was Capelletti in Brodo. New Year's Day required Lenticchie (lentils brings fortune) and Cavolo Agro Dolce. Below are five recipes for these traditional holiday dishes:

Pasta con Sugo di Tonno e Acciughe (Spaghetti with Tuna and Anchovies)
Brodo di Pollo (Homemade Chicken Soup)
Cappelletti in Brodo (Cappelletti Pasta in Chicken Broth)
Lenticchie Brasate (Braised Lentils)
Zuppa di Lenticchie (Lentil Soup)
Cavolo Agro Dolce (Sweet and Sour Cabbage)

Spaghetti con Sugo di Tonno e Acciughe
(Spaghetti with Tuna and Anchovies)
Category: Paste (Pastas)
Origin: Mamma Cortellini
Serves 4–6

This is a great-tasting pasta sauce for an impromptu meal. Even though some may be squeamish about using anchovies, they are essential to the taste of this sauce and blend fabulously with the taste of the tuna. The chili flakes are optional; be careful not to make the sauce too picante. Also be careful not to add too much salt as the anchovies, capers, and tuna should have sufficient salt for the sauce. Mom traditionally served this dish on Christmas Eve, when eating fish was a requirement.

Ingredients:
16 oz. Italian imported spaghettini or fedelini (De Cecco preferred)
Three good-sized cloves garlic, minced
6 fillets anchovies packed in olive oil, chopped (Agostino Recca)
1 can quality tuna packed in olive oil (Genova-Italian or As do Mar-Portuguesa)
? large can or box of Italian Roma tomatoes chopped (I prefer Pomi)
Bunch of Italian flat-leaf parsley (at least 2–3 Tbsp.), chopped
? cup good extra-virgin olive oil (I like oils from Apulia)
1 tsp. capers rinsed and chopped (preferably capers under salt)
Red pepper flakes to taste
Kosher salt and freshly ground black pepper to taste

Preparation:
1. Chop two-thirds of the parsley with the garlic and sauté at medium-low heat in a saucepan with the olive oil for only a few minutes. Do not let the garlic brown or burn.
2. Add the anchovies and capers and simmer until the anchovies melt.
3. Break up the tuna in the can, stirring in the olive oil from the packing.
4. Add the tuna to the sauce and simmer at medium heat until the tuna begins to pop.
5. Add the tomatoes and the juice from the can and the remaining chopped parsley and chili flakes.
6. Add salt and pepper to taste.
7. Simmer for thirty minutes or when the oil surfaces. If the sauce is too thin, add a small amount of quality tomato paste.
8. Cook the pasta in a large pot of boiling water adding salt after it begins to boil according to the cooking instructions on the box but certainly only until it is al dente.
9. Drain the pasta or remove it from the boiling water with tongs or a spider and place in a serving bowl and add to the tomato sauce, and serve immediately.

Reduce juices till the oil rises to the top   Serve with fedelini or thin spaghetti

For Christmas day we traditionally prepared Capelletti in Brodo, which is a fresh egg pasta stuffed with a meat sauce and cooked in a homemade chicken broth. For this dish, three recipes are needed: (1) the fresh pasta, (2) the filling, and (3) the chicken broth. For the fresh pasta, use the recipe in chapter 7 for lasagna. Roll out the dough thinner than the lasagna dough. Thinner pasta is required for Capelletti to ensure tender pasta.

Brodo di Pollo (Chicken Soup)
Category: Minestre (Soups)
Origin: Mamma Cortellini's Traditional Italian
Serves 6–8

Chicken broth is a base for Italian cooking and, according to Mom, medicinal for colds and other ailments. It is used in traditional dishes such as Stracciatella alla Romana, Capelletti in Brodo, and many sauces. The broth can be frozen and used later. Broth will keep in the freezer for up to three months, but it will not keep in the refrigerator for any longer than three to four days. Used alone as a soup it is excellent with small pasta (Pastina in Brodo) such as Tubetti, Anicini di Peppe, or Conchigliette, with a generous topping of grated Parmigiano-Reggiano.

Ingredients:
1 whole chicken, 2½–3 lb. (including neck; gizzards optional)
3–4 celery stalks, quartered, with leaves
1 large onion, peeled and quartered; I leave the peeling on to add flavor
2–3 carrots, peeled and quartered
2 small fresh tomatoes, quartered
4 garlic cloves
2 bay leaves
4–5 parsley stalks in whole
1 Tbsp. black whole peppercorns
Kosher salt

Preparation:
1. Put all the ingredients in a large stockpot; add enough water to fully cover the chicken and then some.
2. Add the salt and bring to a boil. When it reaches a boil, turn the heat down so that it bubbles steadily at a gentle simmer. Cook for one and a half hours, or until the chicken meat can easily be pulled from the bone.
3. Remove the chicken and discard the vegetables. Debone the chicken for other use or freeze for a later date.
4. Allow the broth to cool completely, uncovered.
5. When cool, place the broth in a container in the refrigerator long enough for the

fat to come to the surface and gel.

6. Remove the excess fat and use the broth as needed.

Preparing the broth

Pastina in brodo

Capelletti in Brodo (Capelletti Pasta in Broth)
Category: Paste (Pastas)
Origin: Mamma Cortellini
Serves 6–8

This is a labor of love. Due to the work involved, it is traditionally served only on Christmas Day. I remember being recruited on Christmas morning to stuff the pasta. The keys to this pasta are a good chicken broth, a light filling with a taste of nutmeg, and thin pasta dough.

Ingredients:
Filling:
1 chicken breast or several chicken tenders (1 lb.)
½ lb. pork tenderloin
1 egg
½ cup of ground Parmigiano-Reggiano
Zest of 1 lemon
¼ tsp. freshly ground nutmeg (add more if preferred)
Butter and extra-virgin olive oil for frying the meat and to moisten the filling
Kosher salt and freshly ground black pepper to taste

Fresh pasta (see fresh pasta recipe; roll out to #7 on the KitchenAid pasta machine or one-sixteenth-inch thickness).

Preparation:
1. Cut the pork and chicken into strips.
2. In a frying pan, heat a half stick of butter and three tablespoons of olive oil; over medium heat, fry the chicken and pork until water evaporates and meat is tender.
3. Grind the meat in a food processor, adding the oil from the frying pan.
4. Place the ground meat in a bowl and add the egg, cheese, lemon zest, nutmeg salt, and pepper. Add olive oil or melted butter if the mixture is dry. The filling should be moist so that it sticks together and can be formed into a ball. Place in refrigerator, covered, until ready to use.
5. Roll out the pasta dough to #7 thicknesses on the KitchenAid pasta machine or one-sixteenth-inch thickness. Work with one sheet of pasta at a time, placing the remaining dough in a loaf covered with cling foil and let stand on t

he cutting board until next needed.

6. Place the rolled out sheet of pasta on a cutting board and cut out the dough into circles, one and a half to two inches in diameter; do not let the dough dry out.

7. Place a small amount (half a teaspoon) of filling in the center of the pasta circle.

8. To form the little hat, fold the circle in half forming what is normally ravioli.

9. Pick up the semicircle, using both hands, with the round side down. Holding each end between thumb and index finger, turn the edges inward until they meet and firmly pinch them together until they stick together. Curl the edge up slightly.

10. In a good chicken broth (see recipe for Brodo di Pollo), add a bouillon cube for extra flavor.

11. Cook the pasta in the chicken broth, adding some additional nutmeg and lemon zest to the broth for more flavor, for ten to fifteen minutes.

12. Serve with additional Parmigiano-Reggiano.

Knead the pasta dough to a pliable consistency,
wrap with plastic wrap, and let sit for
twenty minutes

Roll out the pasta to the proper thickness and cut out dough circles two and a half inches in diameter. Stuff the pasta with a small amount of filling and let dry on cookie sheets. Cook in boiling water until pasta rises to the surface, drain, and serve with ample Parmigiano-Reggiano.

Serve as a soup

For New Year's Day, Mom served lentils with ham or sausage as a stew or a soup and Cavolo Agro Dolce, which translates to sweet and sour cabbage. Both are said to bring good luck in the New Year.

Lenticchie Brasate (Braised Lentils)
Category: Verdure (Vegetables)
Origin: Mamma Cortellini
Serves 4–6

Lentils are legumes that Mom traditionally made every New Year's Day. The legend is that eating lentils on New Year's Day will bring you money the rest of the year. In reality, it may only bring you gas for the remainder of the day. However, this is a dish you can make as a stew or as a soup, and it is delicious year round. I normally freeze a ham bone and the leftovers of a honey-baked ham to cook with the lentils, but you can also cook it with sausage or pancetta. Be sure to rinse and clean the lentils before cooking, and some also suggest soaking them, but this may make them too soft after cooking. I like to use the small green lentils; they hold their shape and don't fall apart.

Ingredients:
1½–2 cups green lentils (the smaller the better)
2 Tbsp. extra-virgin olive oil
½ cup (or more) sugar-cured, off the bone ham cut into small pieces; add the bone
    if available; alternatively, use ½ cup of sausage or ¼ cup of pancetta
1 medium onion, finely chopped
1 celery stalk, finely chopped
1 carrot, finely chopped (the onion, celery, carrot trio together is considered a trita)
1 garlic clove, smashed
1 small bay leaf
3 Tbsp. chopped plum or Roma tomatoes
3 Tbsp. chopped Italian parsley
Kosher salt and freshly ground black pepper to taste
Water or broth

Preparation:
1. Rinse and clean the lentils, removing any inedible particles.
2. In a heavy saucepan, sauté the meat in the oil and cook for three to four minutes.
3. Stir in the onions and cook until soft and translucent.
4. Add the celery, tomatoes, and carrots and cook for another three to four minutes.
5. Add the lentils to the saucepan, stirring them to blend with the meat, vegetables, and tomatoes.

6. Pour in some boiling water (or broth) just to cover the lentils.
7. Add the garlic, bay leaf, and parsley and stir.
8. Cook over moderate heat until the lentils are tender, about a half hour to forty-five minutes.
9. Discard the garlic and bay leaf; salt and pepper the lentils to taste.
10. Serve either hot or at room temperature.
11. Drizzle a little extra-virgin olive oil over each plate before serving.

Cook with the bone

Drizzle with extra-virgin olive oil and
serve hot or at room temperature

Zuppa di Lenticchie (Lentil Soup)

Category: Minestre (Soups)
Origin: Traditional Italian
Serves 4–6

This soup is an alternative to Braised Lentils on New Year's Day. It is a tasty soup that satisfies the tradition of serving lentils on this holiday, but it can be served year round. You can use the same small green lentils and the frozen leftover ham to flavor the soup.

Ingredients:
¼–½ cup sugar-cured ham off the bone, cut into bite-size pieces (alternatively, use pancetta)
2 Tbsp. unsalted butter
1 carrot, finely chopped
4 celery stalks, finely chopped
1 large onion, finely chopped
1 lb. (2 cups) small green lentils
1 qt. chicken stock
6 cups boiling water, more as needed to thin the soup
Bouquet of herbs (2 fresh thyme sprigs, 6 Italian parsley sprigs, and one or two small bay leaves), tied together or in a cheesecloth
3 Tbsp. extra-virgin olive oil
1 fresh thyme sprig, chopped, or ¼ tsp. dried
1 fresh rosemary sprig, chopped, or ¼ tsp. dried
1 garlic clove, minced
Kosher salt and freshly ground black pepper to taste

Preparation:

1. In a soup pot, sauté the ham over low heat, stirring occasionally until cooked (five minutes).
2. Pour off any excess fat, turn up the heat to medium, and add the butter.
3. When butter is melted, add the carrots, celery, and onion and simmer until softened.
4. Stir in the lentils; add the stock, boiling water, and herb bouquet and bring to a boil.
5. Reduce heat to medium-low and simmer, partially covered, until lentils are soft (one hour).
6. Remove the herbs. With a slotted spoon, remove two cups of the lentils and vegetables and puree them in a blender or food processor. Return the puree to the soup to thicken the soup. If too thick, thin with the extra boiling water. You can also use a hand blender directly in the soup pot to process some of the lentils and vegetables.
7. Heat the extra-virgin olive oil in a small pan over low heat and add the chopped thyme, rosemary, and garlic. Simmer under low heat for three to four minutes; do not let the garlic burn.
8. Pour the seasoned oil mixture through a strainer into the soup and mix.
9. Season to taste with salt and freshly ground pepper; if you like, add some hot pepper flakes to add more spice.

Blend some of the lentils to thicken

Serve as a soup—drizzle olive oil

Cavolo Agro Dolce (Sweet and Sour Cabbage)
Category: Verdure (Vegetables)
Origin: Mamma Cortellini
Serves 4–6

This is a traditional Cortellini family dish at Christmas or New Year and also Thanksgiving. It has been said that eating this cabbage at the beginning of the year brings you good fortune. This is an unusual dish for Italians as they claim never to mix sweet foods with salt. The legendary good fortune aspect of this dish hasn't worked on me so far, but it goes well with either fowl or game.

Ingredients:
1 whole good-sized head of cabbage, chopped into small pieces
¼ cup extra-virgin olive oil
¼ cup white or apple cider vinegar
¼ cup sugar

Kosher salt and freshly ground black pepper to taste

Preparation:
1. Cut the cabbage in half and then in quarters, and remove the core.
2. Slice the quarters into one-inch-wide strips.
3. In a large skillet, warm the olive oil.
4. Add the chopped cabbage, salt, and pepper and sauté slowly until golden.
5. Start cooking the cabbage over medium heat; then reduce the heat to medium-low.
6. Cook, uncovered, until cabbage is completely cooked. Cabbage will shrink by at least half.. Stir occasionally to cook it evenly.
7. When fully cooked, add the vinegar and sugar; stir and continue simmering till well blended and the vinegar reduces.
8. Season with salt and pepper.
9. This dish can be served hot but is best at room temperature.

Cabbage, halved and sliced   Vinegar reduced and ready to serve

Chapter 9

Uncertain Times

During our adolescent years, Corrado and I lost track of our Italian relatives, partly because of involvement in our day-to-day American lives and a desire to be more American than Italian—and also because international communication was costly. During this period our cousins in Italy were living their Italian lives. It was not until we were older that we became reacquainted with our cousins and established active relationships.

Unlike Mom, Corrado and I lost any trace of our Italian accents. Our time was consumed with high school activities and working to earn spending money to sustain our automobiles. Corrado had a 1953 Oldsmobile, and I had a 1949 Ford coupe, which I bought for seventy-five dollars. Corrado and I had high school sweethearts who happened to be cousins. My girlfriend was Sue Budreau, and Corrado's girlfriend was Karen Cornelius. Sue's father was the brother of Karen's mother.

Corrado and Karen

Sue at the senior prom

In high school Corrado concentrated on mathematics and the graphic arts. I focused on business-related subjects and won an award in bookkeeping. I also participated in drama club and starred in two plays, one as an old man in The Remarkable Incident at Carson's Corner and another as a teenage hoodlum named Tony (what else?) in The Rebel Rousers.

As Mr. Kovalevsky in The Remarkable Incident in Carson's Corner

 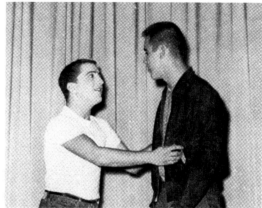

As Tony in The Rebel Rousers

Dad's music consumed his life. He never played games or sports with us, and he did not encourage us to participate in sports. He did take us squirrel hunting, and he fished with us on our annual vacation to Florida's panhandle coast. He hated rock-n-roll in general and had a special dislike for Elvis. I remember listening to the radio when he was away or while under the blankets in my room at night while Dad was practicing. He practiced continuously. I would fall asleep at night listening to his repetitive stanzas.

Dad smoked incessantly and put on weight. He had a smoker's cough that can be heard in some of his recorded performances. Mom felt that his health was weakened from his wartime experience.

Dad and Mom planned an Italian homecoming trip to introduce Douglas to their families. While there, Dad planned to meet some colleagues to tour and perform. In August 1956 Dad, Mom, and Douglas set off for Italy on an Italian Home Lines ship called the MS Italia.

The MS Italia   Sun-bathing on the deck

More sunbathing   A toast by the captain

As this is an epicurean story, it would be remiss of me not to include the menu for dinner aboard the Italia on August 11, 1956.

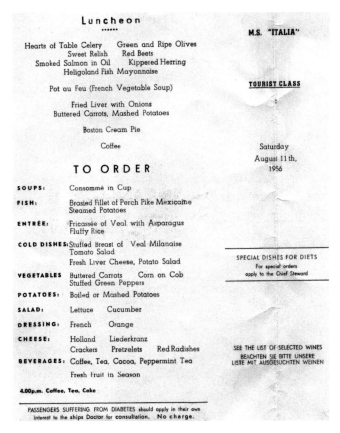

The voyage departed from New York City on August 5, 1956, destined for Plymouth, England, with a further stop at Le Havre, France. From there they took a train to Italy and home. Corrado and I stayed behind in Indianapolis, where Joe and Joan Bellissimo cared for us at our residence on East

38th Street. Joe played first French horn for the Indianapolis Symphony Orchestra. They were great chaperones, and we got to know them well and enjoyed their company. We later became very close friends and spent many good times together.

The Bellissimo family   At a picnic gathering

The Bellissimo family at Christmas

I am told that Douglas, being the center of attention, had a wonderful time in Ancona. Mom and Dad reported that he talked nonstop. It wasn't long until he was speaking Italian. My cousin Maurizio recounts that after another satisfying meal in Ancona; Doug pushed his seat back and announced to everyone, "Io sono finito," which, literally translated, means "I am finished." However, in proper Italian, the phrase means "I am dead." Everyone got a big laugh out of this, and it is remembered to this day. Doug adjusted so well to the Italian language at his age that upon his return to Indianapolis, he spoke only Italian.

Doug with cousins on the beach;   Doug with Anna Maria
and Massimo in Ancona

What was to have been a memorable return to their roots and reunion with family turned sour when Dad contracted pneumonia and was laid up for three months. Instead of it being a vacation of four weeks, it became a three-week vacation and a lengthy recovery and recuperation lasting three months. They returned on the French Line ship named Ile de France, departing on October 4, 1956. Because of Dad's condition, this trip was not jovial like the one from the United States to Italy. Nevertheless, I suspect that they enjoyed dinner while at sea on October 9, 1956. Here is the menu from that day:

Il de France entering the port of New York City

Il de France menue

Dad was never in good health after that trip. He developed a heart valve problem, which, coupled with his addiction to smoking, eventually took his life. He had his first stroke in 1961; it left him temporarily paralyzed on his left side. He did recover from the stroke and actually played again, but his doctor told him that his heart valve needed to be surgically repaired. In April 1962 he underwent open heart surgery at the Indiana University Medical Center in Indianapolis. He did not survive the operation. He died on Friday, April 13, 1962. Open heart surgery at that time was relatively new. The heart and lung machine used to keep a patient alive during surgery was developed at Indiana University but was then in its infancy. This same operation today would have probably had a better outcome.

Dad's surgeon was Dr. H. B. Schumacker, Jr., one of the best heart surgeons in the country at the time. In the following letter, Dr. Schumacker explained to Mom the circumstances that led to Dad's death:

INDIANA UNIVERSITY
Medical Center
1100 WEST MICHIGAN STREET
INDIANAPOLIS 7, INDIANA

NT OF SURGERY   April 16, 1962

Mrs. Ferdinanido Cortellini
3909 Audubon Road
Indianapolis, Indiana

Dear Mrs. Cortellini:

I can never tell you adequately how very sorry indeed I am that we were not successful in getting your wonderful husband through this second operation. Ofcourse this is my objective with every patient. I was particularly anxious in the case of your husband since I had gotten to know him so well and had such admiration for him. As you know from our conversation during the day we had met with these terribly unexpected and dire changes in heart rhythm throughout the operative procedure and had indeed dispaired of ever getting him off the table alive for the greater part of this period. I considered that we were very lucky indeed when we returned him to the recovery room in pretty good condition. I felt, as you also know, that he made some definite improvement throughout the afternoon. Unfortunately, as you know from your conversations with Dr. Hawtof, things began to change for the worse. We were in touch withone another throughout the remaining period of his survival. You know that I would have been out here had there been anything in the world that I could have done over and beyond what Dr. Hawtof and the others were doing for him.

I'm so glad that you had us carry out a post mortem examination. I believe that this gives us an answer to the unexpected troubles with his heart rhythm which we encountered during the operation. In addition to the trouble with his mitral valve for which we were operating, this post mortem examination shows that he had very severe narrowing of the coronary arteries as a result of arteriosclerosis. This was an unexpected finding. The coronary arteries are the arteries which supply the heart muscle itself with blood and it is quite obvious that he had only a marginal supply of blood to the heart muscle. I think this accounts for the rhythm difficulties which initiated the train of events which ultimately led to his tragic death.

We wish we could have gotten him through and restored him to health. I want to express to you and to your family my very deepest sympathy.

Yours sincerely,

H B Schumacker Jr

Harris B Shumacker, Jr., M.D.

HBS/msw

Dr. Schumacker's letter to Mom

Our good friend Bea Fink was kind enough to respond on Mom's behalf to Dr. Schumacker in the following letter:

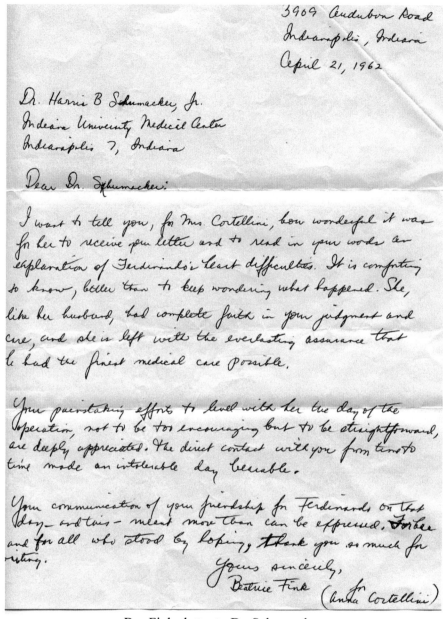

Bea Finks letter to Dr. Schumacker

The Indianapolis symphony society was devastated by Dad's passing. A memorial concert was held in his honor, performing works believed to be Dad's favorites.

The venue was the Broad Ripple High School auditorium, and the program performed by members of the Indianapolis Symphony Orchestra was the following:

Bach chorales
Shubert's "Symphony No. 8" ("Unfinished Symphony")
Delius's "On Hearing the First Cuckoo of Spring"
Ravel's "Closing Movement to His Mother Goose Suite" ("Le Jardin Feerique")
Mascagni's "Intermezzo from Cavaleria Rusticana"

Numerous newspaper articles were written about his passing.

Henry Butler

Cortellini — Our Symphony Lost More Than a Mere Man

THE DEATH OF Ferdinando Cortellini, principal violist of the Indianapolis Symphony, meant not only a loss to the orchestra and the community.

It meant also a loss to the art and the profession of music in terms of a man's sincere devotion.

If there is one thing the serious arts share with religion, it is this kind of devotion, which transcends most worldly concerns and makes the pursuit of gain seem shallow.

Quite possibly Cortellini could have made more money in some other line than music, but certainly he would not have been happy so doing. In fact, he would not have been Cortellini.

His colleagues in the orchestra, who will remember him as a kindly, gently humorous soul, will remember him also as a man satisfied with nothing less than the best achievement within his power.

He was dedicated to perfectionism.

THE FACADE of a musician seldom reveals what goes on inside his personality. Like the rest of us, he has learned to conceal sensitivity, to make a brave and, if need be, comical front.

Unlike the rest of us, the musician lives, moves and has his being in a medium indescribable in words. Even the Italian technical terms like "andante" or "allegro" on musical scores are mere approximations.

At any orchestra rehearsal you learn that the ultimate instructions, the most vital refinements of a conductor's intentions, are not verbally conveyed. The conductor must sing or hum or make the peculiar but universally understood "DEE-da-da-da" musically rhythmic but logically nonsensical syllables which his musicians then will translate into performance.

In the course of performance, both conductor and musicians are quite literally out of this world. They are in a realm of their own which their listeners never com-

pletely penetrate or understand.

EVEN the musicians, with all their technical knowledge and their sharply critical ears for each other's playing, cannot tell you what almost supernatural possession takes hold of an orchestra in a fine performance. In a fine performance, each member of the orchestra may transcend himself. He may do better than he ever thought he could.

One clear memory of Cortellini concerns his playing the wonderful viola solo early in Enesco's A Major Rumanian Rhapsody. It's

like a quotation from a concerto. It briefly combines virtuosity with lyrical intensity in one of the most appealing episodes in either of the Rhapsodies.

Cortellini played it beautifully. And I am sure that Izler Solomon and the orchestra must have felt, as I did, that here was an unforgettable expression of a devoted musician's artistry.

Indianapolis news article on Dad's death

In honor of my father, I dedicate the following recipe in remembrance of the good times we had making and eating pasta together.

Making Ravioli di Magro

The pasta is Ravioli di Magro (ravioli filled with a spinach ricotta). To make the pasta, use the same pasta recipe for the lasagna fresh pasta dough in chapter 7 and roll the dough to #7 thickness on the KitchenAid pasta machine—or one-sixteenth-inch thickness, as for the Capelletti in chapter 8.

Ravioli di Magro (Ravioli with Spinach and Ricotta)
Category: Paste (Pastas)
Origin: Mamma Cortellini
Serves 8–10

Pasta: See fresh pasta recipe

The key to this dish is ensuring that the pasta is thin and delicate. All aspects of the dish are subtleties, from the mild taste of the ricotta filling with a slight accent of nutmeg to the butter sauce infused with sage and shallots. I prefer to drink a good Italian light red wine with this dish.

Pasta filling

Ingredients:
2 boxes frozen chopped spinach
2 Tbsp. butter
1 lb. ricotta cheese (whole milk)
Parmigiano-Reggiano cheese, freshly grated
1 egg
Nutmeg

Preparation:
1. In a skillet, heat the frozen spinach on low heat to eliminate the water from the spinach. When the water is evaporated, add two tablespoons of butter and simmer. Do not let it burn.
2. When the spinach is cool, squeeze it dry and place it in a bowl; add the ricotta cheese and egg.Stir in the Parmigiano cheese and the nutmeg. I like the taste of nutmeg, so I add an additional quarter teaspoon or more. Add salt and freshly ground pepper and mix. The consistency must hold together, so you may need to add more cheese to firm up the mixture.

Stuffing the ravioli

Preparation:
1. As you roll out the pasta sheets and cut the ravioli circles, place a small amount of the stuffing in the center of the circle. Fold in half and press the pasta ends together firmly until sealed.
2. It is important to have a tight seal, or the filling will escape during cooking.
3. You should work one sheet at a time and stuff the raviolis for the sheet you're working immediately after cutting, so that the pasta will not dry, making it difficult to seal. If the pasta dries, you can dip your finger in a glass of water and wet the inside edges of the ravioli to make a better seal.
4. Preferably, this pasta process should be done by more than one person, with one working the pasta and the other stuffing the raviolis.
5. A serving should be between seven and nine raviolis per person.
6. As soon as they are stuffed, lay out the raviolis on a baking sheet to dry. I place parchment paper on the baking sheet and spread either white cornmeal or flour on the paper to prevent the raviolis from sticking to the paper or surface.
7. Let dry for three to four hours, turning them occasionally. Preferably, they should be kept in a cool location to prevent the cheese from spoiling.
8. At this point the raviolis can also be frozen to be used at a later date.

The sauce

Ingredients:
½ lb. unsalted butter
2–3 shallots, finely chopped
A bunch of fresh sage, finely chopped

Preparation:
1. Sauté the shallots in half a stick of butter until soft.
2. Add the remaining butter and chopped sage.
3. Simmer until butter is melted and sage is infused in the butter.

Preparing the pasta:
1. In a large, heavy-bottomed pot, bring water to a boil, adding salt to the water.
2. When water is at a full boil, add the raviolis. (If the raviolis are stuck to the paper, submerge the paper in the boiling water to release them. Do not attempt to pull them from the paper.)
3. When the raviolis surface in the water, continue cooking for one or two minutes and remove them from the boiling water using a large slotted spoon.
4. Place them in a shallow pasta bowl.
5. Add the butter/shallot sauce and stir the pasta gently.
6. Add a ladle of pasta water, if needed.
7. Serve on warm dishes and add grated Parmigiano-Reggiano on top of the ravioli. Serve immediately.

Drying the pasta

Ravioli rising to the surface

Mixing the sauce

Serving the Ravioli

Chapter 10

Life Goes On

Dad's death was a life-changing event for our family. Mom lost the love of her life. And although Dad was an exceptional artist, he was not much of a financial planner. He had only a small term life policy provided by the symphony union. The memorial concert raised a little money, and there were numerous donations from colleagues and patrons. The Lilly Foundation donated $10,000, which was a lifesaver. Mom also sold Dad's viola. When combined, these resources provided a small cushion, but the prospect of continuing to maintain the house, pay the mortgage, and raise three children was daunting.

Mom's parents urged her to return to Ancona to live with them. However, they were aging and were already living with Mom's sister, Zia Marisa, so she did not want to add an additional burden on her family. What's more, Douglas was in the fourth grade, and Corrado and I were finishing high school; so she did not want to uproot us.

Mom decided to remain in Indianapolis with her circle of friends and to try to leverage her dressmaking skills to supplement her social security benefits. She established an in-house seamstress service in the lower level of our home at 3909 N. Audubon Road. Having already established her clientele through the symphony society as a hobby, she now counted on them for our livelihood. Her customer base expanded as word spread of her exceptional talent. Her client list contained well-known names in Indianapolis, including Lilly, Clowes, Goodman, and other symphony patrons. Mom became renowned for making wedding dresses with complex lace veils, evening gowns, and even fur coats.

Mom and symphony friends

As an artisan Mom was extraordinary, but she had no business sense. She refused to charge customers a market rate for her services. Fortunately, her customers always paid her more than she asked. Try as I might, I was never able to convince her to increase the pricing on her dressmaking work. At age seventeen I became Mom's bookkeeper, but she refused to expand her work into a bona fide business. She was a mother and homemaker by day and a seamstress by night. I recall on several occasions waking her from her slouched position at the sewing machine table as I arose for school.

Mom at work

Etching by Corrado

After Dad's death, and with Mom fully consumed in providing for her family, Corrado and I found ourselves left to our own devices. Without Dad's strict discipline, and with Mom's preoccupation with her work and raising Douglas, Corrado and I made immature and misguided decisions that had a significant impact on our personal and professional development.

Corrado dropped out of Purdue University where he was majoring in Aeronautical Engineering. In June 1962 he married his high school sweetheart, Karen Cornelius.

Karen and Corrado's wedding (Mom made the dresses for the wedding) and my wedding
with Sue (Mom also made the dresses)

After high school, instead of starting college, I took a job at Indiana National Bank. One year later, like Corrado, I married my high school sweetheart, Camilla Sue Budreau, Karen's cousin.

In the years that ensued, Corrado and I each had two children. Corrado's son was named Anthony, and his daughter Lea was named after our grandmother. My children were named Tina and Gino. Gino was named after my grandfather.

Tony and Lea   Gino and Tina

Corrado's talents were in art, math, and music, and he eventually pursued a career in the arts. While working at Wolner Associates, Architects (a part of Oxford Development Corp.), as a draftsman designing multi-unit housing complexes, Corrado attended night classes at John Herron Art Institute. He eventually graduated with a degree in sculpture. He also passed the architect licensing test and was certified as an architect outside of the educational requirements. Although he was an architect, his passion was in the arts. He even taught himself to play the classical Spanish guitar.

SUNDAY, APRIL 12, 1992   PAGE G-11

CLOWES MEMORIAL HALL
Conrad Cortellini watches installation of his work.

Cortellini 'Vortex' panels displayed in Clowes Hall

Indianapolis artist Conrad Corrado Cortellini's original art titled *Total Perspective Vortex* has been installed in Clowes Hall of Butler University.

Cortellini created the two-panel piece to honor Dr. Benoit Mandelbrot's discovery and development of the fractal geometry concept in 1989.

Commissioned by Domenic Angelicchio and Dr. Marc Stone, the piece is on loan to Butler and can be viewed before Clowes performances and from 10 a.m. to 6 p.m. Monday through Saturday.

Each panel measures 6 feet square and is divided into 36 sections. Each section has 12 different colored layers stacked one on top of the other.

Cortellini, a native of Italy, came to Indianapolis as a child when his father took the first-chair viola position with the Indianapolis Symphony Orchestra.

He became interested in the application of mathematical concepts to art in the 1980s and used computers to help create *Total Perspective Vortex.*

Total Perspective Vortex is a two-panel piece.

Total Perspective Vortex art piece is still displayed at Clowes Hall

Our early exit from Mom's dependency relieved her of a burden, enabling her to focus her parenting time on Douglas. However, we remained close as a family and frequently enjoyed the fruits of Mom's exceptional cooking. It was during this period that I began collecting her recipes.

After graduating from high school, I received a reference from a symphony patron that led to my employment at Indiana National Bank. I worked as a clerk in the proof and transit department. This group's purpose was to prove each deposit made to a customer's account and to collect deposited checks drawn on other banks. I did this from 1962 through 1969. Today this process is highly automated, with little human intervention. In 1962 it was a manual process, with three shifts working twenty-four hours a day, seven days a week. In this department were two processes that were combined into a single operation. Proving a deposit meant the verification of the dollar amount of a check or draft deposited by the bank's customer. The proof machine verified the amount and simultaneously encoded the amount on the check with magnetic ink (MICR) for automated processing. The checks were also sorted in groupings to be sent as cash letters to corresponding banks, clearinghouses, and the Federal Reserve clearing system. The transit function was the actual distribution of the groupings of checks and drafts in the form of cash letters that were deposited or traded in the banks clearing system. This process occurred day and night at the bank.

The 1961 IBM 803 Proof Machine

Without a college degree, my opportunities for advancement were limited. After having spent several years in the bank's clearing factory and working my way up to shift supervisor, I decided that this sort of work did not fit my long-term aspirations. I enrolled at Indiana University, majoring in accounting. With a wife and two children to support, I attended classes at the Indianapolis campus while I continued to work at the bank. The bank's three shifts afforded me the flexibility of choosing which shift best fit my class schedules. I chose to work the night shift and attend school during the day. Finding time to sleep was a problem. My work day started at 10:00 p.m. and ended at 7:00 a.m., definitely not customary bankers' hours.

I made a number of lasting friends during this period. Jim Fahy, who graduated several years behind me at Scecina, also came to work in the same department at Indiana National Bank. We became the closest of friends and took pride in keeping the department in balance. However, he also tired of the work and left before I did, joining the military in 1966. He went on to graduate from Indiana University after leaving military duty. We later met up again in Europe while working for another Indianapolis bank. The international banking branch of American Fletcher National Bank in Luxembourg provided both of us with work vastly more interesting than what we had been doing in the basement of the headquarters of Indiana National Bank in Indianapolis.

Another close friend from my time at Indiana National Bank was Scott Lyons. We had many good laughs together, and he recalls the time I got my tie stuck in the check entry slot of the IBM proof machine. My tie had to be cut to prevent my death by choking. Who says banking is not dangerous work? I also sang tenor for the Indiana National Bank Christmas choir. We performed in the bank lobby at noon during Christmas season, on Monument Circle, at the Indiana Women's Prison, and once on the radio. Here is a link to the video I created of the 1967 performance on Monument Circle:

http://www.youtube.com/watch?v=JgJLTl-h5Pk.

The work and school commitment took a toll on my relationship with my wife and children. Between work and school, little time was available for anything else. As is common with teenage marriages, Camilla and I grew apart. In April 1971 she filed for divorce, and I became a weekend father.

I left Indiana National Bank in 1969 and went to work at Oxford Development Corporation as assistant controller, with duties more in line with my studies. I continued my education at night and eventually graduated from IU with a BS in accounting. While at Oxford Development, I met the love of my life. Rosalind Grant worked as an administrative assistant to the president. There was a natural attraction between us, and in April 1972, we were married. We recently celebrated our forty-first anniversary.

Our wedding

Graduation, finally!

Being Catholic, Mom was not pleased about my divorce, but she understood the circumstances. She instantly fell in love with Roz the day they met.

Wedding reception

Mom was supportive of our decision to marry, and, of course, she made the wedding dress. Corrado played three roles at our wedding—he was my best man, he was our photographer, and he provided the music.

Shortly after our wedding, I was recruited by Coopers and Lybrand (then called Lybrand, Ross Brothers, and Montgomery; now called Price Waterhouse Coopers) from Oxford Development to join their auditing firm. I assisted Coopers in preparing a registration statement for Oxford's public stock offering. The offering did not make it to market, but the experience was a boost for my career. Coopers was in need of someone with construction/development experience and the opportunity to work in the public accounting field was necessary for me to get my CPA certification. It was during this period that Roz and I developed a close friendship with Jim Kubinski and his wife Cindy. Jim and I worked together on the registration statement for Oxford Development and later worked side by side on audit engagements, which included banks, collieries, wholesale distributors, and food manufacturers. We remain close friends to this day. The years at Coopers were some of the best of our lives; things were finally going our way.

Coopers gang at Kub's house

We moved into a small home on Kessler Boulevard, which still stands today and is as quaint as ever. What a bargain at twenty-five thousand dollars!

Our house on Kessler and Mom cooking in her kitchen

Mom and Roz developed a great relationship. I also became very close with Roz's parents. I felt that Roz's mother, Norma, liked me as much as Roz did. Roz began to pick up Mom's cooking skills and also began journaling her recipes for posterity. The recipes in this chapter and subsequent chapters come from these collections, which were perfected in our weekly get-togethers under Mom's supervision and critique. The recipes that I offer in this chapter include favorites from this period.

Chapter 10 Recipes

Peperonata (Sautéed Peppers and Onions)
Pasta con Sugo di Cotolette di Maiale (Pasta with Pork Rib Sauce)
Pollo alla Cacciatore (Hunter's Chicken)
Pesce al Forno con Rosmarino (Baked Fish with Rosemary Topping)
Mom's Apple Pie and Coffee

Peperonata (Sautéed Peppers and Onions)

Category: Antipasti (Appetizers)
Origin: Mamma Cortellini's Version
Serves 4–6

With this dish, if you like it, you can't get enough. We serve it as a starter with toasted Italian bread to soak up the juices. Roz will sometimes add a sprinkling of balsamic vinegar, any variety of the fine ISOLA's Balsamic Vinegar of Modena, before adding the tomatoes to give it a deeper flavor. I sometimes add a little extra chili pepper flakes or whole chilies to give it more of a bite. This dish works well as an appetizer and can be refrigerated for five to seven days. Whenever I have taken this dish to work functions, I have always, without fail, been asked for the recipe.

Ingredients:
4 red peppers (can mix with yellow and orange)
1 large yellow onion
Bunch of fresh basil, chopped coarsely
1 cup chopped tomatoes (fresh in the summer)

Hot chili pepper flakes to taste
¼ cup extra-virgin olive oil (I use My Brother's by ISOLA, from Puglia)
Kosher salt and freshly ground black pepper to taste

Preparation:
1. Clean the peppers, coring them and removing the membranes and seeds.
2. Cut the peppers into quarters and, crosswise, cut the quarters into half-inch strips or small pieces so that they can be easily placed on crackers (don't make them too thin).
3. Slice the onion into quarters and slice crosswise into same-sized pieces. The key is to make the pieces uniform so they cook evenly.
4. Place peppers and onion in frying skillet with the olive oil.
5. Sauté over medium heat until soft.
6. Add tomatoes, basil, pepper flakes, salt, and pepper.
7. Cook, partially covered, until most of the liquid evaporates.
8. Let cool and serve at room temperature.

Pasta con Sugo di Cotolette di Maiale (Pasta with Pork Rib Sauce)
Category: Paste (Pastas)
Origin: Mama Cortellini
Serves 4–6

This is a sauce that Mom would prepare at the last minute on Sundays when we would drop in on her. I don't know if it has an origin in Italy or not, but there is surely some version in Italy that is similar. In any case, it makes a great pasta sauce. Roz makes a version of this sauce by using baby back ribs; she shreds the meat off the bone and mixes the shredded meat with the sauce. A strong red wine is recommended.

Ingredients:
2–3 lb. pork ribs (off bone, country-style)
¼ cup extra-virgin olive oil for frying the ribs
1 large yellow onion, chopped
Small glass of white wine
1 lb. can or box of Italian chopped or diced tomatoes (I use Pomi by Parmalat)
Marjoram to taste
Red chili pepper flakes (peperoncini), optional but recommended
Small glass of chicken stock
Kosher salt and freshly ground black pepper to taste
Parmigiano-Reggiano, or Pecorino if you want a stronger cheese flavor
1 lb. pasta asciutta (dried pasta) such as spaghetti, penne, fusilli, or other dried pasta

Preparation:

1. If the ribs are too long, cut them in half and remove excess fat.
2. In a large, heavy pot, add enough olive oil to cover the bottom so that the ribs will not stick. Don't add too much oil as the ribs will create their own fat when cooking.
3. Brown the ribs on both sides over medium heat and salt and pepper them.
4. Add the chopped onions and fry until the onions become translucent and soft.
5. Turn up the heat and add the wine to deglaze the pan.
6. Bring the heat down to medium; add the chopped tomatoes and chicken stock.
7. Add the marjoram and pepper flakes; turn up the heat to bring the sauce to a boil.
8. When sauce begins to boil, turn the heat down to medium-low and let simmer for one to one and a half hours, or until the ribs begin to fall apart.
9. Cook the pasta according to package instructions (Nic likes penne); remove the ribs from the sauce, and be sure to skim off the excess oil from the sauce so that it's not too greasy.
10. Serve the meat in a separate dish and add the sauce to the pasta in a suitable pasta bowl.
11. Serve the pasta, adding the Parmigiano-Reggiano—or, if you like a stronger flavor, add Italian Pecorino (Romano; not domestic).
12. Serve with a hearty Italian red table wine such as a Chianti, Monepulciano d' Abruzze, or Rosso di Conero from Ancona.

Pollo alla Cacciatore (Hunter's Chicken)

Category: Carni (Meats)
Origin: Mamma Cortellini
Serves 4

This is another one of those comfort foods that Mom made at least once a week. Make extra sauce, because it is superb with some good Italian or French bread. This was one of Joan Bellissimo's favorite recipes of Mom's. If you are just a white meat eater, this dish is not intended for you. Dark meat such as thighs, legs and wings work best as the meat with bones remains moist when cooking and the inclusion of dark meat makes the sauce tastier. Dad insisted that Mom include the neck of the chicken in the pot.

Ingredients:

1 whole frying chicken, cut into pieces (separate the thigh from the drumstick and include the neck, if you are so inclined)
¼ cup extra-virgin olive oil
4–5 garlic cloves, 3-4 sliced and 1 of which should be minced
2 large sprigs of fresh rosemary
½ box (or 14 oz. can) chopped or crushed Italian tomatoes (the equivalent fresh tomatoes can be used when available)

9090Kosher salt and ground black pepper to taste

Preparation:
1. In a large skillet, fry the chicken in the olive oil until the liquid created by the chicken evaporates.
2. Add the garlic, rosemary, salt, and pepper and brown the chicken, being careful not to burn the garlic.
3. Add tomatoes and turn the pieces of chicken occasionally.
4. Cook, partially covered, until chicken meat comes off the bone (about an hour and a half altogether).

Pesce al Forno con Rosmarino (Baked Fish with Rosemary Topping)
Category: Pesci (Fish)
Origin: Mamma Cortellini
Serves 4–6

Mom often prepared this dish in Florida with fresh grouper or red snapper. There is nothing better. The key is to get the right combination of garlic and rosemary and to not use too much of either, as that may overpower the taste of the fish. You can also use dried rosemary, which may not be as strong-tasting. Roz makes her own bread crumbs with a food processor, using ciabatta or similar Italian bread. My favorite bread crumbs for this dish, however, are panko bread crumbs as they remain crispy throughout cooking.

Ingredients:
1½–2 lb. flaky large white fish (red snapper, sea bass, grouper, halibut, etc.) Use the whole fish, either removing the skin or placing skin side down. Preparation on the outdoor grill adds another dimension.
1–2 long stems of rosemary, chopped
¼ cup extra-virgin olive oil
1 cup bread crumbs (I like to use panko bread crumbs as they remain crispy; you can also use fresh bread crumbs made from Italian bread, but I would avoid store-bought crumbs)
1 large clove garlic, minced
Kosher salt and freshly ground black pepper to taste

Preparation:
1. Rinse fish and pat dry.
2. Remove the needles of the rosemary from the stem and finely chop them along with the garlic.
3. Place the rosemary/garlic mixture in a small bowl and add the bread crumbs.
4. Slowly drizzle the olive oil into the mixture, stirring, mixing, and moistening the bread

crumbs.

5. Spread some of the olive oil in a baking pan and lay the fish in of the oiled dish.
6. Spread the rosemary topping on the topside of the fish, patting it lightly and covering the entire piece.
7. Bake the fish at 375°F for fifteen to twenty minutes. Check fish to ensure that it is fully cooked; when it firms up; make sure that the topping is lightly browned.

The topping

The cooking

The serving

For a lighter touch instead of mincing the garlic and adding it to the rosemary mixture, smash the garlic clove and sauté it in the olive oil until lightly golden. Remove the garlic clove from the oil, let it cool and then add the infused olive oil to the mixture.

Mom's Apple Pie and Coffee

Category: Dolci (Desserts)
Origin: Mamma Cortellini's Adaptation
Serves 6–8

This is the famous "apple pie and coffee" treat that all Italians learned to make fifty years ago when first arriving in the United States. The story goes that as Tony disembarked at New York from

Sicily, he met his cousin Vinnie, and they walked to a nearby café. Vinnie said to Tony, "You will never go hungry in this country if you learn how to say apple pie and coffee." Tony learned his lessons well, and after three weeks of only eating apple pie and coffee, Tony decided to be adventurous. He looked up Bistecca (Italian for "steak") in his Italian/English translation book. He ran all the way to the café and immediately said to the waiter, "Steak." The waiter responded, "Rare, medium, or well done?" to which Tony replied, "Apple pie and coffee." Mom's apple pie was always exceptional, and when served with a good espresso and a scoop or maybe two of vanilla ice cream, it was to die for.

Ingredients:
5–6 apples (Fuji mixed with Granny Smith)
1 cup sugar
¼ cup flour
1 tsp. cinnamon
¼–½ tsp. squeezed lemon juice
½ tsp. salt
Pie crust dough
Unsalted butter to dot over the filling

Preparation:
1. Peel and cut the apples in large chunks so that they do not dissolve when cooked.
2. In a bowl, add the apples and all the other ingredients.
3. Stir and mix thoroughly.
4. In a pie pan, roll out the bottom portion of the pie dough to cover the pan.
5. Layer the filling in the pie pan distributing evenly.
6. Dot the filling with butter.
7. Layer over with the top crust, crimping the edges to seal the pie.
8. Slice air vents in the top to allow for moisture to escape.
9. Bake at 350 degrees for 50 minutes or until crust is golden.
10. Remove from oven and let stand until cool.
11. Serve with good vanilla ice cream (e.g., Haagen-Dazs) and a good espresso e.g., Nespresso).

Chapter 11

Mom Remarries

After Corrado and I left home, Mom continued her dressmaking work to support Douglas. She made a trip back to Ancona in 1963 to visit her aging parents and her brother and sister, accompanied by a family friend, Hugh Matheny, who was then first oboist for the Indianapolis Symphony Orchestra. They traveled on the Italian liner Christoforo Colombo, leaving Douglas, who was ten years old at the time, with Corrado and Karen.

Hugh Matheny (1937–1996)

Mom on her way to New York
to board ship

SS Christoforo Colombo, New York to Genoa, 1963

Luncheon menu

Having lost her beloved Ferdinando a year earlier, this journey to her homeland was less joyful for Mom than the previous journey. In addition, she knew that this visit could be the last time she would see her parents. Nevertheless, she was happy to be headed to Ancona to be reunited with her family.

Zio Raul and family

Zia Marisa and family

Upon Mom's return to Indianapolis, she continued to struggle to make ends meet. Maintaining her house and providing for young Douglas was difficult for her.

In 1964 Mom met Dr. Mathew Cornacchione, formerly a surgeon but then in general practice on the north side of Indianapolis. She met him through one of her dressmaking clients who happened to be Dr. Cornacchione's nurse. His companionship provided Mom with the needed diversion from financial struggles and also gave her a chance for a life of her own. He took great pleasure in Mom's culinary skills. Dr. Cornacchione had an ailing mother, and it became absolutely clear that there would be no commitment or consideration of marriage as long as his mother was living. It reminds me of the Italian mother-and-son relationship in the movie Moonstruck, with Cher and Nicholas Cage. Mom's relationship with Dr. Cornacchione continued for ten years until they finally married on August 13, 1974, after his mother's death. By then Douglas had moved away from home and married Deborah Campbell. After her marriage, Mom sold the house on Audubon Road and moved into Dr. Cornacchione's house on Carrollton Court, near Roz's and my residence on the north side of Indianapolis.

Mom's marriage to Dr. Cornacchione; Mom and Dr. Cornacchione in Florida

Douglas chose not to attend college; instead, he gained fame on the professional miniature golf circuit. He later took a job with DuPont, selling paint, which led to a successful career in the automotive aftermarket business. Deborah, a graduate of Ball State University, chose a career in teaching and is still teaching today. After a series of moves with NAPA, Douglas and Deborah settled in Plymouth, Michigan, near Detroit, where they raised three beautiful children: Christopher, Joseph, and Andrew.

Two of their children graduated from the University of Michigan and the other from Albion College. Douglas is currently district manager for the mid-west district of the LKQ Corporation. Their middle son, Joe, just recently married Allison Mills in a memorable celebration. Attending the wedding from Ancona was my second cousin Francesco Rismondo and his wife Valeria. Francesco is the youngest son of my cousin, Anna Maria Rismondo.

Douglas   Douglas and Deborah

Douglas and Deborah's wedding
Mom made the wedding dresses

FRANCESCO & VALERIA RISMONDO-COUSINS FROM ANCONA

CONRAD & PATTY CORTELLINI-OLDER BROTHER

DOUGLAS & DEB CORTELLINI YOUNGER BROTHER

JOE & ALLISON CORTELLINI DOUG'S MIDDLE SON

CHRIS CORTELLINI DOUG'S OLDEST SON

ANDREW CORTELLINI DOUG'S YOUNGEST SON

ROZ AND I

Joe and Allison's wedding

The twenty recipes in this chapter include one of Dr. Cornacchione's and many of Mom's favorites from our Sunday dinners together. These make up the core of Mom's collection and include:

Antipasto Misto (Mixed Appetizer)
Ciabotto (Ratatouille – Mom's Version)
Pepperoni Arrostiti (Roasted Red Peppers)
Pesce Marinato (Mom's Marinated Fish)
Stracciatella alla Romana (Italian Egg Drop Soup)
Minestrone (Vegetable Soup with Pasta)
Veluto di Verdure (Mom's Vegetable Soup)
Zuppa di Indivia (Endive Soup with Meatballs)
Brodo di Manzo (Beef Broth and Boiled Beef)
Pasta Ceci (Chickpea Pasta)
Mom's Ragu (Spaghetti Sauce)
Rolata di Manzo con Sugo per Pasta (Beef Roll with Pasta Sauce)
Uccelletti con Sugo per Pasta (Little Bird Rolls with Pasta Sauce)
Crocchette di Pollo (Chicken Patties)
Arrosto di Agnello (Roasted Leg of Lamb)
Pizzaiola (Veal Spezzetini in Pizzaiola Sauce)
Pollo con Cipolla e Vino (Chicken with Onion and Wine)
Finocchi alla Parmigiana (Sautéed Fennel with Parmazan)

Fagiolini, Patate, e Pomodoro (Green Beans with Potatoes and Tomatoes)
Uova con Cipolla e Pomodoro (Eggs with Onion and Tomatoes)
Pizzelle (Anise Cookies)

Antipasto Misto (Mixed Antipasto)
Category: Antipasti (Appetizers)
Origin: Mamma Cortellini and Dr. Cornacchione
Serves 6–8

This was Dr. Cornacchione's recipe from Abruzzi, which we have modified over time. The key to the recipe is the quality of the ingredients, some of which may be difficult to find in authentic Italian versions. The tuna used should be a high-quality tuna packed in olive oil, not water. Also, and contrary to Roz's opinion, the order of the placement of ingredients does have a bearing on the taste. Don't change the order, or it won't taste like it should. Don't forget to tell your guests that the olives are not pitted—or make sure the premiums are paid on your liability insurance policy. Fix only what you expect to eat as it is not as tasty the next day.

Ingredients:
Lettuce—leaf type (Romaine)—torn into bite-size pieces
¼ lb. salami (good hard Italian salami, Genoa, Milano, or Filzette), sliced and cut into
    quarters or bite-size pieces
2–3 roasted red peppers, cut into thin strips (see separate recipe for roasting peppers);
    I recommend against the use of store-bought prepared roasted peppers
¼ cup marinated mixed vegetables, normally called Giardiniera (use hot Giardiniera
    or add a chopped jalapeño pepper)
1 small jar good-quality artichoke hearts (I prefer imported from Spain), quartered and
    then sliced into thin slices
1 can quality tuna packed in olive oil
2–3 stalks of celery, cut into small pieces
½ medium red onion sliced, paper-thin, in rings
3–4 fresh Roma plum tomatoes, sliced thin in rounds
3–4 hardboiled eggs, sliced
Italian imported Provolone cheese, grated large/long
Kalamata Greek olives
Capers and anchovies (optional)
Extra-virgin olive oil and balsamic vinegar
Kosher salt and freshly ground black pepper

Preparation:
1. Select a large, flat serving platter, sized according to the number of servings you want
    to prepare. Round platters seem to work better.
2. Cover the platter with the pieces of lettuce. Try not to leave gaps in the coverage.
3. Cover the lettuce with the pieces of salami, again not leaving gaps but also not
    covering the edges of the lettuce on the plate. If the salami is in a large round, cut the
    slices in half for easier serving. Make sure that the salami is cut very thin. Unless
    you have very sharp knives, have your deli slice it for you. I use Volpe brand,
    as Italian imported salamis are currently not available in the United States.
4. Spread the roasted peppers evenly over the salami and sprinkle a few teaspoonsful of
    the juice from the peppers over the platter.
5. Mince the Giardiniera with a mezzaluna (see below) and spread it evenly over the

platter. I use hot Giardiniera to give the dish a bite.
6. Spread the sliced artichoke hearts evenly over the tuna.
7. Flake the tuna in its can and soak up the oil in the can. Spread the tuna evenly over the platter.
8. Spread the celery evenly over the tuna.
9. Separate the onion slices into rings and spread evenly over the celery.
10. Spread the tomato slices over the onions.
11. Spread the hardboiled egg slices over the tomatoes.
12. Sprinkle the grated Provolone cheese over the entire platter, blanketing the platter.
13. Distribute the olives on top of the cheese.
14. Add the capers and anchovies if you desire. (We normally leave them off to lighten the flavor, they could be added separately)
15. At this point you can cover with plastic wrap and keep in the refrigerator prior to serving. This is best served right away but can be refrigerated several hours.
16. Just before serving, salt and pepper to taste and add the oil and vinegar.
17. Serve with a spatula, and be sure to serve all layers in one helping.

Antipasto Misto ready to serve

Ciabotto (Ratatouille – Mom's Version)
Category: Antipasti/Verdure (Appetizers/Vegetables)
Origin: Mamma Cortellini
Serves 4–6

This is a much more substantial version than its French sister ratatouille as it contains potatoes. I like to add chili pepper flakes to give it more zest. Serve as a vegetable to liven up main dishes.

Ingredients:
½ cup extra-virgin olive oil
1 large yellow onion, chopped
2 red peppers and one green pepper, cleaned, seeded and membranes removed, cut into quarters and then into 3 to 4 pieces
2 small eggplants, quartered lengthwise and then cut crosswise into pieces

2 potatoes, peeled and cubed
2 small zucchini, sliced
15 oz. can or ½ box Italian chopped or diced tomatoes
Chili pepper flakes
Bunch of basil, coarsely chopped or torn
Kosher salt and freshly ground pepper

Preparation:
1. In a large skillet, heat the oil and first sauté the onions and peppers together.
2. When the onion is soft and translucent, add the potatoes and eggplants.
3. Continue cooking ten minutes over medium heat.
4. Add the zucchini and cook for another five minutes.
5. Add the tomatoes, chili pepper flakes, and basil; cover partially and cook another twenty or twenty-five minutes or until most of the liquid has thickened.
6. Remove from heat. Let cool and serve at room temperature.
7. Can also be refrigerated and served in the next few days. Keeps well in the refrigerator for five to seven days.

Ingredients

Stovetop cooking

Peperoni Arrostite (Roasted Red Peppers)

Category: Antipasti (Appetizers)
Origin: Mamma Cortellini
Serves 4–6

This antipasto is always a hit and will keep in the refrigerator for five to seven days. I use these peppers in the Antipasto Misto recipe or serve them alone as a starter with Italian bread. Soaking up the oil with the bread is a delight. The hazard in making this dish is peeling the scorched skin. Placing the peppers in a plastic or paper bag seems to steam the skin away from the flesh; however, you still need to have some heat tolerance as you need to do this before the peppers get cool. I usually let Roz do the peeling.

Ingredients:
4 good-quality, medium/large red bell peppers (they should be oval in shape instead of long, and the skin should not be damaged)
¼ cup extra-virgin olive oil
4–5 cloves of garlic, sliced

Preparation:
1. Trim the stems of the peppers so that they will stand on their tops.
2. Wash the peppers, but do not dry them.
3. Place them in a cast iron grill/skillet and turn heat to medium.
4. You need to monitor the cooking and turn them when the skin becomes scorched.
5. When the entire pepper is scorched, take them off and place them in a plastic or paper bag and seal it. Let stand for about five minutes.
6. Slice the garlic and put the slices along with half of the olive oil in a casserole or serving dish.
7. Remove one of the peppers from the bag at a time and take off the scorched peeling. This may be tedious as all the skin needs to be removed, even the skin that is not scorched.
8. Puncture one of the peppers and squeeze it over the serving dish to flavor the oil.
9. Slice open the pepper and remove the core and all the seeds and membrane.
10. Slice the peppers lengthwise in narrow strips and place them in the serving dish.
11. Once this is completed, pour the remaining olive oil over the peppers, enough to coat and provide a marinade for the peppers.
12. Add salt, cover, and refrigerate.
13. To serve, bring to room temperature, sprinkle fresh minced flat-leaf parsley.
14. These can be served alone as a starter or used in other recipes.

Scorching the peppers

Marinating the peppers

Pesce Fresco Sotto Cipolle e Aceto (Mom's Marinated Fish)

Category: Antipasti (Appetizers)
Origin: Mamma Cortellini
Serves 4

Mom would prepare this dish with whatever fish we could catch on the beach in Florida. Pinfish was a frequent catch. Pinfish is similar to perch in taste, but because it is so bony, it is difficult to clean. Nowadays we mostly catch whiting (or gulf kingfish) whenever they are biting, which is not as often as in the past. Our son Nic loves to catch the fish but isn't much on eating them unless I fry them.

Ingredients:
Freshly caught small saltwater fish such as whiting, pompano, or spotted sea trout
Medium sweet onion or a Vidalia onion
2 bay leaves
Whole peppercorns and mustard seeds
White wine vinegar
Kosher salt and freshly ground black pepper to taste

Preparation:
1. Clean the fish, removing scales, head, and intestines, and clean out the cavity thoroughly.
2. In a saucepan, cover the fish with water; add the bay leaves, peppercorns, and mustard seeds and simmer until the fish is thoroughly cooked and the meat begins to fall apart.
3. Remove from heat and let cool.
4. Remove the skin and pluck the meat off the bones, making sure that all bones are removed Only save the white meat of the fish.
5. Place the meat in a small bowl.
6. Slice the onion in very fine slices or slivers and cover the fish.
7. Add the wine vinegar, salt, and pepper, and stir.
8. Place the mixture in a plastic container and let marinate at least overnight. It is best after one or two days.
9. Serve with crackers and white wine as an antipasto.

Stracciatella alla Romana (Italian Egg Drop Soup)

Category: Minestre (Soups)
Origin: Mom's Version—Roman
Serves 6–8

This is another great holiday favorite for an initial serving between the antipasto and the pasta dishes. The traditional recipe calls for putting a pinch of fresh marjoram in the broth before serving. To sharpen the taste, use Pecorino cheese (Romano cheese) instead of Parmigiano-Reggiano. After all, this is a Roman dish.

Ingredients:
1–1½ qt. homemade beef or chicken broth (see separate recipes for broth)
6 eggs (one per person)
Zest of 1 lemon
12 saltine crackers (3 per egg), crumbled
1 cup grated Parmigiano-Reggiano
¼–½ tsp. freshly grated nutmeg
2 chicken or beef bouillon cubes (only if broth requires extra flavor)

Preparation:
1. In a mixing bowl, beat the eggs and add the grated lemon zest, Parmigiano-Reggiano cheese, cracker crumbs, and nutmeg.
2. In a soup pot, bring the broth to a boil; add the bouillon cubes if needed.
3. Before serving, slowly pour the Stracciatella mixture into the boiling broth. Do not stir. The broth will cook the mixture.
4. Once the mixture is firm, break up the egg by stirring over low heat to form small pieces.

Preparing the egg mixture

Serving

Minestrone (Vegetable Soup with Pasta)
Category: Minestre (Soups)
Origin: Mom's Version of Traditional Italian
Serves 4–6

This is the traditional Italian vegetable and pasta soup. When prepared in the summertime, it is good served at room temperature. The vegetables should be roughly chopped to bite size pieces so they retain their identity in the soup. Variations: Instead of adding all the vegetables to the water, heat the olive oil in the soup pot over medium heat, melt one tablespoon of butter in it, add the onion, and sauté over medium-low heat, stirring frequently until well golden (approximately ten minutes). Add the remaining vegetables, spices, salt, and pepper. Continue to cook, stirring frequently with a wooden spoon for fifteen minutes. Add the water and stock or bullion and tomatoes. Bring to a boil, reduce the heat, and simmer, partially covered, for another fifteen minutes. Always add Parmigiano-Reggiano and a helping of your finest extra-virgin olive oil before serving.

Ingredients:
6 cups cold water
1 small onion, coarsely chopped
2 small potatoes, in small pieces
2 carrots, coarsely chopped
¼ head of cabbage, coarsely chopped
2 celery stalks, coarsely chopped
1–2 chicken bouillons (optional)
2 small zucchini, coarsely chopped
2 garlic cloves, minced
Small bunch of basil leaves (or ½ to 1 tsp. dried basil)
½ package frozen peas
2–3 fresh tomatoes, peeled and finely chopped (can also use one 14.5-oz. can of plum
  tomatoes)
1 very small bay leaf
1 small can of cannellini beans or borlotti beans
½ lb. small pasta (Tubetti)
¼ cup extra-virgin olive oil
Kosher salt and freshly ground black pepper to taste
Freshly grated Parmigiano-Reggiano

Preparation:
1. In a large soup pot, add water, onions, potatoes, carrots, cabbage, and celery and boil
   gently until carrots are completely cooked (ten minutes).
2. Add the zucchini, garlic, basil, bay leaf, frozen peas, tomatoes, salt, pepper, and the
   beans and cook for another twenty to thirty minutes. Add the bouillon cubes if needed.
3. Half an hour before serving, cook the pasta separately al dente and add to the soup,
   with a drizzle of extra-virgin olive oil to taste.
4. Serve with a generous sprinkling of Parmigiano-Reggiano.

Chopped vegetables in water

Adding the tomatoes

Serve with olive oil
and Parmigiano-Reggiano

Velutata di Verdure (Mom's Vegetable Soup)
Category: Minestre (Soups)
Origin: Mamma Cortellini
Serves 6–8

This was the first dish that Roz enjoyed of Mom's cooking at our house on Audubon Road when we were dating, and it is still her favorite soup. The simple ingredients make it easy to prepare. The key is to have the water reduced to next to nothing so that the soup is not watery. You can use a hand immersion blender instead of food processor or a stand blender, but be sure it is not lumpy. It should be what Italians call a veluta (which means velvety).

Ingredients:
3 good-sized Roma tomatoes
2 carrots
3–4 celery stalks
2–3 medium potatoes
1 large onion
2 cloves garlic
1 handful of fresh green beans
½ box frozen peas
4–5 cabbage leaves
1 leek, cleaned retaining the white and light green parts
5–6 outer leaves of curly endive lettuce
A few white button mushrooms
Kosher salt and fresh ground pepper to taste
1–2 bouillon cubes (optional)
½ stick unsalted butter

Preparation:
1. Cut larger vegetables in small pieces and place in a large soup pot.
2. Cover vegetables with water.
3. Bring to a boil and let simmer until water is substantially reduced. Water must be
   practically gone.
4. Blend in a blender until a puree.
5. Place the blended vegetables in a saucepan over low heat; add one to two beef bouillons.

6. Add a teaspoon of dried sweet basil or fresh basil.
7. Add half a stick of butter.
8. Stir, reheat gently, and serve.
9. If too thick, add a little water.

The ingredients

The cooking-

The serving after blending

Zuppa di Indivia con Polpettine (Endive Soup with Meatballs)
Category: Minestre (Soups)
Origin: Mamma Cortellini
Serves 4–6

This is a soup our family serves during the holidays. The meatballs can also be simplified by not including the herbs and Parmigiano-Reggiano. It's a great replacement for a starter. It may also be known as the Italian wedding soup, but I've never had it at weddings when in Italy.

Ingredients:
1–1½ lb. fresh endive
½ lb. ground beef
½ egg, beaten
Zest of lemon,
Small garlic clove, minced
Small bunch of flat-leaf parsley, finely chopped
2 Tbsp. Parmigiano-Reggiano

Breadcrumbs, enough to dredge the meatballs
Kosher salt and freshly ground black pepper to taste

Preparation:
1. Boil endive in a pan until tender; chop it, squeeze it, and drain very well.
2. Mix the ground beef, egg, lemon zest, garlic, parsley, and Parmigiano-Reggiano in a
   bowl and form very small meatballs.
3. Roll the meatballs in the bread crumbs and fry in butter or olive oil until browned.
4. Add the endive and meatballs to hot beef broth or chicken broth to warm meat balls
   and then serve topping with Parmigiano-Reggiano.

Brodo di Manzo/Manzo Bolito (Beef Broth and Boiled Beef)
Category: Minestre (Soups)
Origin: Mamma Cortellini's Version of Traditional Italian
Serves 6–8

This recipe serves several purposes. It provides a hearty beef stock to be used for other recipes or
as a soup with minestra and Parmigiano-Reggiano, and it also serves as a mainstay in the Italian family
standard of boiled beef, served either hot or cold. You can serve the meat hot with condiments (extra-
virgin olive oil, lemon drops, a red or green sauce, or horseradish and mustard) and use the broth as a
soup.

Ingredients:
3–4 lb. beef, any combination of chuck, shank, or ribs with bone in
1 medium onion, finely chopped
1 whole ripe tomato, quartered
1 medium carrot, cut in pieces
3 or 4 celery stalks, with some leaves, cut in pieces
1 medium onion, quartered
1 medium potato, cut in pieces
1 bay leaf
Kosher salt and freshly ground black pepper to taste

Preparation:
1. Use a pot that is large and deep enough to hold the beef and also cover the meat with
   water by two inches.
2. Put meat, vegetables, and spices into the pot and bring to a boil.
3. When it begins to boil, reduce heat to a steady, gentle simmer.
4. After one and a half hours, add two tablespoons of kosher salt.
5. Cook another hour and a half to two hours, depending on thickness of beef.
6. Skim off the scum that comes to the surface of the broth.
7. The meat should be tender when poked with a fork.
8. After removing the meat, discard the vegetables and pour the broth through a large
   strainer lined with single-ply paper towel into a bowl. Cover and place in the refrigerator
   until the fat congeals; then remove the grease.
9. This broth can be used a beef stock or beef broth for numerous recipes. It can be frozen in
   cubes or airtight containers and can keep several months.

Similar to the chicken broth (see separate recipe), you can make a beef broth Pastina in Brodo using the
same little pastas. You can also refrigerate the beef and serve at later date; it is also good served cold.

Pasta Ceci (Chickpea Pasta)

Category: Paste (Pastas)
Origin: Mamma Cortellini
Serves 4

This pasta dish is simple but delicious and great for a last-minute idea. If you like the taste of rose-mary, you will love this pasta.

Ingredients:
16-oz. can of chickpeas (I use Goya brand)
2 sprigs rosemary, leaves broken apart
2 garlic cloves, sliced
¼ cup extra-virgin olive oil
Kosher salt and freshly ground black pepper to taste
16-oz. box small pasta (De Cecco; I use Ditalini or Tubetti pasta)

Preparation:
1. Put the chickpeas and the liquid from the can, rosemary, garlic, olive oil, and salt and pepper in a saucepan large enough to hold the cooked pasta; bring to a boil, then reduce to a simmer and cook for ten minutes.
2. When cooked, take a fork and smash about half of the peas to thicken the sauce. You can also use an immersion blender.
3. Meanwhile, cook the pasta al dente and then add to the sauce.

Mom's Ragu (Spaghetti Sauce)

Category: Paste (Pastas)
Origin: Mamma Cortellini
Serves 4

This ragu is based on Mom's recipe, with some additions. It's a simpler and less time-consuming recipe than the Bolognese recipe used for lasagna, and Roz likes it just as well.

Ingredients:
½ lb. Italian pancetta (mild), finely chopped
1 lb. ground sirloin (high-quality, finely ground)
1 medium yellow onion
2 cloves garlic, minced1 small bay leaf and 1 branch thyme

2 Tbsp. extra-virgin olive oil
2 Tbsp. unsalted butter
1 large carrot and 1 large celery stalk, finely chopped
26-oz. box of Pomi chopped tomatoes or good quality San Marzano chopped tomatoes
1 cup white wine
½ cup whole milk
Kosher salt and freshly ground black pepper to taste
Parmigiano-Reggiano for serving
Best pastas to use are Fusilli Lunghi, Fettuccini, Cavatappi, or Penne Rigate

Preparation:
1. In a heavy saucepan, heat the oil and butter together.
2. In a skillet, sauté the pancetta, but do not let it get crispy.
3. Remove the pancetta and set aside.
4. In the same skillet sauté the onions until translucent, add garlic, celery, and carrots
   and sauté until vegetables are soft.
5. Add ground beef and brown; season with salt and pepper.
6. Raise the heat and add wine; cook until wine evaporates.
7. Add milk and let reduce by half.
8. Add tomatoes and their juices, add herbs, bring to a boil then reduce heat to low and
   let simmer for one and a half to two hours.
9. Serve over pasta, adding Parmigiano-Reggiano before serving.

The finished Ragu;   Served with Fusilli Lunghi

Rolata di Manzo con Sugo per Pasta (Beef Roll with Pasta Sauce)
Category: Paste (Pastas)
Origin: Mama Cortellini
Serves 6–8

This is a particularly good red sauce for pasta. It is hardy and is well complemented by Parmigiano-Reggiano. Mom often prepared this for Sunday dinner. If there were leftovers, I enjoyed the meat rolls cold as a late-night snack. Roz and Nic love the sauce but are not too keen on the meat with egg in the middle. The key to making it tender is a substantial pounding of the meat in its preparation. That is why it is important to make sure you pound the heck out of it, the thinner the meat, the more tender it becomes. You can also try substituting sirloin instead of round steak, but the sauce becomes greasier, and it's hard to find a cut of sirloin that can be flattened enough to roll it.

Ingredients:
2 lb. round steak, thinly sliced, without bone
Sliced salami, enough to cover the meat (Milano, Genoa, or Soprasata)
Bunch of fresh Italian parsley, chopped

4 hardboiled eggs, peeled
Medium onion, finely chopped
1½ cans (or large 28-oz. can) Italian plum peeled tomatoes (preferable San Marzano type)
Small bunch of fresh basil
Extra-virgin olive oil to fry the meat
Grated Parmigiano-Reggiano mixed with Pecorino (Romano) cheese
Kosher salt and freshly ground black pepper to taste

Preparation:
1. Lay out the round steak on a large cutting board, removing excess fat around the edges. Using a meat hammer, pound the steak to thin it, enlarging it. Be careful not to put holes in the steak.
2. Lay the sliced salami over the steak, covering it.
3. Sprinkle a layer of chopped parsley over the salami.
4. Pepper the top, but do not salt the inside, as the cheese and salami add plenty of salt.
5. Sprinkle a layer of Parmigiano-Reggiano cheese on top of the parsley.
6. Beginning at the widest end of the flattened steak, line up the boiled eggs in a row, end to end. Bring the edge of the steak over the eggs and roll steak and ingredients into a meatloaf, taking care not to let any of the contents fall out.
7. Using kitchen string, tie the loaf to hold it together for cooking. You may want to tie it once (loosely) lengthwise and then crosswise.
8. In a large, heavy pot (large enough to contain the loaf without bending it), heat olive oil over medium-high heat. Add the loaf and brown on all sides. Salt and pepper the exterior of the loaf to taste.
9. Add the chopped onion and continue sautéing until the onion is soft and golden.
10. Add the tomatoes and some water; the sauce should be thin at first and thicken with cooking.
11. Chop the basil and add to the sauce along with a few flakes of red chili pepper to taste (optional).
12. Let cook for an hour or longer until the sauce reduces and oil rises to the top. If the sauce is still thin, add a couple of tablespoons of good-quality tomato paste.
13. When ready to serve, remove the loaf from the sauce. Cut off the strings and remove.
14. With a sharp knife, slice the loaf into one and a half to two-inch slices. Be careful to not let the meat fall apart; it will be well cooked. What you should have are meat rounds with an inner circle of salami and an egg center.
15. Serve the sauce with either spaghetti or penne and serve the meat with the pasta, adding some flakes of fresh parsley on top of the meat.
16. Serve Parmigiano-Reggiano on top of the pasta.

Ready for slicing

Pasta Serving and Meat Sauce

Uccelletti di Carni con Sugo per Pasta (Little Bird Rolls with Pasta Sauce)
Category: Paste (Pastas)
Origin: Mamma Cortellini
Serves 4–6

The title for this recipe is actually a misnomer as the meat used is beef, not fowl. The Italians call these birds because the pieces of beef are small and resemble bird portions. This is another meat dish that produces a particularly good red sauce for pasta. Using pork instead of beef enhances the sauce taste but may make the sauce greasier. Be sure to remove the toothpicks before serving the meat.

Ingredients:
2 lb. veal, pork, or beef, thinly sliced without bone (see preparation below)
Prosciutto or pancetta, sliced thinly to cover the meat
A bunch of fresh Italian parsley, finely chopped
1 large garlic clove, finely chopped
Medium onion, chopped
1½ large 28-oz. cans of Italian plum peeled tomatoes (preferable San Marzano type)
Small bunch of fresh basil or, as a variation, use marjoram
Extra-virgin olive oil to fry the meat
Grated Parmigiano-Reggiano cheese
Kosher salt and freshly ground black pepper to taste

Preparation:
1. You can use either center-cut boneless pork chops, veal cutlets, or minute steaks. Whichever you use, it should be very thinly sliced. Lay out the slices of meat on a large cutting board, removing excess fat around the edges. Using a meat hammer, pound the steak thin and expand the slices. Pound them as thin as you can without breaking through the meat.
2. Lay the slices of prosciutto or pancetta over the slices of meat, covering them.
3. Mix the chopped parsley and chopped garlic together or chop them together. Put a thin layer of the mixture over the prosciutto/pancetta.

4. Sprinkle salt and pepper over the top.

5. Sprinkle a layer of Parmigiano cheese on top of the parsley.

6. Beginning from the widest end of the meat slice, roll the meat and ingredients into a small meat roll, tucking in any lose edges. Take care not to let any of the contents fall out.

7. Stick a large toothpick through the loose end of the roll so that the meat does not fall apart.

8. In a large, heavy pot—large enough to contain the rolls without overcrowding them— heat the olive oil over medium high heat. Add the rolls and sear them until golden brown (for about five minutes).

9. Remove the rolls and add the onion to the pot. Fry the onion until soft and golden. Place the rolls back into the pot and add tomatoes, a few hot pepper flakes, and basil or marjoram and cook at medium low heat for about forty minutes. Add some water to the tomatoes; the sauce should be thin at first and reduce with cooking.

10. If sauce is still thin, let it cook longer until the sauce reduces and oil rises to the top. If the sauce is still thin, add a couple tablespoons of good-quality tomato paste.

11. When ready to serve, remove the rolls from the sauce and place in a serving dish.

12. Serve the sauce with any form of dried pasta, or even with fresh tagliatelle, and serve the meat with the pasta, adding a generous helping of Parmigiano-Reggiano on top of the pasta.

Preparing the Uccelletti to fry

Frying the Uccelletti

Cooking them in the sauce

Croquette di Pollo (Chicken Patties)
Category: Carni (Meats)
Origin: Momma Cortellini
Serves 6–8

This is one of my favorite ways of eating leftover chicken. I don't actually call this a leftover preparation; I would make the broth just to have the chicken croquettes. For more flavor you can add three tablespoons of Parmigiano-Reggiano to the mixture. The key to this recipe is to not process the chicken meat too finely as the croquettes then become pasty.

Ingredients:
Chicken pulled from the bone from the chicken broth recipe (see Brodo di Pollo)
1 egg beaten
Lemon zest from 1½ lemons
½ tsp. (at least) ground nutmeg
Bread crumbs (preferably homemade and without flavoring)
Frying oil (light extra-virgin olive oil)
Kosher salt and freshly ground black pepper to taste

Preparation:
1. Chop the deboned chicken by hand into very small pieces that can be formed together into a patty. Do not use a food processor as the meat will become too pasty.
2. Put chicken in a bowl and add lemon zest, nutmeg, egg, salt, and pepper.
3. Mix thoroughly and test for moisture. The mixture should hold together when compressed into a patty. If too dry, add a touch of chicken broth or olive oil.
4. Form into small patties and coat in the bread crumbs.
5. Fry in enough heated oil to cover the bottom of the frying pan. As the chicken is cooked, you need only brown the patties to add color and heat thoroughly.
6. Serve immediately.

Mixing the chicken

Frying the patties

Arrosto d'Agnello (Roasted Leg of Lamb)
Category: Carni (Meats)
Origin: Mamma Cortellini
Serves 6–8

At Easter the traditional serving at our home was leg of lamb. However, this meat dish is ideal for a cookout or as a Sunday roast at any time. This roast can be fixed using a bone-in or butterflied leg of lamb. Check the proper cooking times for each. Ideally, you might cook some potatoes with the roast by adding them to the juices of the roast for the last half hour or so of the cooking. Let the roast stand at least ten minutes before cutting. Untie the roast and slice it into slices that are not too thick. Serve with a hearty red Italian wine such as Barolo or Amarone.

Ingredients:
3–4 lb. leg of lamb, butterflied
2 large garlic cloves, sliced in wedges
Extra-virgin olive oil
Sprigs of fresh rosemary
Kosher salt and freshly ground black pepper

Preparation:
1. Slice the leg of lamb so that it lies flat (butterfly the roast).
2. Trim the excess fat from the roast but leave enough to flavor the roast.
3. Salt and pepper the lamb.
4. Spike the lamb with a small wedge of garlic combined with small twigs of fresh rosemary. Do not overdo, as the garlic and rosemary may dominate the flavor of the lamb.
5. Roll the lamb together and tie it together to form a roast.
6. Chop some of the rosemary leaves, mix with olive oil, and brush to coat the roast.
7. Brown the roast at a high temperature (400°F) for about ten minutes or until lightly browned.
8. Cook the roast at 340°F for approximately one hour or as indicated in the meat cooking instructions.

Ready to cook

Pizzaiola (Veal Spezzettini in Pizzaiola Sauce)
Category: Carni (Meats)
Origin: Mamma Cortellini
Serves 4–6

This is one of my favorite of Mom's dishes, and I can easily eat the entire dish by myself. Bread is a must, along with a glass of Chianti or Dolcetto.

Ingredients:
2–2½ lb. of veal scaloppini (the thinnest possible) or you can buy a veal loin and slice your own scaloppini
¼ cup extra-virgin olive oil

1 tsp. (or more) dried Italian oregano
3 cloves garlic, one minced and two sliced
½ box (2 cups plus) of Pomi Italian plum tomatoes
Kosher salt and freshly ground black pepper to taste

Preparation:
1. The veal must be paper-thin. Flatten the scaloppini pieces one at a time. Place a scaloppini piece on a cutting board, cover with cling foil, and pound the meat with a meat mallet, tenderizing and spreading it into paper-thin pieces. Cut the scaloppini into bite-size pieces.
2. In a heavy skillet, place the oil, meat, garlic, oregano, salt, and pepper and simmer until the liquid from the meat evaporates.
3. Add the tomatoes and cook fifteen to twenty minutes until the sauce is thickened slightly. Don't let the sauce dry out as you need to have sauce to serve with the meat.
4. Serve with plenty of Italian bread.

Pounding the scaloppini   Serving the Pizzaiola

Pollo con Cipolle e Vino (Chicken with Onions and Wine)
Category: Carni (Meats)
Origin: Mamma Cortellini
Serves 4–6

Slow! Slow! Slow! The key to cooking this dish is cooking the chicken very slowly until fully cooked. This is a dish Mom frequently prepared for the family and is one of those recipes that Roz wrote down from her everyday cooking.

Ingredients:
2 lb. chicken pieces (I use thighs and breasts without skin)
1 medium yellow onion, cut in pieces
½ cup of dry white wine
½ stick of butter

Preparation:
1. Fry chicken pieces in the butter in a heavy frying skillet until they are golden (and until all the water is evaporated).
2. Add the onion and continue frying until the onion is golden and soft.
3. Add the wine and simmer slowly, covered, until wine is evaporated.
4. Continue to cook very slowly until chicken is cooked.

Finocchi alla Parmigiana (Sauteed Fennel with Parmesan)
Category: Verdure (Vegetables)
Origin: Mamma Cortellini
Serves 6–8

This makes a great side dish. I serve this at Thanksgiving as one of the vegetables with turkey and also with our Christmas dinner. Scatter the fennel fronds as an accent to the top of the dish before serving.

Ingredients:
5 bulbs fennel
3 Tbsp. butter
1 Tbsp. extra-virgin olive oil
½ cup whole milk, or add cream to skim milk
¼ cup grated Parmigiano-Reggiano
¼ lb. Italian fontina cheese
Kosher salt and freshly ground black pepper to taste
Fronds from the tops of the fennels

Preparation:
1. Cut the tops off the fennel bulbs and remove outer stalks. Retain the fronds.
2. Cut the bulbs lengthwise into eighths, making sure that the core stays intact for each piece.
3. In a frying pan, melt the butter and then add the olive oil. Add the fennel slices and sauté them until golden brown (cook very slowly).
4. Add salt and pepper to taste.
5. Add the milk to the skillet and continue cooking slowly until the milk is nearly evaporated and the fennel is tender.
6. Remove the fennel slices from the skillet and place them in an ovenproof casserole dish along with all the drippings in the skillet.

7. In a bowl mix the grated Parmigiano-Reggiano and bread crumbs and sprinkle the mixture over the fennel evenly.
8. Add dots of the fontina cheese on top.
9. Bake in the oven at 350°F for ten to fifteen minutes or until cheese melts and begins to brown on top.
10. Garnish with some fennel fronds.

Frying the fennels

Prior to baking

Fagiolini, Patate, e Pomodoro (Green Beans with Potatoes and Tomatoes)
Category: Verdure (Vegetables)
Origin: Mamma Cortellini
Serves 6

This is a great vegetable side dish to serve with all meats.

Ingredients:
1 lb. fresh green beans (not too large), boiled but not fully cooked
¼ medium onion, finely chopped
2 cloves garlic, minced
2 red potatoes, cleaned and cut into small cubes, boiled but not fully cooked
¼ cup extra-virgin olive oil
½ box Pomi Roma tomatoes with juices
Small bunch of fresh basil
Kosher salt and freshly ground black pepper to taste

Preparation:
1. Clean and boil the green beans in salted water for eight to nine minutes, depending on the size of the beans; do not overcook.
2. Drain the beans and retain some of the water in case the sauce needs thinning.
3. In a separate pot, boil the potatoes for ten minutes, not letting them overcook.
4. In a skillet, add the oil and sauté the onions and garlic until they soften and are golden.
5. Add the tomatoes and juices, basil, green beans, potatoes, salt, and pepper; cover and simmer.
6. Taste to see when beans and potatoes are fully cooked; set aside and let cool. Can be served warm or at room temperature.

Uova con Pomodoro e Cipolla (Eggs with Tomatoes and Onions)
Category: Vari (Other)
Origin: Mamma Cortellini
Serves 4

These eggs should be eaten with a loaf of good Italian bread for dipping in the sauce. This is a great dish for lunch or for whenever you want something quick.

Ingredients:
4–6 eggs
Medium yellow onion
4 cups chopped tomatoes (Pomi or San Marzano)
1 tsp. dried oregano, or more to taste
3 Tbsp. extra-virgin olive oil
2 Tbsp. unsalted butter
Kosher salt and freshly ground black pepper to taste

Preparation:
1. Slice the onion thinly.
2. In a large skillet, add the olive oil and sauté the onion until soft.
3. Add the tomatoes and oregano and sauté fifteen to twenty minutes, until juices reduce.
4. Add the eggs on top of the sauce—do not break the yolk or stir in the eggs.
5. Add salt and pepper.
6. Cover and cook until the eggs are firm.
7. Remove and serve. If you like the yolk to be soft or liquid, serve before the eggs are fully cooked.

Pizzelle (Anise Cookies)
Category: Dolci (Dessert)
Origin: Mamma Cortellini
Makes Six Dozen Cookies

These cookies are a must at Christmas. Nic used to take them to school for his teachers. They take a long time to make, so it is a labor of love. The house has a fragrance of anise for the longest time after cooking them, so we cannot hide them from Nic or surprise him. The first few cookies may stick to the iron until it is cured, but the rest should come off easily.

Ingredients:
6 eggs
3½ cups of all-purpose flour
1 cup (two sticks) of unsalted butter
1½ cups of granulated sugar
4 tsp. baking powder
2 tsp. anise extract
Electric Pizzelle iron

Preparation:
1. Melt the butter in the microwave; add the anise to the butter and let cool.
2. In a large bowl, beat the eggs and sugar; mix well until smooth.
3. Add the cooled butter and anise mixture to the eggs.
4. Add the baking powder to the flour and slowly add to the egg mixture until fully blended.
5. Heat the Pizzelle iron until the "ready" light turns on.
6. Add a teaspoon of the mixture to each pattern and let cook thirty to forty-five seconds.
7. Remove and let cool on a cookie cooling rack.
8. Store in a dry, airtight container (don't refrigerate).

Making Pizzelle

Chapter 12

Return to Ancona

In the year that followed my marriage to Roz, Mom and I decided that we needed to introduce Roz to our Italian family in Ancona. At the time I was in the middle of busy season at Coopers, studying for the CPA exam, and Roz was still working at Oxford Development. For these reasons we decided to delay our trip until August 1972. As it turned out, my cousin Anna Maria had planned to marry Paolo Rismondo that summer. When she heard we were planning a visit, Anna Maria changed the wedding date so it would take place during our visit to Ancona. We were able to combine a belated honeymoon with a family wedding and a reunion. It's not common to bring your mother on your honeymoon, but then it should be apparent by now that I had an uncommon mother.

We arrived in Milan, where Anna Maria's brother Maurizio and his wife Anna Grazia picked us up at Malpensa Airport, just north of Milan. The next day Maurizio drove us to Ancona in his Alfa Romeo, which was our first experience on the autostrada with an Italian driver. Anna Maria was the last of Zia Marisa's (Mom's sister) children to marry. Zia Marisa had five children. The oldest is Gabriella, and her husband then was Roberto Dameno. They lived in Monza (near Milan) and had houses in Ancona and Marcelli (Ancona's Riviera). Maurizio married Anna Grazia and lived in Milan. They had a summer home in Numana near the beach and Monte Conero. Claudio married Serenella Alessandroni, and they lived on a farm near Ancona. Their vineyard produced a fine Verdichio. Massimo and his then-wife Angela Alessandrini lived in Ancona. All had children, so you can imagine the casino (Italian for chaos or confusion) when we all got together. After the wedding Anna Maria and Paolo Rismondo planned to live with Zia Marisa in Ancona, only a block from where I was born. Mom, Roz, and I stayed in Zia Marisa's home during our visit. Today, Gabriella is married to Franco Rismondo (Paolo's brother), and they live in Ancona with a summer home in Numana. Maurizio still lives in Milan with Anna Grazia. Claudio passed away a number of years ago after a long battle with cancer. Massimo is now married to Doriana and lives in Ancona. Zia Marisa lived with Anna Maria and Paolo in Numana until she passed away in 2012 at the age of ninety-seven.

All five cousins at Gabriella's wedding, starting from right to left:
Massimo, Maurizio, Gabriella, Claudio, and Anna Maria

Mom and Roz in front of Anna's flat

Bottling Claudio's Verdichio
(what I didn't drink)

Claudio, Serenella, daughter Antonella, and Roz   Mom, Roz, and Raul, Mom's brother

As this was my first visit back after leaving at age six, and Roz's first visit to Europe, Maurizio volunteered to show us Florence and Venice. Unfortunately, we did this as day trips. Realistically, Ancona to Florence and back and then to Venice and back are not considered day trips because of the considerable distances. However, Maurizio's Alfa Romeo and his driving made the day trips possible. The drives were memorable, to say the least, considering the couple of hours we spent in each city.

Maurizio and Anna Grazia and Florence panorama

Ponte Rialto, Venice

Anna Maria's wedding was a huge success. Mom made the wedding dress, and Roz played the organ at the wedding. I failed to mention earlier that Roz studied music at Stephens College in Columbia, Missouri, majoring in piano. She also was the church organist for the Castleton Methodist Church on the northeast side of Indianapolis. I actually sang tenor in the church choir where she played. Paolo and Anna Maria were married in the church across the street from where I lived as a child. Zia Marisa prayed in this church every morning. One of the pieces of music that I remember Roz playing at the wedding was the "Adagio in G Minor" by Albinoni.

The reception was held in the garden of Gabriella's home in Marcelli. It was a beautiful Mediterranean day, without a cloud in the sky.

Roz, Mom, and Mom's brother Raul and wife Rita
on another beautiful day at Marcelli,
where the reception was held

Anna and Paolo leaving the church

Reception in Gabriella's garden

Maurizio and Roz

Anna and Christina

Anna, Mom, and Zia Marisa

Claudio, Roz, and Paolo

It was a marvelous vacation, one we will never forget. Roz fell in love with Italy: the people, the food, Italian coffee, and my family. Upon returning home to Indianapolis, we longed to make a return trip to Italy. We wondered why anyone would ever want to leave such a wonderful life.

Rocky waterfront of Ancona

Work back home with Coopers was demanding and challenging. I found working in public accounting exciting as it required an understanding of what it was that made each client's business tick. I actually gained a reputation within the firm as having the most elaborate and complex test work papers. At Coopers I gained the experience I needed to qualify for licensing as a certified public accountant. In June 1974 I received my certification from the state of Indiana.

I loved working for the firm and the camaraderie that accompanied the team assignments. It was a difficult decision to leave public accounting, but the offer of a position with American Fletcher National Bank, managing its branch in Luxembourg, could not be refused. After spending nearly three years with the firm, I was approaching manager level, and making the change would mean I would never return to public accounting. In retrospect, I chose adventure over professional development.

In the spring of 1975, Roz and I moved to Luxembourg.

The recipes that I offer below are some of my favorites that were prepared by Zia Marisa and Anna Maria during our visit to Ancona.

Pomodori Ripieni al Forno (Roasted Stuffed Tomatoes)
Carciofi alla Giudia (Sautéed Artichokes with Parsley and Garlic)
Bucatini alla Amatriciana (Bucatini with Tomatoes, Pancetta, and Onion)
Brodetto (Zuppa) di Pesce (Fish Soup Anconetana)
Canocchia (Nocchia) *al Limone* (Scientific Name: *Squilla Mantis* or Mantis Shrimp)
Muscioli alla Marinaia (Moule Munier, Italian Style)

Pomodori Ripieni al Forno (Stuffed Roasted Tomatoes)
Category: Verdure/Vegetables
Origin: Zia Marisa and Mama Cortellini
Serves 4–6

This is a great summer side dish and goes well with grilled meats. I could eat a half dozen myself. Sometimes Mom would go a little heavy on the garlic, ruining my chances for kissing anyone after dinner. Oh well, these are life's choices. These tomatoes are great for an antipasto and can also be cooked on the grill. This well-known recipe was prepared perfectly by Zia Marisa. The availability of authentic Italian ingredients certainly helped. Perfectly ripe (still firm) tomatoes are the key to the successful preparation of this dish.

Ingredients:
10–12 medium tomatoes, mature but still firm
Homemade bread crumbs (enough to form the stuffing)
2 garlic cloves, minced
Kosher salt and freshly ground black pepper to taste
Large bunch of Italian parsley, minced
Extra-virgin olive oil to moisten the stuffing mixture

Preparation:
1. Cut the tomatoes in half.
2. Place a strainer over a mixing bowl and clean out the cavities of the tomatoes, letting the juices flow through to the mixing bowl and straining the seeds. Discard the seeds.
3. In the mixing bowl, mix the bread crumbs, garlic, olive oil, parsley, salt, and pepper with the strained juices, creating a semi-moist mixture (not a paste).
4. Stuff the mixture into the tomato cavities, avoiding pressing the mixture too hard into the cavities, and cover the tops of the tomatoes with the stuffing.
5. Preheat the oven to 350°F and bake.
6. After the tomatoes become wrinkled and well cooked, place them under the broiler to brown the tops.
7. Serve either warm or at room temperature.

On the outdoor grill   Even in the oven, always delicious

Carciofi alla Giudia (Sautéed Artichokes with Parsley and Garlic)
Category: Verdure/Vegetables
Origin: Zia Marisa and Mama Cortellini
Serves 4

One of my favorite vegetables is the artichoke because of its unique delicate taste and sweet after-taste. Many Americans are familiar with the large globe artichoke, which is normally served boiled or roasted with its petals removed one at a time and dipped in a sauce. The artichoke I advocate is called carciofini (baby artichoke) in Italy. It is best when the stem is still attached. Although you can find baby artichokes in good produce stores and Italian markets, they are seldom available with the stem and leaves still attached. The stems have as much flavor as the artichoke itself. Below are photos of how carciofini are sold in Italy.

Once prepared, this dish combines the sweet flavor of the artichoke with accents of garlic and parsley. Potatoes can be cooked with the artichokes to fortify the dish. The potatoes will take on the flavor of the artichokes and seasoning. Serve as a vegetable with meat or fish. This is a good spring-time vegetable dish.

Ingredients:
15–18 baby artichokes
1 large potato (optional)
Large bunch of Italian parsley, finely chopped
3 large garlic cloves (one minced, the other two sliced)
Juice of ½ large lemon
½ cup white wine
½ cup extra-virgin olive oil
½ cup water
Kosher salt and freshly ground black pepper to taste
(Optional) a couple of potatoes cut up in pieces similar in size of the artichokes

Preparation:
1. Clean the artichokes by removing outer leaves until you reach the tender, pale green leaves. Trim the base lightly and cut off the top third of the artichoke, which is still hard and prickly.
2. Slice the artichoke in half. As these should be very young artichokes, they should not yet have formed the choke. If the choke exists, you need to remove it.
3. Place the artichoke halves one at a time into a mixing bowl with the squeezed lemon juice and a quarter cup of water. Rub the artichokes' cut faces down into the lemon water to prevent them from turning brown.
4. If adding potatoes, cut them into inch-and-a-half cubes so they are small enough to have the same cooking time as the artichokes. This is optional, to make the serving larger and diversify the flavors.
5. In a medium-sized heavy pot, add the olive oil, artichokes, garlic, parsley, potatoes, and one cup of water.
6. Add salt and pepper to taste.
7. Bring contents of the pot to a boil and then turn the heat down to medium/medium low. Let simmer for fifteen to twenty minutes.
8. When water reduces, add the wine and continue to simmer for another ten minutes or until wine reduces and the artichokes are tender. If wine evaporates before the artichokes are tender, add a little more water and complete the cooking.

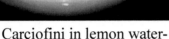

Carciofini in lemon water-   Sauté with parsley, garlic, and potatoes

Bucatini alla Amatriciana (Bucatini Pasta with Tomatoes, Pancetta, and Onion)
Category: Paste (Pastas)
Origin: Traditional Roman
Serves 6–8

This pasta is easy to make and, normally, a big hit. We served it to our visiting cousins from Italy, and they were surprised by its delicious taste. The origin of this recipe is Amatrice, a small town near Rome known for its pork and pancetta. It is well-known throughout Italy, but in my experience, it is not served much in the United States. In Italy, the recipe calls for the use of guanciale, this is bacon from the cheek of wild boar. However, a quality pancetta will suffice. Roz and I first had this pasta at Gabriella's garden in Marcelli for a midday meal after a morning at the beach. I don't know if it was the appetite from swimming or the exquisite taste of the pasta, but I remember that afternoon even today. I would not recommend using American smoked bacon as a substitute for the pancetta. The key for the success of the pasta is using quality pancetta and cheeses. Using bucatini instead of spaghetti is also important as bucatini tends to hold more sauce and cheese than spaghetti. Kids love to eat these pastas and treat them like straws. I last served this pasta dish with a Rosso di Conero from the region of Ancona, but it will go well with any good Italian red wine.

Ingredients:
4 oz. Italian pancetta (not smoked), cut into very small cubes
1 large yellow onion, finely chopped
1 stick butter
1½ cans chopped (or crushed), peeled San Marzano Italian plum tomatoes (28-oz. can)
2 cups of a mixture of grated Parmigiano-Reggiano and Pecorino-Romano imported cheese.
Kosher salt and freshly ground black pepper to taste
½ tsp. chili pepper flakes (peperoncini flakes) or more to taste
2 lb. bucatini or perciatelli (De Cecco brand)

Preparation:
1. The pancetta should be about one-half inch thick. Slice it into very small cubes.
2. In a large, heavy-bottomed saucepan, melt the butter and add chopped onion.
3. Fry the onion until it softens and starts to turn golden.
4. Add the pancetta and fry until it shrinks, but remove from heat before it gets crispy.
5. Take the tomatoes out of the can and chop or crush them (if they are still whole).
6. Add the tomatoes and the peperoncini flakes to the pan.
7. Add salt and freshly ground pepper to taste.
8. Cook slowly over medium-low heat until the oil rises and separates (about forty-five

minutes).

9. At this point you can set aside or even refrigerate the sauce if you are serving later.
10. Otherwise, cook the bucatini very al dente (half a minute before al dente).
11. Add the cooked bucatini to the sauces over low heat, add the cheese, and stir.
12. Turn the heat off, cover, and let stand for several minutes to infuse the flavors in the pasta.
13. Serve immediately and add more cheese at the table.

Serving Bucatini alla Amatriciana to LJ, Clelia, and family at Easter

Brodetto or Zuppa di Pesce (Fish Soup Anconetana)

Category: Pesci (Fish)
Origin: Zia Marisa and Traditional Marche
Serves 6–8

One of Ancona's most famous recipes is Brodetto, which is similar to Bouillabaisse or fish soup. Ancona, being a port city, has access to some of the Adriatic's best-known fish and shellfish. The fish for this dish must be fresh! When making this in Ancona, we added canocchia, which to my knowledge is not found in the United States. Serve with plenty of bread for dipping in the broth. Serve with a good Verdichio from the Marche region of Italy.

Ingredients:
¼ cup extra-virgin olive oil
½ yellow onion, finely chopped
2–3 cloves garlic, minced
½ box of chopped plum tomatoes removing the seeds
Herbs: small bunch of parsley, chopped; 2 celery tops, chopped; 1 bay leaf
1 glass white wine
Red pepper flakes, salt, and ground pepper to taste
White wine vinegar (small amount)
4–5 lb. white fish for the soup, such as monkfish, haddock, cod, snapper, swordfish, red mullet, or other white-meat fish, cleaned and cut in bite-size pieces.
A few small fish to be left whole, such as perch and mullet.
Crustaceans and shellfish: shrimp, scampi calamari, and mussels–and, if you can find them, canocchia.

Preparation:
1. In a large, heavy pot, sauté the garlic and onion to a golden tone.
2. Add the celery, parsley, and bay leaf and simmer for five minutes.

3. Add tomatoes, pepperoncino, salt, and pepper.

4. After fifteen minutes add the white wine.

5. Clean and cut the fish while the sauce is cooking. In addition, clean the shellfish and the shrimp, leaving the shell on the shrimp. Remove the feet and whiskers from the shrimp and cut the back to remove the mud vein.

6. Clean some small fish but leave whole, with the heads, to be cooked with the soup for added flavor.

7. Add the fish first and, after ten to fifteen minutes, add the shellfish and the crustaceans.

8. Let cook for another five minutes and then serve, placing a proportionate amount of varied seafood on each plate.

Red mullet

Serve with plenty of bread

Canocchia (Nocchia) al Limone (Squilla Mantis or Mantis Shrimp in Lemon)

Category: Pesci (Fish)
Origin: Paolo Rismondo
Serves 6–8

The name "mantis shrimp" is actually a misnomer, because despite its appearance, it isn't shrimp. It resembles its namesake, the mantis, and is an equally ferocious predator. What look like eyes on the mantis shrimp's carapace are spots on its tail, which serve to make it look like a possibly dangerous fish to other animals that might prey upon it.

The problem making this dish in the US Midwest is that these mantis shrimp are not easily found. They are quite common in the Adriatic and all around Australia but are only caught in the Chesapeake Bay in the United States. However, if you can find it, you will have the finest experience in crustacean eating. This is by far my favorite!

This is what they look like live

Ingredients:
18–20 canocchia (they should be bought only in the winter months, October through March, and only if they are alive)

Extra-virgin olive oil for dressing
½ lemon for dressing
Small bunch of Italian parsley

Preparation:
1. Place the canocchia in a skillet without water.
2. Cover them with a dishcloth soaked in water.
3. Cover the skillet and cook over medium heat for five or six minutes.
4. Remove the lid and cloth; if the canocchia have turned red, they are cooked.
5. Remove from heat and let cool.
6. With scissors, cut off all the legs and remove the gills under the stomach, the head, the points of the tail, and the two fins on the sides.
7. Remove the outer shell by cutting two lateral lines on the back and gently removing it.
8. Put them on a large serving tray and dress them with a little salt, olive oil, lemon, and parsley.

This is what they look like on the table

Muscioli (Cozze) alla Marinaia (Moule Meunière Italian Style)
Category: Pesci (Fish)
Origin: Paolo Rismondo
Serves 4–6

Mussels are a specialty of Ancona due to its rocky shorelines, which make a natural breeding ground for these shellfish. This dish is easy to make. The key to its success is high-quality fresh mussel. Discard mussels that don't open in cooking. For additional flavor, a clove of finely chopped garlic can be added to the parsley.

Ingredients:
1½ lb. very fresh mussels
Bunch of Italian parsley
¼ cup extra-virgin olive oil
Juice of 1 lemon
Pepper, freshly ground

Preparation:

1. When cleaning the mussels, remove the beard and scrub the shells.
2. Place the mussels in a large, deep skillet; add the oil and half of the lemon juice along with the parsley and ground pepper.
3. Cover pot and cook the mussels for five minutes until the mussels open and the juices release from the mussels.
4. After mussels open, place them on a serving dish. Remove half of the shell to make them easier to serve and eat. Add some of the cooking water to the remaining lemon juice and drizzle over the mussels.

Chapter 13

Luxembourg Days

One of my largest clients at Coopers was American Fletcher National Bank. Jim Kubinski and I were assigned to this client. I audited the mortgage company and the international division. American Fletcher had an established branch in the Grand Duchy of Luxembourg to fund its international and foreign currency portfolios. The year preceding my arrival in Luxembourg, a German bank named Herstatt Bank failed due to lack of internal controls, causing discomfort in the international banking community. American Fletcher became concerned about its own controls at foreign branches. The position of branch manager at American Fletcher's Luxembourg office was opening due to an assignment rotation. The bank chose to replace its branch manager with someone having more control experience than business development. Accordingly, I was offered the position; I reported to the head of the international department, George Hull, based in Indianapolis.

With significant trepidation, I resigned my position at Coopers. Roz and I began an international journey that would keep us living abroad for more than fifteen years. We moved from our home on Kessler Boulevard to a small town just west of the city of Luxembourg called Nospelt. This was our first move across the Atlantic, and, needless to say, we had no idea of what was to come.

During most of my tenure at the Luxembourg branch, I had the pleasure of working with my close friend, Jim Fahy, the head of business development at the branch. It was a remarkable coincidence that we were both living in Luxembourg and working for the same bank. We had been friends and cohorts at Indiana National Bank. Jim and his wife Rebecca were two of our closest friends. They married in Jonesville, Indiana, on August 19, 1972, and I was in the wedding. Mom made Becky's wedding dress. Our close relationship made the transition to Luxembourg much easier as they were already living there when we arrived.

Mom, Karen and Roz and Fahy's wedding

At Indiana National years earlier, Jim and I had a totally different work experience. We had been grunts in the bank's basement in downtown Indianapolis. In Luxembourg we were executives in a European banking community, with a posh office structure complete with a basement wine cellar.

The city of Luxembourg is picturesque. It straddles a gorge that separates the old from the new city. The Grand Duchy of Luxembourg dates back over one thousand years and has many scenic areas, which attract lots of tourists.

Luxembourg is an independent constitutional monarchy, bordered to the northwest by Belgium and the Ardennes, to the southwest by France, and to the east and south by Germany. The border between Luxembourg and Germany is formed by three rivers: the Moselle, the Sauer, and the Our River.

Map of Luxembourg

With approximately a half million inhabitants, it covers an area of only about one thousand square miles (about the size of Rhode Island). Its capital, Luxembourg Ville, is the site of the European Court of Justice, the European Court of Auditors, the Statistical Office of the European Communities ("Eurostat"), and other vital EU organs. The Secretariat of the European Parliament is located in Luxembourg, but the Parliament usually meets in nearby Strasbourg.

French is the legal language, but three languages are recognized as official in Luxembourg: French, German, and Luxembourgish. Apart from being one of the three official languages, Luxembourgish is also considered the national language of the Grand Duchy; it is the mother tongue or "language of the heart" for nearly all its citizens. Luxembourgers are deeply appreciative of the sacrifices made by American troops that led to the country's liberation in the two world wars of the twentieth century. More than five thousand American soldiers, including General George S. Patton, are buried at the American Military Cemetery near the capital, and monuments stand in many towns in honor of the American liberators.

Luxembourg's food scene reflects its geographic location between the Latin and Germanic worlds, drawing on the cuisines of neighboring France, Belgium, and Germany. More recently it has been influenced by the country's many Italian and Portuguese immigrants. As in Germany, most traditional everyday Luxembourg dishes are of peasant origin, in marked contrast to the more sophisticated French fare. Along the banks of the Moselle, where most of the Luxembourg Riesling is grown, local menus abound with fritures, meaning a fried river fish, like you have never tasted before. These fish resemble perch, but they are fried to the point that the entire fish can be eaten. Similar to anchovies and sardines the small bones of the fish soften with the intense cooking that they can be eaten. On many occasions Roz and I drove to the banks of the Moselle with Jim and Becky to partake of Friture de la Moselle and a cold bottle of Luxembourg Riesling. By the way, Luxembourg Riesling in no way resembles the German counterpart. The Luxembourg Riesling is extra dry, whereas the German Riesling is considerably sweeter. Luxembourg makes a lot of wine for a little country—some 17 million cases a year. The Luxembourgers drink most of what they make but share what's left with their neighbors, the Belgians and the Germans, with just an errant bottle or two finding its way into France. I don't believe I have ever tasted a drier wine. For years I have tried without success to find Luxembourg Riesling in the United States.

Friture de la Moselle, Riesling, and vineyards on the Moselle

In keeping with the city's international flavor, the restaurants in the Luxembourg Ville mostly feature French and Belgian cooking. We also found several fine Italian restaurants due to the large Italian community and its influence on the restaurant business. The most interesting restaurants were usually found in neighboring small villages in conjunction with countryside hotels called auberges, or hostelries. One of our favorite of these restaurants was Hostellerie a La Bonne Auberge. Located on the Belgian border, it was in a beautiful setting and had magnificent French and Belgian cuisine as well as local dishes with an emphasis on game. My favorites were frogs' legs, escargot, venison, and sole meunière.

Hostellerie a La Bonne Auberge near the Belgium border and the Ardennes

In the Luxembourg economic expansion, favorable tax laws, especially for holding companies and finance companies, attracted financial institutions such as American Fletcher, creating a boom town. We arrived during this expansion and consequently could not find an apartment in the city. We found a newly built home in the neighboring farming village of Nospelt, about five miles northwest of the city. This distance was not much of a commute for me as an American, but little did I know that I would have to deal with roadways blocked by cattle and sheep.

1 Rue Leck, Nospelt, Luxembourg, and our neighbors

The bank provided us with a company car, and we purchased an Italian sports car for Roz to drive. As branch manager of American Fletcher National Bank, I was a part of the banking community, which meant invitations to banking events, membership to the golf club once frequented by Dwight D. Eisenhower, and other benefits. The American Fletcher offices were located in an attractive, old, three-story home in a luxurious section of the city. It was furnished with exquisite antique English furniture selected by my boss, George Hull, who was an English antique enthusiast. The branch even had a wine cellar in the basement instead of a vault holding its liquidity. It was stocked with fine aged French wine, including Gevrey-Chambertin, Nuits-Saint-Georges, Pomerol, and more. We also stored a supply of Mirabelle Liquor-Eau de Vie Plum (local plum liquor) for the times we entertained Luxembourg's national banking commissioner.

Luxembourg's renowned Mirabel plums and liquor

The branch was better equipped for entertainment than for banking operations. It had an active dealing room where we funded foreign currency positions for the head office in Indianapolis. It really came to life when Jim Fahy and I hosted numerous luncheons for banking clients, the Luxembourg banking commissioner, and the US ambassador. All in all, it was an enviable position, one I was unable to duplicate in my later career.

The bank building   Josianne, (admin assistant), and Dick Spikerman, my predecessor, at my welcoming reception

George Hull, Frank McKinney, CEO of American Fletcher, and the banking commissioner-

Reception with the banking commissioner and the US ambassador, serving prosciutto and melon

The staff at the branch was composed of a combination of local talent and experienced staff from the European community. Jim and I were the only expatriate staff. There was high demand for banking experience in the community because of the rapid expansion in banking, forcing us to attract staff from other European communities. The chief accountant, Alex Rozencwajg, was from Germany, and our two traders, Derek Canning and Nick Jones, were both from the United Kingdom.

Our accounting staff was made up of Gaston Givier, Nico Bartholomey, and Sylvain Kirsch. Nowadays I communicate with Sylvain through Facebook. Alex Rozencwajg is now CEO of a Swiss bank in Luxembourg. Other staff members not shown were Germaine Bodeving, who had a crush on Jim; Rujiza Milkovicz; and Mark Jacobs.

Nico Bartholemy, Sylvain Kirsch, and Alex Rozencwajg

Because there was an active Italian community in Luxembourg, I was able to befriend a number of Italians assigned to branches of Italian banks in Luxembourg. Two such friends were a couple named Mario and Lalla Molino. Mario was branch manager for the Banca Commerciale Italiana of Milano.

We also enjoyed good times with Marco and Rita Biffi. Marco was branch manager for Banco di Roma. These friendships provided me the opportunity to practice my Italian. What's more, they provided firsthand information on the best Italian restaurants in town. We became close friends with both couples during our three years in Luxembourg. We especially enjoyed our travels to Italy together.

Mario and Lalla Molina, taking a coffee break
en route to Keukenhof in Holland

As one might expect, we also formed close bonds with the American community in Luxembourg. Our friendship with Jim and Becky Fahy grew deeper. We frequently socialized with our counterparts at other American banks. John Sandvig was branch manager for a Minneapolis bank. We took several trips with John and his wife Jan, including a very memorable one to Russia.

Jim and Becky Fahy with John and Jan Sandvig at our home in Nospelt

Most weekends were spent traveling outside of Luxembourg. The border was only ten minutes away in all directions except to the north. We took full advantage of the car provided by the bank. Probably the most memorable excursions were the long ones to Italy. We loaded the car in Luxembourg, picked up the autobahn at Strasbourg, crossed into Germany, and then crossed the Swiss border at Basel. The San Bernardino Pass took us through the Alps. Once past San Bernardino, we entered the Italian-speaking region of Switzerland. From Ticino it is a short ride to Italy, passing first through Lugano Switzerland and then through Como, and finally entering Milano.

Approaching the Alps; The German side of San Bernardino Pass, and then the Italian side

As our travels from Luxembourg occurred before there was a European Union, each border crossing was a challenge, especially the German and Swiss borders. My US passport, showing that I was born in Italy, drew considerable scrutiny at each crossing. It took an especially long time at border crossings when traveling with the branch accountant Alex Rozencwajg and his wife. He had a refugee-status passport from Germany, and his wife had an Israeli passport. We were relieved on those infrequent occasions when no questions were asked.

At a border crossing into Switzerland with Jim and Becky Fahy

In 1977, our trip to the Soviet Union with the Sandvigs was especially interesting. Miami University of Ohio offered classes in Luxembourg. Fifty students of Russian political science needed chaperones for a trip to retrace the Russian revolution. As part of the American community in Luxembourg, we were offered the opportunity to help keep the students in line. It was a tough job, but someone had to do it. With the Vietnam War having ended only two years earlier and the Cold War still warm, we were apprehensive as to how we would be treated.

The trip was an adventure. We flew to Moscow and back on Aeroflot, aboard a Tupolev Tu-154. The pilot on our return trip must have been a former fighter pilot. On one of the descents before landing, the pilot had the plane dropping so quickly that the door to the luggage compartment burst open, and luggage rolled down the aisle.

Passing through customs on arrival took forever. One of the students attempted to sneak in a bible, and a few other students wore jeans under their outer clothing, intending to trade the jeans on the black market. We traveled on student fares, making our accommodations primitive. Our hotel room in Moscow had only a radio with one channel playing patriotic music. Our showers were in the basement, with the lighting provided by a single bare light bulb on the end of an electrical cord. However, the many incredible sights provided to us during the visit more than made up for the lack of amenities in our accommodations. The trip started in Moscow and ended in Leningrad. In the Kremlin there were seven immaculately preserved Orthodox cathedrals and churches, even though Christianity was outlawed.

Miami University tour group (Russian political science professor on the left)

We also attended a performance of La Tosca (in Russian) at the Bolshoi Theatre

We followed the evolution of the Russian revolution to the Hermitage, which was the Czar's winter palace. Immediately after the revolution of 1917, the Hermitage was proclaimed a state museum.

The train ride from Moscow to Leningrad was stark. After boarding in Moscow, all the doors to the coach were locked. The coach was heated—not well—with a coal-fired stove. The inside temperature felt like it was freezing. Along the way we stopped in the lesser-known town of Novgorod, three hundred miles from Moscow. The trip to Novgorod was overnight, and we wondered why such a short distance required overnight travel. It must have been a way to provide the tour group overnight accommodations without incurring a hotel expense. During the restless night, I looked out at one point to see that we were passing through blizzardlike conditions. However, when we arrived in Novgorod, we were greeted by sunny skies and very little snow on the ground, causing us to joke that the train must have been routed through Siberia. Novgorod was a farming community with picturesque cathedrals and wooden structures in the classic Russian style. We attended a local dance party, but when the locals started drinking heavily, we were asked to leave by the local watch guard that were ever present.

In the three years that we lived in Luxembourg, in addition to the Soviet Union, we were fortunate to see much of Western Europe, most of it by car. On many of these trips, we were accompanied by friends and family

Jim and Cindy Kubinski from Indianapolis

Tina and Gino from Indianapolis

Bob and Linda Thopy from Indianapolis

Some of our most memorable visits in Europe included:

Getting out of the rain at Harry's Bar
in Piazza San Marco, Venice

and a gondola artisan shop
in Venice

Visits to Ancona

Salzburg Austria

Calabria with Lalla

Como on the lake

Candles in Notre Dame of Paris

We left Luxembourg with the expectation that I would be reassigned to Geneva to manage the operations of American Fletcher's joint venture with Cummins Engine Company, subsequently called AFNB Swiss. During this period it was popular for large corporations to invest in private banks in nations with favorable tax laws. In order to place management control in the hands of experienced bankers, Cummins sold two-thirds of its interest in its Swiss private bank to American Fletcher National Bank. I was tasked to assist the Cummins general manager with improving the bank's internal controls. Unfortunately, the Swiss were stingy in issuing work permits and concluded that only one work permit would be issued to a bank the size of AFNB Swiss. Therefore, Cummins and AFNB management had to choose whether to utilize the work permit for the Cummins general manager or the AFNB operations manager. As Cummins was the single largest customer of AFNB, the bank deferred to Cummins. As my replacement at Luxembourg, George Elliott, had already been announced during my wait for the work permit, once the Swiss denied my work permit, I was repatriated to Indianapolis in the early months of 1978.

Going away reception

Going away parties

We accumulated a number of recipes while in Luxembourg. Some of the Italian recipes were from Lalla Molino and Rita Biffi, and others were from our visits to Ancona and cousins. Lalla provided a Piemonte (Piedmont region of Italy) influence while Rita was classic Roman. Other recipes were derived from the local Luxembourg cuisine. Below are the recipes that I remember collecting during the Luxembourg period of our lives.

Bruschetta (Garlic Toast)
Bagna Cauda (Garlic Fondue)
Peperoni Arrostiti con Tonno (Roasted Pepper with Tuna)
Toasts aux Champignon (Toast with Mushrooms)
Avocat aux Crevette (Avocado with Shrimp)
Spaghetti con Sugo di Pesce (Spaghetti with Fish Sauce)
Cannelloni alla Nizzarda (Cannelloni Pasta, Nice Style)
Saltimbocca alla Romana (Veal Scallops with Prosciutto and Sage)
Vitello Tonnato (Veal in Tuna Sauce)
Moules a la Luxembourgeoise (Mussels Luxembourg Style or Mariniere)
F'rell am Rèisleck (Trout in Riesling Sauce, Luxembourg Style)
Crostata (Italian Marmalade Pie, Ancona Style)
Grolla di Buon Amici (Grolla of Good Friends)

Bruschetta (Garlic Toast)
Category: Antipasti (Appetizers)
Origin: Italian Traditional
Serves 6 to 8

Bruschetta is derived from the Italian verb bruscare, which means "to rub." Rubbing fresh garlic on bread is the essence of basic bruschetta. However, this toasted bread has evolved with the addition of numerous toppings to the toasted bread. Possible toppings are endless, but the most common is a mixture of fresh chopped tomatoes, fresh basil, and olive oil. The rubbing of the garlic is often forgotten. Bruschetta is not to be mistaken with the American version of garlic bread, which is often made with less than ideal doughy bread soaked with butter and sprinkled with dehydrated garlic leaving an unpleasant aftertaste.

Ingredients:
Italian or French bread slices, cut into bite size pieces (one loaf makes enough for 6 to 8)
1–2 cloves of garlic, peeled and kept whole
Extra-virgin olive oil
Kosher salt

Preparation:
1. Place the sliced bread on baking sheet and lightly sprinkle olive oil over the bread.
2. Salt lightly with kosher salt.
3. Broil in the oven using the broiler. Watch the cooking closely so the bread does not burn. Turn bread over and broil until both sides are browned.
4. Let the bread cool on a drying rack.
5. Lightly rub the garlic on one side of the toasted bread.
6. Serve as a starter or during the meal.

Toasting the Bread

Topping:
The traditional topping for bruschetta is a tomato and basil topping.

1. Use plum tomatoes or Roma tomatoes. Slice them in very small cubes and place them in a small mixing bowl.
2. Wash and spin a small bunch of Italian basil; julienne the basil by rolling the leaves and slicing then in very thin strips.
3. Add salt and pepper to the topping.
4. Add the basil and some good extra-virgin oil to the bowl and mix well.
5. Add the topping to the bruschetta and serve as an appetizer.

Bruschetta

Bagna Cauda (Garlic Fondue)
Category: Antipasti (Appetizers)
Origin: Piedmont, Italy, Traditional
Serves 4–6

The origin of Bagna Cauda is the Piedmont region of Italy, which is known for its antipasti. In fact, we would order only antipasti when eating in places like Torino and Cuneo. Like fondue, Bagna Cauda is popular in the mountains or in cold weather. There are many different versions of this wonderful hot dip; however, we learned our recipe from Lalla, who is from Cuneo, in the heart of Piedmont near the French border. We refined it with Etta and Italo, who are from Torino. Bagna Cauda is Latin; in Italian it is Bagna Calda, meaning "hot bath." The traditional serving is with toasted bread and blanched vegetables. The dish is so called because the mixture of garlic and anchovies is traditionally kept warm in a chafing dish or fondue pot. Bagna Cauda is served with small pieces of assorted vegetables for dipping and crusty bread to catch the drips. Among the possible vegetables are raw Jerusalem artichokes, cardoons, bell peppers, carrots, spinach, green onions, or celery; cooked potatoes; roasted onions or beets; and blanched cauliflower or broccoli. Some cooks prefer to simmer the garlic first in a little milk to tame the flavor. Don't be put off by the amount of garlic that is called for and the use of anchovies. The flavor is incredible.

Ingredients:
1 cup extra-virgin olive oil
1 bulb (8–10 cloves) garlic, very finely chopped
12 anchovy fillets (the ones packed in salt are best), rinsed and chopped
4 Tbsp. (½ stick) unsalted butter
About 8 cups trimmed, cut-up vegetables
Slices of coarse country bread for serving
½ pint cream
Milk to soak the garlic
Freshly ground black pepper
Pinch of crushed red pepper flakes (optional)
1 Tbsp. wine vinegar

Preparation:
1. Before chopping, soak the garlic in the milk for six hours or overnight. Discard the milk.
2. In a suitable saucepan that will retain the heat for the fondue over low heat, combine the chopped garlic, olive oil, and cream.
3. Cook slowly over low heat.
4. Rinse, dry, and chop the anchovies, or mashing them until they form a paste and add to the mixture.
5. Simmer until smooth, about five minutes.
6. Remove from the heat and stir in the butter and the spoon of vinegar.
7. Pour the mixture into a warmed fondue pot set over a warming candle or sterno can.
8. Serve immediately with vegetables for dipping. Pass the bread slices at the table.

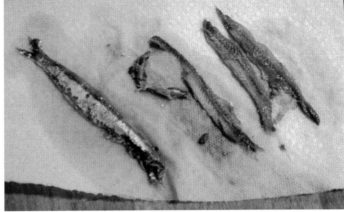

Plenty of garlic					and must have anchovies

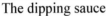

The dipping sauce				and lots of vegetables and bread

Peperoni Arrostiti con Tonno (Roasted Red Peppers with Tuna Topping)
Category: Antipasti (Appetizers)
Origin: Lalla Molino/Piemonte
Serves 4–6

This is another antipasto from the Piemonte (Piedmont) region of Italy taught to us by Lalla Molino while we were in Luxembourg. It contrasts the sweet taste of the roasted red peppers with the salty taste of tuna mixed with parsley and garlic. It also makes an attractive presentation, well suited for the Christmas holidays.

Ingredients:
4–6 roasted red bell peppers depending on size (see how to roast on the recipe for
    Peperoni Arrostiti (Roasted Peppers)
Extra-virgin olive oil for marinating the peppers
Large bunch of Italian parsley finely chopped
2 large garlic cloves, sliced for marinating the peppers
1 small garlic clove for the topping
I can good-quality tuna packed in olive oil
Kosher salt and freshly ground black pepper to taste

Preparation:
1. Roast the peppers as you would for the roasted peppers recipe.
2. After peeling and seeding the peppers, cut them into four sections lengthwise, following the natural shape of the peppers.
3. Slice the garlic into a dish with sides, such as a pie dish, and place the pepper slices in the dish. Top with olive oil and salt.
4. Cover with plastic wrap and let the peppers marinate overnight.
5. Cut each quarter piece in half or in thirds, depending on the size of the pepper, so they form smaller pieces, large enough to hold the topping.
6. In a small bowl, break up the tuna in the packed oil from the can; add the chopped parsley and minced garlic. Add more olive oil as needed to moisten.
7. Add salt and pepper to taste and mix until the topping forms a moist mixture.
8. Spread the marinated pieces of pepper on a serving tray.
9. Dollop a small amount of the tuna topping on each piece of pepper and serve.

Roasting the peppers and serving

Toasts aux Champignon (Toast with Mushrooms)
Category: Antipasti (Appetizers)
Origin: Traditional French/Luxembourg
Serves 4–6

This is a simple dish that we often enjoyed at lunchtime in Luxembourg. Its origin is probably French, but it is well-known in Luxembourg where woodlands provide an abundance of mushrooms. The cream makes it rich and the bread substantial, so it was all we needed for a hearty lunch accompanied by a fine Luxembourg Riesling.

Ingredients:
1 lb. wild mushrooms (shiitake, oyster mushrooms, or fresh, thinly sliced portobello mushrooms)
6 (or more) slices crusty Italian bread, such as a large ciabatta
½ pint crème fraîche or whipping cream
2 Tbsp. of butter and 1 Tbsp. of extra virgin olive oil
2–3 finely minced French shallots
Fresh parsley
Kosher salt and freshly ground black pepper to taste

Preparation:
1. Clean mushrooms and slice them.
2. Melt butter and olive oil over medium heat in a skillet.
3. Sauté the mushrooms with the shallots and a little salt and pepper; stirring occasionally.
4. Cut bread into large slices and rub both sides with olive oil.
5. Broil the bread in the oven until golden brown.
6. Pour the cream on the mushrooms and let reduce.
7. Finish parsley, finely chopped.
8. Pour generous quantities of mushrooms on the toast and serve hot.

Sautéing the mushrooms and
adding the crème fraîche

Serving on toast

Avocats aux Crevette (Avocado with Shrimp and American Sauce)
Category: Antipasti (Appetizers)
Origin: Traditional French/Luxembourg
Serves 4

This was a starter frequently served in Luxembourg restaurants and one we often chose. It is especially good with miniature bay shrimp. Make sure that the shrimp are wild-caught, not farmed, and have no other artificial flavors or preservatives. The only ingredients should be shrimp. If using cooked frozen shrimp, follow the thawing instructions on the package. Thaw the shrimp completely in a strainer over a bowl and place them in a clean, dry dishtowel and gently squeeze them to make sure that all the excess water is removed. I am surprised that this dish is not often seen in American restaurants given the abundance of avocados in the United States.

Ingredients:
2 avocados
½ lb. cooked, very small shrimp
1 shallot, chopped
Extra-virgin olive oil
½ lime (optional)
4 Tbsp. mayonnaise
2 Tbsp. ketchup
About 12 lettuce leaves
Kosher salt and freshly ground black pepper to taste

Preparation:
1. Cut the avocados in half lengthwise and remove pits.
2. Carve out avocado flesh and cut in large chunks. Mash some of the chunks with a fork or muddler. How much you mash depends on how chunky you want the avocado puree to be. Add chopped shallots, lime juice (optional), and a dash of olive oil. Salt and pepper to taste.
3. In a small bowl, mix mayonnaise and ketchup to make the American cocktail sauce.
4. Line the carved-out avocados with lettuce leaves. Using a spoon, evenly divide the avocado chunky puree among the avocado halves.
5. Place the shrimp evenly on each avocado and top with a teaspoon of American cocktail sauce.
6. Serve shortly after preparing.
7. Add a pinch of cayenne pepper to the American cocktail sauce to give it a bite (optional).

There are variations of this dish worth consideration. You may want to add half a celery stalk, chopped in very small pieces, and add capers and flat leaf parsley, also chopped very fine. You can replace the Ketchup sauce with a Dijon mustard, lemon juice, dried tarragon sauce with a healthy pinch of Old Bay Seasoning. To blend these flavors, you can mix all the ingredients including the shrimp (except the avocado) in a bowl before placing it in the avocado.

Spaghetti con Sugo di Pesce (Spaghetti with Fish Sauce)
Category: Paste (Pastas)
Origin: Paolo/Ancona
Serves 4–6

This is a traditional dish typical of a port town such as Ancona, where large and small fish are abundantly available. The flavors are simple and pure, using fish in a simple marinara sauce. I use a large fish such as haddock, halibut, or red snapper so that the sauce is free of bones when the fish blends into it.

Ingredients:
1 box of thin spaghetti or fedelini
2 lb. large fish fillets such as haddock, halibut, or red snapper
¼ cup extra-virgin olive oil
2–3 cloves garlic, sliced
1 chili pepper or the equivalent of chili pepper flakes

1½ lb. tomato pulp, passed through a strainer, or Pomi Passato
1 Tbsp. Italian parsley, roughly chopped
Flour to coat the fish
½ small onion, finely chopped
Kosher salt and freshly ground black pepper to taste
2–3 sprigs thyme (optional but recommended)

Preparation:
1. In a skillet place the oil, garlic, onion, and chili pepper and sauté until the onion it is translucent.
2. Add the tomato pulp, thyme, salt, and pepper and cook for half an hour over moderate heat.
3. At the same time, pour the remaining oil in a skillet and add the sliced fish, salted and lightly floured.
4. Fry the fish over medium high heat for a few seconds, until they become lightly browned on both sides.
5. Place the fish on paper towels to absorb the excess oil.
6. After oil is absorbed, place it in the sauce and let simmer until the fish is well cooked (fifteen to twenty minutes), occasionally covering the fish with the sauce.
7. Cook the spaghetti in plenty of boiling, slightly salted water, ensuring not to overcook, as it must be al dente.
8. Place the spaghetti in a large, heated, concave dish; cover the spaghetti with fish sauce and some small pieces of the fish. Sprinkle with parsley and serve immediately.
9. Serve the remaining slices of fish (if any) that remain, with a little of the sauce, as a main dish.

Placing the fish in the sauce, cooking the fish in the sauce, and serving

Cannelloni alla Nizzarda (Cannelloni Pasta, Nice Style)
Category: Paste (Pastas)
Origin: Lalla Molino
Serves 6–8

This is a dish that Lalla Molino taught us in Luxembourg. Its origin is the Ligurian coast, which is adjacent to the Cote d'Azur in France—once part of Italy. Hence it is named Nizzarda, the Italian pronunciation of Nicoise. It is a delicate homemade pasta dish, utilizing the flavors of sage, rosemary, and nutmeg.

Timing is important in preparing this pasta dish. You can prepare the chicken in advance to the point of grinding the chicken, which then can be refrigerated. However, you need to time the preparation of the veluta and the pasta so that the veluta will not stiffen and become lumpy. As some of the veluta is needed for the filling, it should be prepared before the cannelloni are filled. We normally prepare the veluta while the pasta sheets are drying.

Ingredients:

Filling:
2 full boneless chicken breasts
1 medium yellow onion, finely chopped
1 large or 2 medium garlic cloves, minced
Needles of a branch of fresh rosemary, finely chopped
A bunch of fresh sage, finely chopped
4 oz. pancetta, finely chopped
3 Tbsp. extra-virgin olive oil
6 oz. unsalted butter (one stick)
1 cup heavy cream
Kosher salt and freshly ground black pepper to taste
1 cup whole ricotta cheese
2 eggs
½ cup Parmigiano-Reggiano

Salsa Veluta:
? cup all-purpose flour
3 Tbsp. unsalted butter
2¼ cups chicken broth
Kosher salt and freshly ground black pepper to taste
¼ tsp. nutmeg

Preparation:
1. Finely chop together the onion, garlic, sage, and rosemary.
2. Finely chop the pancetta.
3. Slice the chicken breasts into strips.
4. In a large skillet, add the olive oil and butter and sauté the onion mixture and pancetta over medium heat until the onion is golden and tender.
5. Add the chicken strips and cook over medium heat until chicken is well cooked.
6. When the chicken is golden, add the cream.
7. Add salt and pepper and let cook until the cream reduces (about ten minutes).
8. Put the contents of the skillet in a food processor, pulse the chicken into fine grain, and set aside in a bowl; this is the base of the filling.
9. Prepare the Veluta:
   a. Melt the butter in saucepan.
   b. Sprinkle in the flour slowly; add salt and pepper and simmer until golden.
   c. Add the broth slowly and stir to avoid lumps, and cook for approximately fifteen minutes.
   d. Add salt, pepper, and nutmeg (freshly ground is preferable).
10. Add about two tablespoons of the veluta to the chicken mixture.
11. To the filling add the eggs, ricotta cheese, and Parmigiano-Reggiano, which concludes the filling. Set aside and make the pasta.
12. Make fresh pasta (see pasta recipe). I use three eggs to make approximately twenty one large cannelloni.
13. Cut the pasta sheets into 5x5-inch squares and let dry.
14. Boil the pasta but do not overcook. Remove from water when the pasta surfaces.
15. Lay out the pasta and, on one end, apply a generous strip of the filling.

16. Roll the pasta into long tubes and place them into a buttered lasagna dish (13x9-inch dish). You can vary the size by cutting the past sheets accordingly.
17. Apply the veluta on top of the cannelloni, making sure that the pasta is fully covered.
18. Sprinkle additional Parmigiano-Reggiano on the surface as well as dots of butter.
19. Cover until ready to bake.
20. Bake at 400°F for fifteen minutes (if refrigerated, it may need to bake longer).

Sautéing the chicken

Filled and ready to bake

Saltimbocca alla Romana (Veal Scallops with Prosciutto and Sage)
Category: Carni (Meats)
Origin: Rita Biffi/ Traditional Roman
Serves 4–6

This is a Roman dish introduced to us by Rita Biffi. It is commonly found on the menu of many Italian restaurants. The dish combines the saltiness of the prosciutto with the savory taste of sage to enhance the veal taste.

Ingredients
4–6 (5-oz.) thinly sliced veal cutlets (scallopini)
4–6 slices thinly sliced prosciutto
8–12 fresh sage leaves, plus more for garnish
All-purpose flour, for dredging
Kosher salt and freshly ground black pepper to taste
2 Tbsp. extra-virgin olive oil
2 Tbsp. unsalted butter
2 Tbsp. dry white wine
¼ cup chicken broth
Lemon wedges, for serving

Preparation:
1. To ensure that the cutlets are not too thick you may need to pound them with a meat mallet to achieve the right thickness, which should be no more than a quarter inch.
2. Put the veal cutlets side by side on a sheet of plastic wrap. Lay a piece of prosciutto on top of each piece of veal and cover with another piece of plastic.
3. Gently flatten the cutlets with a rolling pin until the prosciutto has adhered to the veal.
4. Remove the plastic wrap and lay a couple of sage leaves in the center of each cutlet. Weave a toothpick in and out of the veal to secure the prosciutto and sage.
5. Put some flour in a shallow platter and season with a fair amount of salt and pepper; mix with a fork to combine.

6. Dredge the veal in the seasoned flour, shaking off the excess.
7. Heat the oil and one tablespoon of the butter in a large skillet over medium flame.
8. Put the veal in the pan, prosciutto side down first. Cook for three minutes to crisp it up and then flip the veal over.
9. Sauté the other side for two minutes until golden.
10. Transfer the saltimbocca to a serving platter, remove the toothpicks, and keep warm.
11. Add the wine to the pan, stirring to bring up the browned bits in the bottom; let the wine cook down for a minute to burn off some of the alcohol.
12. Add the chicken broth and remaining tablespoon of butter; swirl the pan around.
13. Season with salt and pepper.
14. Pour the sauce over the saltimbocca and garnish with sage leaves and lemon wedges; serve immediately.

Veal cutlets (scallopini) and prosciutto di Parma

Pounding the cutlet and covering with prosciutto

Adding the sage

Frying in a skillet

Vitello Tonnato (Cold Veal or Turkey with Tuna Sauce)
Category: Carni (Meats)
Origin: Traditional Piemonte
Serves 4–6

This is a traditional Piedmont dish taught us by Rita Biffi, a Roman. It makes a great summer dish served cold. It is traditionally made with veal but turkey breast can be substituted. Both work very well. It is great for entertaining, as it can be prepared in advance and refrigerated before serving. The dish can be kept for up to three days in the refrigerator.

Ingredients:
1¾ lb. boneless roasting veal, in one piece, or similar size skinless turkey breast
1 carrot, peeled
1 stalk celery
1 small onion, peeled and quartered
1 bay leaf
1 clove
1 tsp. whole peppercorns

For the tuna sauce:
14 oz. good-quality canned tuna, packed in olive oil
4 anchovy fillets, preferably packed in salt
2 tsp. capers, rinsed and drained
3 Tbsp. fresh lemon juice
1¼ cup mayonnaise
Kosher salt and freshly ground black pepper to taste
Capers and pickled cornichon, to garnish

Preparation:
1. Place the veal or turkey, vegetables, and spices in a medium saucepan. Cover with water, bring to a boil, and simmer for fifty to sixty minutes.
2. Skim off the scum that rises to the surface. Do not overcook as the meat may fall apart when slicing.
3. Allow it to cool in its cooking liquid for several hours, or overnight.
4. Drain the tuna. Place it in a food processor and add the anchovies, capers, and lemon juice.
5. Process to a creamy paste. If too thick, add two or three tablespoons of the cold water.
6. Place the tuna puree into a mixing bowl and fold in the mayonnaise..
7. Slice the veal as thinly as possible without having the meat fall apart.

8. Spread a little of the tuna sauce on the bottom of a serving platter.
9. Arrange a layer of the sliced meat on top of the sauce and cover the meat with
   another layer of sauce.
10. Make another layer of meat and sauce and continue until all is used, ending with
    a topping of sauce.
11. Garnish with capers and cornichons.
12. Cover with plastic wrap and refrigerate until needed.

Cooking the veal or turkey and covering the layers

The serving

Moules a la Luxembourgeoise (Mussels, Luxembourg Style, or Mariniere)
Category: Pesci (Fish)
Origin: Josianne/Luxembourg
Serves 6–8

Ingredients:
4–6 lb. mussels, scrubbed and de-bearded
2 leeks, washed and finely chopped
1 carrot, scraped and finely chopped
1 onion, peeled and finely chopped
2 shallots, peeled and finely chopped
1 large celery stalk (with leaves), finely chopped
1 bunch Italian parsley, finely chopped
5 cloves garlic, crushed
1½ cups of very dry Riesling or Pinot Grigio
5 Tbsp. butter
Kosher salt and freshly ground black pepper to taste
1 sprig of thyme, finely chopped
2 sprigs tarragon leaves, finely chopped

Preparation:
1. Pick over the cleaned mussels and throw away any that are not closed. Place in a bowl of water and wash the mussels further, rubbing them together and changing water several times.
2. Clean all vegetables and chop finely.
3. Allow the butter to reach room temperature.
4. Lightly fry the onion and shallots in two ounces of butter in a large pot.
5. Add all the chopped vegetables, thyme, and tarragon.
6. Pour in the wine and allow it to simmer for fifteen minutes.
7. During this time, crush the garlic, and mix with five tablespoons of butter.
8. To this add a little freshly milled pepper.
9. With the pot over a very high heat, drop the mussels into the boiling contents, pouring in the rest of the wine.
10. Cover firmly. Every two minutes, stir with a circular movement to make sure the mussels do not remain at the bottom of the pot.
11. After ten minutes, almost all the mussels should have opened.
12. Put the garlic butter in the pot.
13. In two or three minutes, with regular stirring, the sauce should have mixed thoroughly.
14. Sprinkle with freshly chopped parsley and serve immediately.

F'rell am Rèisleck (Trout in Riesling Sauce)
Category: Pesci (Fish)
Origin: Traditional Luxembourg
Serves 4

With an abundance of free-flowing streams, trout is readily found in Luxemburg. A dish that I preferred, and which was often served at banking luncheons, was Trout in Riesling Sauce. The key to the sauce is tarragon, which is used frequently in French and Luxembourg dishes. The sauce can be served over the fish or separately for those wanting a more delicate accent.

Ingredients:
4 good-quality trout (about ½ lb. each)
7 fluid oz. dry Riesling (or Elbling, or other dry white wine)
Flour for dusting fish
10 fl. oz. fresh cream
2 oz. unsalted butter
3 Tbsp. Italian parsley, chopped
3 shallots, finely chopped
Pinch of chervil
1 sprig of tarragon
3 Tbsp. chives, chopped
Kosher salt and freshly ground black pepper to taste
paprika to taste

Preparation:
1. Clean, scale, wash, and dry the trout thoroughly, leaving them intact.

2. Sprinkle with salt and black pepper; then dust with plain flour.
3. Melt the butter in a frying pan, add the trout, and fry over low heat for about three minutes per side.
4. Liberally butter a casserole dish and add the trout.
5. Add all the herbs and shallots to the frying pan; then add the Riesling or wine.
6. As soon as it comes to a boil, stir in the cream and season with salt, black pepper, and paprika. Pour the sauce over the trout.
7. Transfer to an oven preheated to 400°F and bake for fifteen minutes.
8. Remove the trout from the dish and place on a warmed plate.
9. Put the casserole dish on the cooktop, bring the sauce to a boil, and whisk constantly until thick.
10. Pour the sauce over the trout or serve separately.

Fry in butter after dredging in flour and salt and pepper

Create sauce in herbs

Pour sauce over fish and serve with potatoes

Crostata di Marmelatta (Italian Tart with Preserves)
Category: Dolci (Desserts)
Origin: Traditional Italian/Ancona
Serves 4–6

The prefix crosta in the Italian word crostata means crust. And in fact the most important aspect of a crostata is getting the crust right. Unlike American pies, where the emphasis is on the filling, the Italian crostata requires a sweet, flavorful crust, usually using marmalade for the filling. Mom would make this simple, sweet dessert to accompany a good cup of coffee after dinner or when we were in the mood for a good comfort food.

Ingredients:
2 cups all-purpose flour
½ cup sugar
1 tsp. packed grated lemon zest
½ tsp. salt
½ cup plus 2 Tbsp. (¼ sticks) chilled unsalted butter, diced while cold
2 large egg yolks
1 large egg
1–1½ cups cherry, raspberry, or blueberry preserves
Confectioners' sugar
½ tsp. baking soda
½ tsp. baking powder

Preparation:
1. Preheat oven to 350°F. Blend flour, sugar, lemon zest, and salt in processor for ten seconds.
2. Add butter and process until coarse meal forms.
3. Add yolks and egg and process until moist clumps forms.
4. Transfer dough to work surface. Gather dough into ball and knead for one minute.
5. Divide dough into two pieces, one slightly larger than the other.
6. Press larger dough piece evenly onto bottom and halfway up sides of a round 9-inch tart pan with removable bottom.
7. Spread one to one-and-a-half cups preserves in crust.
8. Cut remaining dough into eleven or twelve equal pieces. Roll pieces between hands and work surface into pencil-thin ropes.
9. Arrange five or six ropes over preserves, spacing evenly and pressing ends to seal at crust edge; trim extra dough.
10. Arrange remaining five or six ropes in opposite direction, spacing evenly and forming a lattice pattern. Press ends to seal at crust edge; trim extra dough.
11. Bake the Crostata until crust is golden brown, about forty or forty-five minutes.
12. Cool tart in pan on rack.

The crostata can be prepared eight hours ahead. Let stand (at room temperature.) Remove pan sides. Lightly sift powdered sugar over the crostata, cut into wedges, and serve.

Crostata with raspberry marmalade or preserve filling

Grolla di Buon Amici (After Ski Drink)
Category: Dolci (Desserts)
Source: Mountains of Italy
Serves 4–6

I was first introduced to this after-ski drink while attempting to ski for the first time in Biella at the cabin of relatives of Roberto (who was then Gabriella's husband, in the early 1980s). This was during one of our extended weekend trips from Luxembourg to Milan. The custom in this Italian Alps town is to drink Grolla after a hard day of skiing and a hearty mountain meal. Believe me; my skiing day was hard, especially on my rear. They made the Grolla in an iron pot over a wood-burning fire. Nowadays I prepare it on a stovetop, but it still has the same effect. As there are no skiing mountains in the Chicago suburbs, I serve it on cold nights after a hearty meal. It is called "of good friends" because you drink it out of a wooden bowl with multiple spouts and pass it around for the next person to drink out of the next spout. The key is remembering which spout you drank out of. And don't worry if you happen to forget—you are among friends. The objective is to drink it all without putting it down. It is bad luck if you pass up a drink or you put the bowl down before it is empty.

Ingredients:
2 cups grappa and 1 cup genievre grain alcohol (made from Juniper berries). The grappa
    need not be your most expensive, unlike what I display below.
Rinds of ½ orange and 1 lemon.
¼ cup of sugar.
Pot of stovetop espresso coffee (6 cups), normally made in a Bialetti or Carmencita-type pot.

Preparation:
1. Place the grappa, genievre, orange and lemon peels, and sugar in a small saucepan
    and heat at medium-high heat over the stove.
2. Heat it just to the boiling point. Do not let it boil, or you will evaporate the alcohol.
3. In the meantime, prepare the pot of coffee and heat the Grolla bowl either in the
    microwave or oven. Heating the bowl releases the juices from the wood, which

adds to the flavor of the Grolla.

4. Pour some sugar around the opening on the top of the Grolla bowl and around each spout. With a teaspoon, take some of the alcohol and drizzle it over the sugar around the openings. Pour the finished coffee into the hot Grolla bowl and then add the grappa mixture, including the rinds.

5. The Grolla is ready to pass around, but be careful because the first few sips will be very hot.

6. For effect turn down the lights, open the Grolla lid and ignite the fumes for a glowing image. Don't let it burn too long as you will be burning off the alcohol.

7. Pass it around, remembering which spout is yours, and let the aroma overwhelm you.

Coffeemakers and the Grolla bowl

Genievre and Grappa Nardini

Joe and Chris Cortellini enjoying the Grolla

The three brothers mellowing after Grolla

Chapter 14

Chicago to Milan

We returned to Indianapolis during one of the Midwest's most fierce winter storms on record, the Blizzard of '78. One evening while Roz was in Bloomington with her parents, I was in Indianapolis entertaining Alex and Wendy, colleagues from Luxembourg. Alex was chief accountant at the bank's branch in Luxembourg, and Wendy was the credit analyst. As the storm was developing, Alex, Wendy, and I were dining at the Stouffers Hotel on Meridian Street. After dinner we returned to the Columbia Club on Monument Circle where they were staying. Due to the storm's severity, I needed a room for myself. I spent the next three days stranded as the entire city of Indianapolis shut down. Fortunately, the Columbia Club had plenty of supplies on hand.

Wendy and Alex with me on the deserted streets of Indianapolis
We eventually made it to Bloomington to rescue Roz

After residing for a short time at Riley Towers in downtown Indianapolis, Roz and I found an older fixer-upper home on East 44th Street in the Meridian/Kessler neighborhood. We hung wallpaper in most of the rooms, remodeled the master bathroom, and closed off the dungeon basement. The effort tested our marital bonds, but in the end we had a pretty nice house.

House on 44ᵗʰ Street

Professionally, I returned to AFNB's international division, which, unfortunately, had no suitable position available for me. I was welcomed back by the staff, and, after a period of debriefing, I secured an appointment as assistant controller in the bank's general accounting group. Although appreciative of the opportunity to revive my general accounting skills, I soon became discontented and began to look for other opportunities.

During this period Mom and Dr. Cornacchione sold their house on Carrollton Court and moved to Sarasota, Florida. Mom loved Florida and her garden of tomatoes, basil, and other herbs. However, she felt isolated from her family and cherished our visits. Time spent with Mom after she moved to Florida was limited, like it was during our Luxembourg days. My efforts to make a record of her recipes during these periods dwindled.

While in Florida, Dr. Cornacchione's health, affected by emphysema and lifelong history of smoking, continued to fail. He died in 1981. After his death Mom was fortunate to have dear friends, Dr. Bennett Kraft and his wife Margo, nearby. Missing her family, she ultimately returned to Indianapolis, where she bought a house on the north side.

Mom with Dr. Bennett Kraft and Margo

While serving as assistant controller at AFNB, my search for a new position resulted in a new job with a French-owned bank named Banque de L'Indochine et de Suez as operations manager at its Chicago branch, located on South Wacker Drive. Banque de L'Indochine had its origin in Southeast Asia in 1875 with the opening of its first branch in Saigon. It was called Banque de L'Indochine et de Suez after a merger between Banque de Suez et de L'Union des Mines and Banque de L'Indochine in 1975. Initially set up as a note-issuing bank in French Indochina, it quickly expanded to serve French settlements in Oceania, New Caledonia, French Somaliland, and other parts of Asia that were outside French control. The merger in 1975 combined Banque de Suez's merchant banking skills and its established European presence with Banque de L'Indochine's established commercial banking expertise and its established networks in Asia and the Middle East. In 1981, the bank's name was shortened to Banque Indosuez.

In 1979, the Chicago branch of Banque Indosuez was heavily involved in the financing of trade between US suppliers and Saudi Arabian customers. I became knowledgeable in letter-of-credit operations, including documentation requirements, payments, and financing at execution. I also learned about governmental regulations concerning embargos imposed upon blacklisted companies. I reported to the bank's finance director, Rudy Schwegler, a Swiss expatriate. It was a great learning opportunity, but I grew to understand how (and why) locals dislike working for expatriate staff. I discovered I'd rather be an expatriate manager in an overseas assignment as opposed to a subordinate of a foreign expatriate in the States.

The Indosuez Chicago staff

Our Home in Lake Forest

The bank's staff was young and talented, and it was fun working with them. Roz and I enjoyed our modest home in Lake Forest, a lovely suburb north of Chicago along the lakeshore north.

Wanting to work in Europe again, I responded to a *Wall Street Journal* ad for a position as operations manager in a bank's European network. Within a short time, I received an offer from Continental Illinois National Bank and Trust Company to serve as the operations manager of its branch in Milan, Italy. We arrived in Milan in mid-November, 1980.

In the December 1978 issue of the *Dun's Review*, Continental Bank was named one of the top five best-managed companies in the United States. I felt privileged to have been selected for an assignment by such a respected employer. I still find it difficult to believe that only six years later, the bank failed.

My initial impression of Milan, formed in part by the time of the year and the weather upon arrival, was a dark city, noisy, with maddening traffic and cars parked on sidewalks for lack of parking space. Over time, however, Roz and I grew to love it.

We rented an apartment as temporary quarters near the Linate airport. The commute on the underground to work in the city's center was nightmarish. It was always crowded and hot.

Finding permanent accommodations was a difficult task. We were facing a deadline as we needed to find something before our furniture arrived. Most places were too expensive, too old, or too small. We finally selected an apartment on the third floor (no elevator) of a beautiful villa near the Castello Forzesco area of town on Via Ariosto. It was situated on the edge of Piazzale Baracca, with wonderful coffee bars and pastry shops, and near the well-known shopping street of Corso Vercelli. The apartment was centrally located, with a short tram ride to the office, which was located on Via Montenapoleone. The apartment needed considerable renovation, including refinishing floors, wallpapering, hanging drapes, and installing new appliances. Fortunately, bank management accepted my contention that it was less expensive to make renovations to this apartment with lower rent then for us to continue searching for permanent accommodations. When finished, it was a beautiful apartment and comfortable, except for the lack of an elevator and air conditioning. We were located only a few blocks away from the famous church of Santa Maria delle Grazie where Da Vinchi's Last Supper is painted.

Italo and Etta visiting us at our temporary quarters in Milan

Via Lodovico Ariosto, our apartment
on the third floor (top floor)

Corso Vercelli, on my ride to work and the coffee shop where they made the best coffee.
They roasted their own coffee beans. Imagine the aroma upon stepping into the shop

Santa Maria delle Grazie, bombarded during the war,
and what it looks like today with the Last Supper

The Milan branch of the Continental Bank had a staff of about one hundred, providing commercial and trade financing for US Multinational companies (large US companies having operations in Europe) and indigenous customers. My primary goals for this assignment were to strengthen the internal control and procedural framework for the banking operations, which was staffed by local talent. Additionally, I was also to implement its worldwide bank operating system, known as IBSPS, twice aborted previously. Prior to my arrival, the branch was given a derogatory management letter from its external auditors; they had refused to sign off on the branch balance sheet because it could not be validated. In reviewing the task ahead of me, I concluded that new local, qualified talent was needed, as well as temporary assistance from the Continental network by individuals who were familiar with Continental operating procedures. I hired a local chartered accountant by the name of Generoso Gallucio to strengthen the accounting staff. I brought in Jack Sebesta, a seasoned Continental accountant who was on temporary assignment in Amsterdam, to rationalize the branch procedures; Peter Howard from the London branch and, later, Michele Kahn from the Paris branch for credit policy; and Hardy Gunther from the Frankfurt branch to strengthen the bank operations. To implement IBSPS I brought in Toon Broyland, an IT specialist, from Amsterdam. This blitz was successful as we resolved the audit deficiencies and normalized operations in less than six months and implemented IBSPS with the help of the IBD team from Chicago. We also relocated the branch with the assistance of head office architect, Jay Gentile, transferring it from the incongruent fashion street of Via Montenapoleone to a very effective, yet stylish, building in the commercial district of Via Turati. By the end of this assignment, the Milan branch was considered the most profitable branch in the Continental Bank's European network.

From Montenapoleone to Via Turati

There were long work days—and many nights—but there was also a lot of fun with such a diverse staff. We found lots of reasons to celebrate.

Scenes from staff Christmas party at our apartment

Visiting the Rome representative office and Thanksgiving in Milan

Generoso Gallucio and I made one very memorable business trip to Rome. When we landed in Rome, we were greeted by an impromptu strike (which happened often) of luggage handlers. The pilot refused to let us off the plane until the raucous passengers, including Generoso and me, insisted. Relenting, the pilot allowed us to exit at the back of the aircraft onto the runway. Knowing that the luggage handler strike meant that we would have no luggage at the gate, Generoso jumped through the open luggage compartment door of the airplane and retrieved our luggage. We then took a triumphant stroll, luggage in hand, along the tarmac to the gate.

Generoso and me in Rome
visiting the Bank of Italy

My office at Via Turati

With the help of the IBD unit operations team from Chicago, including Ron Bacci and Mark Greco, we successfully implemented the worldwide system.

Continental Bank's IBD unit operations team

On a personal level, living in Milan was ideal, at least for me, as I spoke the language and had numerous relatives living in Italy. One of my relatives, Maurizio, lived minutes away from our apartment. It is not often that an expatriate can live in his birth country and be paid a bonus for doing so. We took advantage of traveling the country with weekend trips to places including the Ligurian Coast, Monte Bianco and Aosta, the Veneto, and Emilia Romania. We visited Ancona as often as possible and toured in southern Italy for vacations. We regret not having visited Sicily.

We had a frightening experience on a weekend trip to Imperia on the Ligurian coast. In early spring Roz and I decided to take a few days to visit this beautiful coastal area. At about six o'clock on a Monday morning, we were awakened by a banging on the hotel door. As I opened the door in my pajamas, two policemen, holding machine guns at the ready, forced their way into our room. While Roz watched from under the bed covers, I was told to dress and was then whisked away to the local police station. There was no indication of a warrant or a reason for the intrusion. I found myself yearning for those rights we Americans take for granted in the Bill of Rights to our constitution. It was good that it was a Monday and someone would be coming to work at the police station to deal with the situation. Otherwise, I surely would have spent the weekend in jail, and Roz would have been left alone in the hotel. At the jail I waited in a room, luckily not a cell, for a short time until I was escorted to the Uffici Stranieri (Foreign Office). Once again, I was lucky to have my American passport, Permesso di Soggiorno, and Permesso di Lavoro (residency and work permits) in my possession. I carried these with me at all times. Eventually I was told that I was arrested for being *"renitente della leva."* In US terms, I was accused of being a "draft dodger."

In Italy, military service is mandatory. When I reached eighteen years of age, I received a demand to serve in the Italian military. At that time I was in Indianapolis finishing high school and had no intention of becoming an Italian soldier. I ignored the demand and later gained my US citizenship. In Italy, once an Italian, always an Italian, so the military headquarters in Ancona issued a warrant for my arrest. At Italian hotels at check-in, the hotel requires a guest to present his or her passport to run a background check for outstanding warrants. In the countless times that I had previously stayed in Italian hotels, this was apparently overlooked. Because our visit occurred during a very light tourist season, and the hotel's clerk probably had nothing better to do, the check was run, and I was nabbed.

As all my papers were in order, there seemed to be some confusion at the foreign office. How could I be a fugitive from justice, yet have all the needed permits? The foreign office in Imperia decided that this was a federal military issue and not a civil matter, so the *carabinieri* (the famous federal police) were called. The carabinieri came for me and took me to their local headquarters. After explaining my situation all over again and producing my papers, someone placed a call to the military office in Ancona. The military office in Ancona explained the origin of the complaint. After what seemed like forever, a decision was made to release me on my own recognizance, on the condition that I would get in touch with the Italian consulate in Detroit, which had jurisdiction over my case, to resolve my military status. This eventually required, upon a return trip home, a meeting with the Italian consular officer in Detroit. I received a letter, which I carry with me to this day, stating that I have satisfied the requirement for Italian military service.

At about noon I was released. Without an apology or the offer of a ride back to the hotel, I made my way back to Roz.

Stormy weather in Imperia in March

Milan is not known as a tourist destination. On the surface one could conclude this because of the commercial and industrial appearance of the city, the traffic, and the climate, which is influenced by the surrounding mountain ranges. In my opinion, Milan is a gem in disguise. The city is the fashion capital of the world; the restaurants rival those in Paris and Rome. The architectural attractions, including the Duomo, the Galleria, la Scala, Castello Sforzesco, Brera, and the Navigli (canals), are some of the most beautiful in Europe.

Mom, Corrado, Roz, and Jane in the foreground and the Duomo lit at night

The Galleria, which is the Piazza Duomo, next to the church with the same group

La Scala, where we attended a performance
by Chicago Symphony Orchestra in 1981
and other performances

Little known are the Navigli (canals) of Milan,
which at one time in Milan's history rivaled those in Venice

Summing up Milan, there is a song written and sung by Lucio Dalla titled "*Milano che Fatica,*" which translates to "Milan, what a struggle." That title pretty much sums up living in Milan. Lucio Dalla was an artist whose talents we grew to love while in Milan. He was more of a poet than a singer, and his songs cried out the themes of the times. This YouTube video of his song "Milano" tells the story of Milan.

http://www.youtube.com/watch?v=FiuVKux_HhY&feature=youtu.be

Milan summers can be steamy due to little movement of air in the Po Basin. The absence of air conditioning in the apartment was an inconvenience. Restful sleep on the hot summer nights was difficult. A couple of our favorite getaways during these hot periods were the Dolomite Mountains and St. Moritz, Switzerland. Our favorite town in the Dolomites was Cortina d'Ampezzo. Summertime in the mountains was a refreshing break from the hectic pace of Milan.

Taking a break in Cortina and St. Moritz

As this is a cookbook, I need to devote some time to discussing the cuisine and restaurants of Milan. The city's culinary foundation is straightforward "casalinga" (or housewife) style cooking, influenced by the meats of Lombardy and the grains of the Po valley. The staples are rice and polenta. Red sauces are certainly found, but they are not the tradition. One of our favorite restaurants in Milan was the Trattoria Milanese, located in the old town section of Milan on Via Santa Marta, where not even a tiny Fiat could fit. This restaurant is a superb classical Milanese eatery run by an old man and his son. It was our favorite hangout. The menu read like a Milanese cookbook: salad of nervetti (which is a salad of pork cartilage); tiny onions and vinegar dressed cold veal cutlets; minestrone soup served with pasta or, more traditionally, rice, and in the summer served chilled with olive oil topping. Also on the menu were risotto Milanese; polenta with braised beef (brasato) and osso buco so tender that the meat fell off the bone, with plenty of marrow. Other Milanese classics were zampone with lentils, fried eggs, and Gorgonzola cheese atop polenta. For the more adventurous, there was mondeghîli, which I never had. It is some sort of fried hash cake of chopped beef, meaty Milan sausage, liverwurst, parsley, bread crumbs, and grated Parmesan cheese. The tripe soup-stew, busecca, is offered with the other fried or stewed innards (not my favorite).

To die for was the zabaglione, a soup-like dish served warm and thick with a taste of Marsala wine. I remember meeting Generoso, Jack, and other friends there on a weekly basis to share a plate of spaghetti, aglio, olio e pepperoncino, and always, always, a bowl of zabaglione. The zabaglione served at Trattoria Milanese was the best Roz and I ever enjoyed. The eggs were prepared in a bowl beaten with the Marsala; and to thicken it, the zabaglione was steamed in the bowl with pressure from the cappuccino nozzle before serving. It was amazing.

I returned to this restaurant many years later, and it was still vibrant after seventy-six years. The old man had passed away, but his wife was still there. The wife and son were then running the restaurant, which had grown in size, was more chic than before, and was decorated with romantic watercolors, copper pots, and faded posters. At our later visit, it was attracting an international clientele and no longer had a local clientele or feeling. However, the food was still excellent.

Via Santa Marta and Milan's old district

Trattoria Milanese waiters at work

Another of our favorite restaurants in Milan was named Boccondivino. I entertained the IBD visitors at this unique eatery that I had been introduced to by Gallucio. It served a different wine with each course ending with a variety of grappas to insure your inebriation. This restaurant is still successful today and is worth a visit. The atmosphere is rustic and the food exceptional.

Boccondivino, famous for its wine selection with a different wine for each course

The Italian cheese selection was outstanding

Other notable Milanese restaurants that we frequented, both for luncheons and dinners, during that period and still existing today are Bagutta on Via Bagutta; Bice on Via Borgospesso (which had a sister restaurant in Chicago); Boeucc on Piazza Belgioioso; and Paper Moon on Via Bagutta, all near the original location of the Continental Bank branch on Via Montenapoleone.

Bagutta, rich in tradition and dating back to 1926, serving Milanese cuisine

Ristorante Bice, which had a location in Chicago, serving Tartufo Bianco in season

Paper Moon, our favorite luncheon restaurant

Generoso also introduced me to a Tuscan restaurant called Terza Carbonaia, located on Via Scipioni, which I try to frequent whenever I return to Milan.

Garden seating and a multitude of antipasti at the Terza Carbonaia

It is famous for its rich buffet of antipasti, grilled vegetables, fried eggplants with zucchini flowers, and bruschetta with fresh porcini mushrooms. Its pastas include Tufoli al ragu di filetto, gnocchi al gorgonzola, penne all'arrabbiata, and *tagliatelle ai funghi porcini*. The restaurant's claim to fame as a Tuscan restaurant is its meat dishes grilled on an open fire, including Tagliata, T-bone steak fiorentina, filet, chops accompanied by oven-baked potatoes, grilled radicchio trevisana, mushroom, and mixed salad. Its desserts include homemade tiramisu and apple pie, served hot with gelato alla crema.

Dinner at Terza Carbonaia during my visit in 2004
with Generoso's staff and my Motorola staff

We also frequented many restaurants outside of Milan. We actually sought out restaurants that were participants in the Italian Touring Club's marketing program called *"Ristoranti del Buon Ricordo."* Restaurants (normally well-known restaurants) in this program presented a diner with a special plate as a souvenir if he or she ordered the featured specialty, which was painted on the plate. We collected over fifty plates out of the hundred restaurants participating in this program throughout Italy during our stay in Milan. I earned the plates; Roz only nibbled at most of the specialty dishes. These plates hang on a wall in our home today.

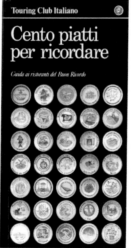

The program brochure and one hundred plates to remember

Some of the more interesting dishes we ate at these restaurants were:

- *Pastissaoa de Caval*—horsemeat at Ristorante Dodici Apostoli in Verona
- *Piccione alla Ghiotta*—pigeon at Ristorante Umbra in Assisi
- *Trippa al Pisana*—tripe at Ristorante Sergio in Pisa
- *Stoccafisso all'Anconatana*—salt cod at Ristorante Villa Amalia in Falconara (Ancona)

Milan is the capital city of the province of Milano and the principal city of the Lombardy region of northern Italy. Milan as a city dates back more than 2,500 years and has been controlled by many conquerors. Today it is the leading financial center and the most prosperous manufacturing and commercial city of Italy. Milan is one of the major financial and business centers of the world. It also enjoys fame as one of the world capitals for design and fashion. It is a premier location for motorsports and football (soccer).

Milan is located in the Po Basin of northern Italy, four hundred feet (122 meters) above sea level. Snowfalls are relatively common in winter. Due to its proximity to the Alps to the north and the Apennine to the west and south, the city is often shrouded in the fog typical of the Po Basin. Flights into Milan are often diverted to either Venice or Genoa. Nevertheless, it provided us a convenient starting point for our travels throughout Italy. The road infrastructure leading from Milan was good, with many fantastic destinations only a few hours away. We could drive to Ancona from Milan in five hours.

We were fortunate to spend almost three years in Milan, and we certainly took advantage by getting to know our relatives and their families and seeing the incredibly beautiful sights of this wonderful country.

We traveled to Portofino and Cinque Terre with friends from Lebanon, Indiana, who were assigned to work in Milan by Dow Chemical. We became friends with Joe and Marilee Mollelo, Rita and Jerry DeVriese, and Bob and Sue Fike, all expatriates with Dow Chemical. Portofino is uniquely beautiful in its magnificent marina. It's known for its fish and pesto dishes. We learned the local version called Trenette al'Pesto. South of Portofino is Cinque Terre (five lands), which is a series of towns along the Ligurian coast, each more spectacular than the previous. The highlight was a walking trail along the rocky coast that connected each town. This is a must-see for anyone visiting Italy.

Portofino, one of the most picturesque coastal towns of Italy, was a short ride from Milan

Cinque Terre (Five Lands), just south of Portofino,
is a coastal walk from town to town

Just north of Milan in the Lake District is Como, on Lago di Como, with beautiful homes along the lake and a fantastic shopping district. An unusual feature of the lake is that it has so many palm trees despite being so near the Alps. We enjoyed taking many visitors to this area.

In front of Isola Bella with Jim Fahy,
holding on to the palm trees

One of our favorite eating spots in the mountains was La Maison de Filippo,
located on the Italian side of Monte Bianco. It is only an hour-and-a-half ride from Milano

My cousin Italo DiSanto lived less than forty-five minutes south of Milan in the very well-known town of Cremona. Cremona is famous for its violin making—it was the home of Stradivarius. A local candy called Terrone (almond and sugar wafer bars) is highly prized. Italo and his wife Etta lived in a historic renovated apartment. Both were teachers in Cremona, and Italo was also an architect and designer of furniture. They had a marvelous apartment in the historic center of Cremona. Etta made up for Mom's absence by providing me with many excellent recipes.

Dinner in Italo's apartment in Cremona and Roz is playing the piano in their family room

Strolling along the Po River that runs
through Cremona with Etta's mother

Outside their apartment in front
of our Alfretta (Alpha Romeo)

We also had the chance to visit Lalla Molino, who was then living with her family in Cuneo, a mountain town near the French border. Cuneo, like Torino, is famous for its antipasti, white truffles, and the Gianduiotti candy.

Gianduiotti candy and Roz and Lalla in Torino

Either by train or automobile, Verona and Venice are each easily accessible from Milan for a weekend jaunt. Verona is a beautiful medieval town known for the balcony scene in Romeo and Juliet and for having an intact coliseum where we attended a performance of the Aida. Venice has no equal; the best time to visit is late winter when tourists are absent.

Venice, off season, with Alex and Yetti visiting from Luxembourg. Notice the lack of tourists

The famous Romeo and Juliet balcony in Verona and at the spectacular
Verona coliseum to attend Verdi's opera Aida with bank colleagues

Near Verona there is a lovely town that is the grappa capital of Italy, producing what I believe is the best grappa available, Nardini. The town is named Bassano del Grappa and is also known for its beautiful ceramics and good food.

Bassano del Grappa and Nardini

We visited Ancona often, of course. Mom visited us on several occasions, once with Corrado and his wife Jane.

Mom and Corrado arriving in Milano and hiking on Monte Conero

Paolo Rismondo with Mom, Italo, and Etta in Ancona

The bank granted leaves to its expatriate employees once a year. This provided us a chance to get back to our families in the United States. Although Mom did visit us on several occasions, Roz's parents never had the opportunity to visit us in Italy. So once a year, we flew to Indianapolis to see as many of our relatives as would have us. We also arranged to meet them in Florida to combine a vacation with the reunion.

Visiting Roz's parents in Bloomington and Mom in Sarasota

In late 1982, with the Milan branch operations normalized, I was asked to take another assignment in either Buenos Aires or Paris. As Buenos Aires is considered the Paris of South America, I chose to take the position in the real thing. After many farewell parties and a sense of loss at having to leave my country of birth, I said good-bye to Milan and my family and colleagues who had named me "nostro Americano" (our American). Fortunately Mom was with us during this transition to Paris and was a lot of help in preparing our Paris apartment.

Going-away dinner with staff

Going away party at Irv Knox (branch general manager)
and his wife Josephine's place with Generoso and Roz

Giulio Lazzaroni on the left, who replaced me as
operations manager, and dancing with the staff

Crossing the Alps by train on our way to Paris

Arrival in Paris in early December

As you can imagine, I was able to collect many recipes during our stay in Milan. Some were provided by relatives and others by colleagues and friends. Roz attended a cooking school while in Milan. Below are my favorite recipes from this period. As you will see, most of them involve pastas.

- *Spaghetti Aglio, Olio, e Pepperoncino* (Spaghetti, Garlic, Oil, and Hot Peppers)
- *Pasta con Carciofi,* (Pasta with Fresh Artichokes)
- *Trenette al Pesto* (Linguine with Pesto, Green Beans, and Potatoes)
- *Penne all'Arrabiata* (Penne with Hot Tomato Sauce)
- *Pasta con Zucchine* (Pasta with Fresh Zucchini and Basil)
- *Risotto con Radicchio* (Rice with Radicchio)
- *Pasta Fagioli* (Fazul) (Pasta with Bean Soup)
- *Spaghetti al Limone* (Spaghetti with Lemon Sauce)
- *Pasta alla Putanesca* (Pasta with Hot Olive and Tomato Sauce)
- *Spaghetti/Linguine con Vongole* (Linguini with Clam Sauce)
- *Spaghettini all Checca* (Spaghetti with Fresh Raw Tomato and Herbs)
- *Pasta alla Norma* (Spaghetti with Eggplant)
- *Polenta alla Griglia con Ragu di Funghi* (Grilled Polenta with Mushroom Ragu)
- *Osso Buco Milanese* (Stewed Veal Shank Milanese)
- *Cotoletta Milanese* (Breaded Veal Cutlet Milanese)
- *Tagliata* (Grilled Sliced Beef Sirloin with Rosemary)
- *Arrosto/Codone al Tartufo* (Veal or Pork Roast Stuffed with White Truffles)
- *Melanzane Parmigiana* (Eggplant Parmesan)
- *Bietole Soffritto* (Sautéed Beet Greens or Endive)
- *Insalata Caprese* (Caprese Salad)
- *Insalate di Carciofi* (Fresh Artichoke Salad)
- *Tiramisu* (Pick-Me-Up Dessert)
- *Castagne al Carbone* (Chestnuts over Open Flame)

- *Zabaglione* (Egg Custard)

Spaghetti Aglio, Olio, e Peperoncini
(Spaghetti Olive Oil, Garlic, Chili Pepper)

Category: Paste (Pastas)
Origin: Traditional Italian
Serves 4

This is a staple in Italy and comfort food for many Italian families. Like the hamburger in America, it is easy and quick to prepare. Because of its simplicity, the quality of the ingredients is most important. I normally leave the garlic in the sauce and eat it with the spaghetti. You can, of course, remove the garlic before mixing the oil if you don't care to eat the delectable fried garlic.

We liked to order this dish at our mom-and-pop restaurant in Milano, La Trattoria Milanese. Friends, family, and business colleagues we introduced to this dish found it difficult to limit themselves to only one helping of this pasta. It is especially good with a bottle or two of Oltra Po Pavese wine. The oft-repeated joke is to say you want a plate of this after having eaten a large meal.

Ingredients:
1-lb. box Italian imported spaghettini (use spaghetti, spaghettini, or fedelini,
  but do not use capellini or vermicelli)
3–4 cloves of garlic, sliced
Bunch of Italian flat leaf parsley (at least 1 Tbsp.)
½ cup extra-virgin olive oil (I like oils from Puglia)
Red pepper flakes to taste (at least ¼ tsp.); I sometime substitute whole
  tiny cayenne peppers and crumble 3 or 4 instead of the pepper flakes)
Kosher salt and freshly ground black pepper to taste
Grated Pecorino or *Parmigiano-Reggiano* (optional)

Preparation:
1. The important aspect of this sauce is the frying of the garlic. If you get it too
   brown or burn the garlic, you will need to start over.
2. Put the oil in a large skillet and warm the oil.
3. Add the garlic over medium heat or lower.
4. When the garlic's color begins to change (golden) add the red pepper flakes,
   salt and pepper.
5. Stir well and remove from heat.
6. Drain the pasta (either retain a small portion of the boiling water or do not
   over drain the pasta, in order to maintain some moisture in the pasta). I

normally lift the pasta from the boiling water when done with tongs as opposed to draining the pasta through a colander.

7. Return the skillet with the oil to low heat and either add the drained pasta into the skillet or mix both the oil and pasta in a large pasta dish and add the parsley.

8. Serve immediately and add grated cheese at the table.

Pasta con Carciofi Freschi *(Pasta with Fresh Artichokes)*

Category: Paste (Pastas)
Origin: Traditional Milanese
Serves 4

The sweet aftertaste of fresh artichokes is a dining experience you will remember. The *Parmigiano-Reggiano* cheese is an outstanding complement to the artichokes. The key to this preparation is ensuring that you have removed the tough outer leaves of the artichoke and all remnants of the choke. Otherwise, your guests will be forever removing artichoke fragments from their mouths. The risk of leaving a few remnants, however, is well worth it. This is one of the best vegetable sauce pastas around. Serve with a Pinot Grigio or Vernaccia. Artichokes with their stems and leaves as found in Milan are best but, unfortunately, are hard to find in the Midwest.

Ingredients:
7–8 medium/smallish fresh artichokes, sliced, with choke removed
¼ cup good-quality Italian extra-virgin olive oil

4–5 cloves garlic, thinly sliced
Handful of fresh Italian flat-leaf parsley chopped
¾ cup white wine
1 whole lemon, used to maintain the color of the artichokes
¼ tsp. chili pepper flakes
Kosher salt and freshly ground black pepper to taste
1 lb. pasta (penne or fusilli)
Parmigiano-Reggiano

Preparation:

1. Clean the artichokes by removing outer leaves until you reach the pale green leaves that are tender. Trim the base by slicing odd the dark portion reaching the tender meat of the heart and cut off the top third of the artichoke, which is still hard and prickly.
2. Slice the artichoke in half. It is preferable to use young artichokes that have not yet formed a choke. If the choke exists, you need to remove it.
3. Place the sliced artichokes one at a time into a mixing bowl with the squeezed lemon juice and three-fourths cup of water. Dip cut artichokes into the lemon water to prevent them from turning brown.
4. Just before cooking, slice the artichoke quarters in thin slices.
5. Add the olive oil to a large, heavy-bottomed saucepan.
6. When oil is hot, add the garlic slices and cook for about one minute to flavor the oil.
7. Add the artichoke slices, chopped parsley, three-fourths cup of water and cook for fifteen to twenty minutes over medium-low heat.
8. Add chili pepper flakes (optional).
9. Turn up the heat and add the wine; let evaporate. Then simmer until the artichokes are tender. You may need to add some water if the artichokes become too dry.
10. Salt and pepper to taste
11. Cook the pasta al dente; and, when cooked, add the pasta to the saucepan with the artichokes and mix well.
12. Add Parmigiano-Reggiano on servings.

Place them in lemon water
to keep their color

Sauté the sliced baby artichokes

Serve with Parmigiano-Reggiano

Trenette al Pesto (Linguine with Pesto, Green Beans, and Potatoes)
Category: Paste (Pastas)
Origin: Traditional Ligurian
Serves 4

One of our favorite places in Italy—and a gem of a city—is Portofino (which in Italian means "elegant port," which it is). It is located about an hour and a half from Milano in the heart of Liguria. An advantage to living in Milan was having a beautiful place like Portofino nearby with its Mediterranean climate. Food wise, Portofino is famous for fresh fish and, more importantly, its aromatic basil plants and its pesto. We have never experienced better pesto than that of Portofino. The local version is called *Trenette al Pesto* and combines small potatoes and green beans with pesto and pasta. Trust me, it's excellent. Although pesto can be saved in the refrigerator under olive oil and can even be frozen, it is best consumed within twenty-four hours of being made.

Portofino

Ingredients:
1-lb. box linguini or *linguini fini*
4–6 oz. fresh basil leaves (broad leaves are better)
2 oz. Italian parsley leaves
1 large clove garlic, minced
2 Tbsp. *pignoli* (pine nuts)
½ cup extra-virgin olive oil
Kosher salt and freshly ground black pepper to taste
1 cup grated *Parmigiano-Reggiano*
½ lb. fresh green beans

2 small potatoes

Preparation:

1. In a food processor, place the basil leaves, garlic, parsley leaves, pignoli, salt, and pepper; gradually add the olive oil, scraping the sides of the processor to ensure that the pesto is fully blended. The parsley helps retain the green color.
2. Transfer the blended pesto to a container to store in the refrigerator, topping it up with the olive oil to seal the contents.
3. Boil the green beans five minutes or longer, depending on the size. They must be al dente. Skim off the foam from the green bean water and submerge in ice water to stop the cooking.
4. In the same cooking water as the beans, boil the potatoes ten or fifteen minutes, depending on the size. Remove and let cool, peel, and cut into one-inch cubes.
5. In a large boiling pan cook the pasta al dente.
6. In a large warmed pasta bowl place the potatoes and add some butter. Add the green beans and half the pesto sauce and sprinkle with *Parmigiano Reggiano*.
7. Mix gently, taste, and add more pesto if needed.
8. Serve immediately, topping with more cheese at the table. You can add more pesto as desired.

Potatoes and green beans are boiled
and placed in a bowl

Pesto is layered on top and then linguini
is added with more pesto
and some pasta water

Add *Parmigiano-Reggiano* and serve immediately

Penne all'Arrabiata (Penne with Hot Tomato Sauce)

Category: Paste (Pastas)
Origin: Italian Traditional
Serves 4

Arrabia in Italian means "anger." This dish takes its name from the hot, angry sauce. It is a well-known dish throughout all of Italy, with a number of variations. I took this particular recipe from our cousins from Cremona (Italo and Etta DiSanto) when we lived in Milano.

To make sure that the sauce is amply *hot*, you may need to add chili pepper flakes or another chili pepper, if one alone does not do the trick.

Ingredients:
1 stick butter
½ lb. fresh mushrooms, sliced
2 cloves garlic, smashed
1 chili pepper (or the equivalent in pepper flakes)

¼ lb. (or more) lean pancetta, cut in small cubes
1½ lb. can or box chopped Italian plum tomatoes
1-lb. box penne pasta
Parmigiano-Reggiano or Pecorino Romano cheese
Kosher salt and fresh ground black pepper to taste
Fresh basil to taste

Preparation:
1. Fry the pancetta in a large saucepan over medium heat in half a stick of butter until the pancetta is golden and begins to become crispy.
2. Strain the pancetta and set aside.
3. In the same pan, adding half of the remaining butter (one-fourth of a stick), fry the mushrooms until all the water evaporates from the mushrooms and the oils becomes clear.
4. Strain the mushrooms and set aside.
5. Add the remaining butter and fry the garlic and chili pepper until the garlic begins to turn golden.
6. Add the chopped tomatoes, basil, salt, and pepper and bring to a boil; then turn down heat and simmer.
7. Add the mushrooms and pancetta and cook for half an hour or until the sauce reduces and oil rises.
8. Remove the garlic and chili pepper to serve the sauce.
9. Cook the pasta al dente, add the sauce and the *Parmigiano-Reggiano* cheese, and serve immediately.

I like to serve this pasta with a good red table wine such as a Dolcetto or a Barberra d'Alba.

Preparing the mushrooms and the pancetta

Serving the pasta

Pasta con Zucchine (Pasta with Fresh Zucchini and Basil)
Category: Paste (Pastas)
Origin: Anna Grazia—Milanese
Serves 4

This is a great summer pasta to make when zucchinis are ripe and plentiful. The key is finding very green zucchini and using only slim ones, which contain less water. Topping the pasta with fresh basil and garlic accents the flavor and complements the zucchini. Be sure to add the *Parmigiano-Reggiano* when serving. This recipe was given to me by Anna Grazia Mosci, Maurizio's wife.

Ingredients:
4 good-sized zucchini (narrow, not big around) sliced in rounds of ¼-inch thickness, cut evenly
2 small cloves of garlic, chopped fine, saving half of the chopped garlic for the topping
1 small yellow onion, sliced very thin
1 good-sized bunch of broad-leaved basil (julienned); set aside a small amount for the topping
1 small bunch Italian parsley, chopped
Extra-virgin olive oil (to fry the zucchini)
Kosher salt and freshly ground black pepper to taste
Grated *Parmigiano-Reggiano* for serving

Preparation:
1. In a large skillet, sauté the onion with the olive oil over medium-low heat, being careful not to let the onion brown (golden only).
2. Add the first part of the chopped garlic and let sauté for one minute (again, do not let brown).
3. Add the zucchini and parsley and cook until the zucchini are soft and begin to turn golden. Do not overcook, as this will cause the zucchini to fall apart.
4. Add the larger portion of the basil, retaining a small amount for the topping, and sauté for a minute; then remove from the stove.
5. Cook the pasta al dente.
6. Drain the pasta and stir it into the skillet of zucchini.
7. Add the remaining basil and garlic and stir gently.
8. Serve, adding the grated *Parmigiano-Reggiano*.

Risotto/Pasta con Radicchio (Rice or Pasta with Radicchio)
Category: Paste (Pastas)
Origin: Northern Italian
Serves 4

   The bitter taste of radicchio is mellowed by cooking and makes for a remarkable taste with risotto or short pasta. This creates a blend of sweet and bitter that results in a very interesting taste. The dish can be made with a risotto in a base of chicken stock or pasta in a base of fresh cream. The rice and radicchio are typically Northern Italian flavors associated with Milan. The radicchio found in the Midwest is the round-shaped bulb. The radicchio found in northern Italy is long in shape and is called Trevisiano, after the town of Treviso in the Veneto region.

Ingredients:
2–3 small radicchio heads (at least 1½ cups), rinsed and patted dry, quartered, cored,
   and coarsely chopped
2 Tbsp. extra-virgin olive oil
2 Tbsp. butter
1 small onion, finely chopped
½ cup fresh cream at room temperature
5–6 cups chicken stock
½ cup dry red wine
2 cups Arborio or long grain rice or short pasta
Kosher salt and freshly ground black pepper to taste

Preparation:
1. Sauté the radicchio and onion in the olive oil/butter mixture, being careful not to
   burn the butter.
2. When onions are soft, add the wine and continue cooking for several minutes.
3. If cooking risotto, add the chicken stock to cook it.
4. If making pasta, cook the pasta, drain, and add the fresh cream to the pasta.
5. Add the radicchio sauce as well as a few uncooked radicchio leaves.
6. Toss and garnish with *Parmigiano-Reggiano* or *Pecorino-Romano* cheese.

Pasta Fagioli or Pasta Fazul in dialect (Bean and Pasta Soup)
Category: Paste or Minestre (Pastas or Soups)
Origin: Etta Di Santo and Traditional Italian
Serves 4–6

This is a recipe provided to me by Etta DiSanto. It is commonly prepared throughout Italy. In Milan, in the summer, it is served at room temperature with extra-virgin olive oil drizzled on top. I like to add pepperoncino to give it a little bite. For best results use dried beans, as instructed in this recipe. As dried Borlotti or cranberry beans may be hard to find in the Midwest, canned beans may be substituted. If using canned beans, sauté the onion, tomatoes, and oil with a little water to form the sauce before adding the beans to ensure you don't overcook the beans. Etta likes to add fresh cream and *Parmigiano-Reggiano* cheese on top of each serving instead of olive oil and cheese. This is a great comfort food served hot, on cold, foggy days in Milan.

Ingredients:
2 medium yellow onions, finely chopped
6 Tbsp. (or more) extra-virgin olive oil
2 cloves garlic, minced
A handful of dried porcini mushrooms (soaked in hot water)
1½ cups dried cranberry beans or other red beans (like Borlotti)
1 lb. peeled fresh Roma tomatoes, chopped
2 sprigs fresh rosemary and three sprigs of fresh thyme (a lesser amount if using dried)
Sea salt or kosher salt and freshly ground black pepper to taste
Parmigiano-Reggiano
Pasta (Etta makes this with gnocchi, but you can use tagliatelle, fettuccini, or ditallini)

Preparation:
1. Soak the beans overnight in cold water over, covering the beans by three inches.
2. Drain the beans and put them in a large soup pot with three quarts of water.
3. Add three tablespoons of olive oil, onions, and tomatoes and bring to a boil.
4. Reduce the heat and simmer, partially covering the pot, for three hours.
5. Remove two-thirds of the beans and puree them in a food processor, or use an immersion blender to puree some of the beans.
6. Return the puree to the soup and continue simmering for fifteen minutes or until beans are fully cooked.
7. Season with salt and pepper and some pepperoncino flakes (optional).
8. In a small pot, heat the rest of the olive oil on low heat and add the thyme, rosemary, and garlic.
9. Cook slowly, being careful not to brown or burn the garlic (three to four minutes). Pour the heated oil into the soup through a sieve, filtering out the herbs.
10. In a separate pot, cook the pasta al dente and add the pasta to the soup.
11. Serve very hot, sprinkling the *Parmigiano-Reggiano* and a few drops of olive oil on the serving.

Etta makes this with gnocchi (not potato gnocchi), which is made as follows:
1. Take two cups of all-purpose flour and place on wooden cutting board and form a volcano with the flour.
2. Add boiling water in the center of the volcano and form the dough by stirring the flour into the water.
3. Kneed to a doughy mixture.

4. Roll into thin strands, cut into one-and-a-half-inch pieces, and push a thumb print into each piece.
5. Cook separately about ten to twelve minutes.
6. When cooked, drop them into the soup.

Etta also adds some cream in the soup to make it richer.

Sautéing the onions

Cooking the beans with the diced tomatoes

and Sautéing the herbs

Serving with pasta and *Parmigiano-Reggiano*

Spaghetti al Limone (Spaghetti with Lemon Sauce)
Category: Paste (Pastas)
Origin: Etta DiSanto
Serves 4–6

Etta DiSanto also provided this recipe, which, like *Aglio, Olio, e Pepperoncino*, is simple and easy to prepare and can be fixed on short notice. If you like the taste of lemon, you should like this dish, which is delicate and satisfying.

Ingredients:
Zest of 2 lemons
2 cups heavy cream
2 Tbsp. unsalted butter
Kosher salt and freshly ground black pepper to taste
3 Tbsp. or more of *Parmigiano-Reggiano*
1-lb. box spaghettini or fedelini

Preparation:
1. In a large skillet, place the cream, butter, and the lemon zest and heat, but do not let it boil.
2. Salt and pepper to taste.
3. Cook the spaghetti and, when al dente, drain or lift into the skillet. Save some of the cooking water to add to the pasta if too dry.

4. Mix thoroughly in the skillet and add the *Parmigiano-Reggiano*.
5. Serve immediately on a heated plate and top with *Parmigiano-Reggiano*. Add some chopped parsley for color.

Grate the lemon and *Parmigiano-- Reggiano* and heat the cream

Mix in the skillet and serve immediately on a heated plate

Serve immediately on a heated plate

Spaghetti alla Puttanesca (Pasta with Hot Olive and Tomato Sauce)
Category: Paste (Pastas)
Origin: Traditional Italian
Serves 4–6

Puttanesca means "in the style of the prostitute." There are differing stories as to the origin of this recipe and its name, but it is a well-known Italian dish. Some say it was prepared by the ladies of the night to seduce their clients. Others say that it was prepared by the ladies for their families after a day of hard work as it is simple to make, uses basic ingredients, and is delicious. You can choose whatever explanation or make up your own. In any respect it is a quick, easy recipe and a delicious pasta dish for workdays—or any day. Serve it with spaghettini, penne or fusilli and a red Italian wine. No cheese is added to this dish. You may want to chop some fresh Italian parsley and add to the top of servings.

Ingredients:
2 garlic cloves, minced
1 small onion or large shallot, finely chopped
¼ cup extra-virgin olive oil for frying
6 anchovy fillets, chopped, or 1 Tbsp. anchovy paste
3 cups canned chopped Roma tomatoes in their juice or fresh tomatoes
14–16 Kalamata black olives, pitted and sliced lengthwise
1–2 Tbsp. (quantity to taste) capers (I use the kind packed in salt, not brine), rinsed and drained
Small bunch of fresh basil, sliced chopped

Kosher salt and ground fresh black pepper to taste
1 tsp. red pepper flakes (pepperoncini)

Preparation:
1. In a medium-sized saucepan, heat the olive oil and sauté the onion/shallot until it softens.
2. Add the anchovies and garlic and continue to cook until the anchovies dissolve.
3. Add tomatoes and let cook until the juices reduce and a sauce is formed.
4. Add salt and black pepper to taste.
5. Add the capers, pepperoncini, and basil and let cook until the oil surfaces.
6. When sauce is done, cook the spaghetti al dente, drain, add sauce, and serve.

Spaghetti/Linguine con Vongole (Spaghetti/Linguini with Clam Sauce)
Category: Paste (Pastas)
Origin: Etta DiSanto (Cousin)
Serves 4–6

Spaghetti con Vongole is a traditional Neapolitan dish. However, it is popular throughout Italy and the United States. Italians prepare this dish two ways: with tomatoes (in rosso) and without (in bianco). The other traditional ingredients are limited to spaghetti, live clams, garlic, olive oil, parsley, salt, and pepper, so it is relatively simple to make. However, the key is having fresh small clams that are alive and open during cooking. The live clams open during cooking, releasing a liquid that serves as the primary flavoring agent. In the Ligurian region of Italy, east of Genoa, "*Spaghetti alle Vongole Veraci*" means spaghetti with tiny baby clams in the shell, no more than the size of a thumbnail, with a white wine/garlic sauce. Cheese is never added to this dish.

Soaking the clams to extract the sand

Whole clams still in the shell must be sold live. Fresh, un-shucked clams should be stored in a porous bag made of burlap or other natural material in the refrigerator. If you have no cloth bags, store in a bowl covered with a wet cloth in the refrigerator, not on ice. Never store them in sealed plastic or submerged in water, or they will die from lack of oxygen.

Ingredients:
2–3 lb. of fresh, un-shucked small clams (the best are *vongole veraci*, which probably
    can't be found in the United States except in bottles); use the smallest little neck clams
    you can find, the smaller the better
5 Tbsp. extra-virgin olive oil
3 cloves garlic, sliced thinly
4 Tbsp. finely chopped Italian parsley
½ cup dry white wine
Kosher salt and freshly ground black pepper to taste
1 tsp. or more chili pepper flakes (pepperoncino)
1 lb. quality Italian spaghettini or fedelini

Preparation:
1. Clean the clams. This is probably the most important step as no one wants a mouthful
    of sand. Use fresh clams, preferably within twenty-four hours of purchase—although
    if truly fresh, they will last a few days under refrigeration. Discard any fresh, live
    clams with shells that are open or those that do not close when tapped, along with any
    that have broken shells. If you can jiggle the shell halves from side to side, it is a sure
    clue the clam is no longer living.
2. Just before cooking, soak the clams for twenty minutes in fresh water. As the clams
    breathe, they filter water. When the fresh water is filtered, the clams push salt water
    and sand out of their shells. After twenty minutes, the clams will have cleaned them-
    selves of much of the salt and sand they have collected. Instead of pouring the clams
    and water into a strainer, pull the clams out of the water with tongs. Sand has sunk to
    the bottom of the bowl; pouring the water into a strainer will pour it back over the clams.
3. Bring a large pot of water to a boil for cooking the pasta; add salt.
4. Meanwhile, heat the oil in a large skillet over medium heat. Add the garlic and sauté,
    stirring often, until just golden. Add the chili pepper flakes and cook for another fifteen
    seconds.
5. Add the clams and the wine to the skillet; increase the heat to moderate, cover the
    skillet, and cook until the clams open and release their juices (three to six minutes,
    depending on the size of the clams).
6. As the clams open, use tongs to remove them from the skillet; place them into a
    bowl and set aside.
7. Add the spaghetti to the boiling water and cook until two minutes before its recom-
    mended cooking time on the box so that they are very al dente. Remove the spaghetti
    from the pasta water with tongs, place in a bowl, and set aside, re taining at least a
    half cup of the pasta water.
8. Add one-fourth cup of the reserved pasta water to the skillet, bring to a boil,
    and add the spaghetti to the skillet. Cook over high heat, tossing continuously until the
    spaghetti reaches al dente and has soaked some of the sauce from the pan.
9. Add the clams back into the skillet and any juices remaining in the bowl, along with the
    chopped parsley, and toss to combine. Add more pasta water if the spaghetti seems dry.
10. Transfer pasta to a warm bowl or serve directly on the serving plates and sprinkle with
    olive oil.

Tossing with spaghetti and serving

Spaghettini alla Checca (Spaghettini with Fresh Raw Tomatoes and Herbs)
Category: Paste (Pastas)
Origin: Traditional and Etta
Serves 4

These are great dishes for the summer. The key to success is the flavor of the tomatoes. The second dish is a bit simpler to make but may not have as nice a presentation. A white wine, such as a *Soave* or *Vernaccia*, is recommended for both. They are both easy and quick to prepare and, because of their simplicity, can rescue you when you have nothing else prepared. Both are uncooked sauces, but the first version is a bit more complex, using mozzarella, while the second version is more of a cream sauce, made with *Parmigiano-Reggiano*.

Version #1 with Mozzarella

Ingredients:
1-lb. box Italian imported spaghettini or fedelini
2 lb. fresh plum tomatoes, cut into ¼-inch pieces
½ lb. whole-milk Italian mozzarella, or use mozzarella bocconcini or ciliegine again
    cut into ¼ inch cubes
Small bunches of the following fresh herbs, chopped:
    1 Tbsp. fresh basil
    1 Tbsp. fresh oregano
    1 Tbsp. fresh marjoram
    ½ Tbsp. fresh thyme (leaves only)
1 garlic clove, smashed
Kosher salt and freshly ground black pepper to taste
½ cup extra-virgin olive oil

Preparation:
1. Begin cooking the pasta water and add spaghetti when water boils, as usual.
2. While the spaghetti is cooking, place the mozzarella, tomato pieces, chopped herbs, salt, and pepper in a large serving bowl (preferably one that is wide and shallow) and mix well. The bowl needs to be large enough to contain the pasta when cooked.
3. Heat the olive oil and garlic until the garlic begins to turn golden; then remove and discard the garlic.
4. Continue to heat the oil until it is smoking hot. Then pour it over the herb and tomato mixture.
5. When the spaghetti is cooked (very al dente), drain it and add it to the bowl. Mix vigorously until the spaghetti is well coated.

6. Cover the bowl with a plate or lid; let stand for two minutes so that the mozzarella melts before serving.

Version #2 with *Parmigiano-Reggiano*:

Ingredients:
1-lb. box Italian imported spaghettini or fedelini
Large bunch of fresh sweet basil
2 lb. of fresh plum tomatoes, cut into pieces
½ or ¾ cup grated *Parmigiano-Reggiano* cheese
Kosher salt and freshly ground black pepper to taste
½ cup extra-virgin olive oil

Preparation:
1. Begin heating the pasta water; add the spaghettini when the water boils as always.
2. While the spaghetti is cooking, put the tomatoes, basil, and cheese in a food processor or a blender, add salt and pepper, and blend, adding the olive oil a little at a time as blend the sauce.
3. Blend into a creamy mixture, adding more cheese to thicken, depending on the juice content of the tomatoes.
4. When the spaghetti is cooked (very al dente), drain it and add the uncooked sauce to the spaghetti. Mix thoroughly until the spaghetti is well coated.
5. Serve immediately and add more cheese at the table.

Pasta alla Norma (Pasta with Eggplant and Tomato Sauce)
Category: Paste (Pastas)
Origin: Traditional Sicilian with Variations by Anna Grazia and Mamma Cortellini
Serves 4–6

This is a recipe that Mom occasionally made, but we learned a new twist on her recipe from Anna Grazia Mosci while living in Milan. It is simple to make and yet classy enough to serve as a first course to dinner guests. Pasta alla Norma received its name in nineteenth-century Sicily after the popular opera by composer Bellini.

Norma from Bellini's opera Norma is played
in the below YouTube link by Maria Callas.
She sings "*Casta Div*a," in 1958

http://www.youtube.com/watch?v=gZrao_GX4nk

Important for this dish is to find firm young eggplants, free of the many seeds contained in older eggplants. Cut the eggplants crosswise in one-half to three-quarters-inch-slices, uniformly sized to promote even cooking.

Avoid using too much olive oil when frying the eggplant. Initially the eggplant will absorb the oil, so it may appear that more is needed. However, the eggplant will release the oil as it continues to fry. The sauce is made like a marinara sauce, using garlic, basil in olive oil, and either fresh Roma tomatoes or a large can of peeled, chopped Roma tomatoes.

Ingredients:
2 medium-sized young eggplants (thinner rather than fatter in shape)
Tomato Sauce:
    1 large clove of garlic, smashed
    A dozen fresh Roma tomatoes or a large can of peeled, chopped Roma tomatoes
    ½ lb. grated ricotta salata
    ¼ cup extra-virgin olive oil
    Small bunch of fresh basil leaves, sliced chopped
1 lb. dried pasta such as penne or rigatoni

Preparation:
1. Slice the eggplant into quarter-inch slices, salt, and let drain for thirty to forty-five

minutes.

2. Without a little olive oil, just covering the bottom of the frying pan, fry the eggplant until golden on both sides, and set aside. Keep in mind that when frying eggplant the eggplant will first absorb the oil and then release it as it finishes frying, so don't add more olive oil.

3. Prepare a simple tomato sauce (see *Sugo di Pomodoro Semplice* (Simple Tomato Sauce) in chapter #3 or the sauce for *Spaghetti al Pomodoro Fresco e Basilico* (Spaghetti Tomatoes and Basil) in chapter #17) and cook the sauce until the oil rises.

4. Cook the pasta al dente.

5. Put three quarters of the sauce in the pasta and set the rest aside.

6. On a serving plate, place two of the eggplant slices on the bottom of the plate. Add the pasta and put another two slices on top of the pasta. Add a spoonful of the sauce, sprinkle with the grated ricotta salata, and serve.

Blotting the eggplant and placing in the serving dishes

Grating the ricotta salata and serving

Polenta alla Griglia con Ragu di Funghi
(Grilled Polenta with Mushroom Ragu)
Category: Vari (Other)
Origin: Etta DiSanto, Traditional Mountains
Serves 4–6

Etta DiSanto provided this recipe. It is a typical plate served in the mountains of Italy where mushrooms are plentiful. Fresh porcini is ideal, but it is not found in the United States, so dried porcini can be used after soaking in hot water. Making your own polenta is preferred, but if you need to save time, you can use prepared polenta, found in most Italian grocery stores. This would probably be the Italian equivalent of Toast aux Champignon.

Ingredients:
Polenta:
5 cups cold water
1 cup cornmeal or yellow polenta flour (medium grind)
2 Tbsp. extra-virgin olive oil
1½ tsp. fine sea salt
1 bay leaf

Mushrooms:
5 Tbsp. extra-virgin olive oil
2 garlic cloves, minced
Unsalted butter
1 tsp. dried thyme
½ cup dried porcini soaked in hot water, drained and strained and sliced
½ lb. fresh shiitake mushrooms, cut in quarters
¼ lb. fresh chanterelle, cut in half
¼ oyster mushrooms, cut in two-inch slices
Slices of fontina cheese, one for each slice of polenta
2 Tbsp. Italian parsley, finely chopped
Kosher salt and freshly ground black pepper to taste

Preparation:
1. Prepare the polenta: pour the water and olive oil into a heavy pot, add the salt and bay leaf, and bring the water to a boil.
2. Add the polenta flour to the water by sprinkling it into the water a little at a time, sifting it through your fingers. Whisk steadily with a wire whisk until it is well incorporated. Return to a boil over medium heat, continuing to whisk it. When large bubbles begin to burst, lower the heat to keep it warm, leaving the lid ajar.
3. Stir it frequently, scraping the bottom and sides as the polenta thickens. Cook for about twenty-five minutes until it becomes glossy and begins to pull away from the sides as it thickens.
4. Spread over a wooden cutting board in a layer, one-half to three-fourths inch thick. Let it set so that it can be sliced when cool.
5. For the Ragu, sauté the mushrooms in a mixture of olive oil, butter, and garlic and then add the chopped parsley and thyme.
6. Cut the polenta in squares or ovals that would fit on the bottom of a serving plate.
7. Grill the polenta slices on a stovetop grill. Make sure the grill creates grill marks and only turn once.
8. Place a slice of fontina on top of the polenta while still grilling it to let it melt.
9. Place the polenta on a hot serving dish, add the mushroom ragu on top, and serve immediately.

Slicing and frying the mushrooms

Slicing and grilling the polenta

Serving the polenta with mushroom ragu

Ossobuco Milanese (Veal Shank Milanese)
Category: Carni (Meats)
Origin: Traditional Milanese
Serves 4

This well-known Milanese dish is one of my favorite meat dishes if prepared properly. It takes a while to prepare, so Roz doesn't fix it too often. The key to this dish is enjoying the bone marrow spread over a piece of Italian bread (it may be high in cholesterol, but it is delicious). You should try to find shanks that have larger, round bones, which will contain larger quantities of marrow. The Ossobuco can be served with or without the *gremolata*. *Gremolata* is a combination of lemon zest, garlic, parsley, and olive oil. Traditionally an addition to *Ossobuco* (braised veal shanks), it is also great as a garnish on grilled or roasted lamb, pork chops, beef, and even roasted potatoes. Gremolata is best made fresh; it doesn't keep for more than a day, but is also best if it has an hour or so before serving for the flavors to meld.

Ingredients:
½ cup extra-virgin olive oil or as needed
4 veal shank pieces, cut into medium slices
Kosher salt and freshly ground black pepper to taste
Flour for dredging
3 celery stalks, finely chopped
2 small carrots, finely chopped
1 large onion, finely chopped
¼ pound shiitake or porcini mushrooms
½ cup dry white wine
1½ cups canned crushed or chopped Italian tomatoes

2–4 cups hot chicken or beef broth
Fresh thyme

For the gremolata *(herbs finely chopped and blended together as a topping):*
1 tsp. finely chopped or grated lemon zest
1 small garlic clove, minced
2 Tbsp. chopped flat-leaf parsley
2 tsp. chopped fresh basil
1 tsp. chopped fresh rosemary

Preparation:
1. Heat one-fourth cup of the olive oil over medium heat in a heavy skillet large enough to hold the shanks in a single layer.
2. Salt and pepper shanks to taste (use kosher salt).
3. Coat with flour, shaking off excess.
4. Brown them over medium heat, turning them only once (ten to fifteen minutes).
5. Take out the shanks and set aside.
6. Add three tablespoons of olive oil and heat over medium heat.
7. Add the celery, carrots, onion, thyme, and mushrooms. If using dry porcini, soak them in hot water to soften and discard the water.
8. Cook vegetables till soft (fifteen minutes).
9. Turn up heat and add the wine, stirring till wine evaporates.
10. Add the chopped tomatoes and two cups of the broth.
11. Arrange the shanks in the skillet and add some of the sauce over the veal shanks. If the liquid does not cover the meat, add more broth.
12. When sauce comes to a boil, reduce heat, cover, and simmer gently for two to two and a half -hours until the meat on the shank is very tender. Uncover the skillet the last thirty minutes to thicken the sauce.
13. While the meat is cooking, prepare the gremolata.
14. Prior to serving (ten minutes), remove the meat and continue to cook the sauce, reducing it further. Stir in the gremolata and continue cooking for a few minutes more.
15. Serve meat in a large platter and pour the sauce over the meat.
16. Serve with Risotto alla Milanese or Risotto *Parmigiano-Reggiano*.

Cotoletta alla Milanese con Rucola e Pomodoro
(Breaded Veal Cutlet, Milanese Style, with Rucola and Tomatoes)

Category: Carni (Meats)
Origin: Traditional Milanese
Serves 4

Probably the best known Milanese dish in America is the breaded veal cutlet. In Milano I like it best served with the cutlet paper-thin, rib bone intact, and lots of rucola and tomatoes. In the United States it is not often found fried with the rib bone intact. This is by far one of my most favorite Milanese dishes.

Ingredients:
4 veal chops with full rib bone, about ¾ inch thick
Kosher salt and fresh ground black pepper to taste
Flour for dredging
2 large eggs, lightly beaten
1 cup plain (unseasoned) bread crumbs or panko
3 Tbsp. unsalted butter
2 Tbsp. of extra-virgin olive oil
1 lemon, cut into wedges
Arugula (more commonly called rucola salad or rocket salad) and chopped tomatoes as topping

Preparation:
1. Prepare the chop by cutting away all excess fat; remove meat and fat from the bone so that the bone is clean.
2. Pound the meat portion of the chop to a thickness of approximately one-quarter inch I like to make them very large and very thin.
3. Dust the cutlets with flour on both sides.

 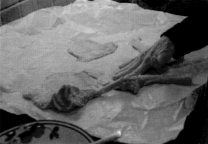

4. Salt and pepper the cutlet; coat in the flour and beaten egg and cover with bread crumbs, pressing them into the meat.

5. Use two frying pans to cook the chops. Heat the butter and olive oil together in

each pan until the butter begins to foam.

6. Immediately add the chops until a golden crust forms on the underside (about four minutes). Be careful with the cooking heat as it must be high enough to cook the meat quickly but not so high as to burn the butter.

7. Turn the chops carefully with a spatula, add more butter if needed, reduce the heat to low and cook until a golden crust forms on the other side (three or four minutes)

9. Repeat until all the chops are cooked. If using the same pan for the next chops, you will need to wipe the pan clean and add new butter and oil.

10. Add olive oil to the rucola and tomatoes and serve the cutlet with a wedge of lemon.

Tagliata di Manzo (Grilled, Sliced Sirloin Steak with Rosemary and Garlic)
Category: Carni (Meats)
Origin: Terza Carbonanio Restaurant in Milan and Traditional Italian
Serves 4

This dish is for meat lovers and the meat should be eaten rare. Its origin is Tuscany, where *Bisteca Fiorentina* (Florentine T-bone steak) is famous. The Florentines are known for their love of red meat. The key flavor in this dish is the rosemary. To accent this dish, I like to serve it with oven-roasted rosemary potatoes. Other vegetables that typically go well are breaded and fried eggplant, fried zucchini flowers, and sautéed artichokes.

There is a Tuscan restaurant in Milan, to which I return every chance I get, by the name of Terza Carbonaia. It serves Tagliata and an endless variety of antipasti and vegetables. If you're a meat lover, I highly recommend this restaurant and this dish. I also suggest pairing it with a bottle of Brunello di Montalcino or other Tuscan red wine such as a Tignianello or Chianti Classico.

Ingredients:
Two large New York strip steaks (2–3 inches thick) or similarly thick T-bone or porter-
    house steaks (excess fat trimmed)
Marinade:

¼ cup extra-virgin olive oil
2 cloves garlic, sliced
3 branches fresh rosemary, chopped
3 shallots
2 Tbsp. of balsamic vinegar
1 tsp. red pepper flakes or to taste
Kosher salt and freshly ground pepper to taste

Preparation:
1. Blend the marinade ingredients in a baking or casserole dish large enough to fit the steaks, but not too large for the marinade content.
2. Place the steaks in the marinade and turn to soak the steaks in the juices.
3. Cover with cling foil and place in the refrigerator overnight, turning the steaks occasionally.
4. Heat the grill to 450°F and cook the steaks one side at a time, turning only once.
5. Brush the steaks with the marinade and if the fire is to hot or flames up turn the heat down so as to not scorch the steaks.
6. Grill for four to five minutes on each side. The steaks should be pink and moist, with some blood in the middle.
7. Remove from the grill and place the steaks back in the baking dish, salt and pepper to taste, cover with aluminum foil, and let stand for five minutes.
8. Slice the steaks across the grain in thin slices (like roast beef) and serve immediately.

Arrosto/Codone al Tartufo (Veal or Pork Roast Stuffed with White Truffle Paste)
Category: Carni (Meats)
Origin: Etta DiSanto
Serves 6–8

This can be made with a veal roast (*codone*) or a pork roast (*arista*). Etta and Italo DiSanto taught us this recipe, with the key ingredient being white truffles from Alba. Actually, truffles are difficult to find, expensive, and may be wasted if used in a roast. As an alternative, use white truffle paste found in most good Italian specialty food stores. This is a great holiday main dish and a good substitute for turkey. Let the roast stand at least ten minutes before serving. Untie the roast, remove the rosemary, and carve the roast into slices that are between one-half and three-quarter inch thick. Serve with a hearty red Italian wine.

Ingredients:
3 lb. pork loin roast
Lean boiled ham, baked ham, or prosciutto
½ tube white truffle paste
Fontina cheese
Sprigs of fresh rosemary

Preparation:

1. Slice the roast so that it lies flat (butterfly).
2. Trim the excess fat, but leave enough to provide flavor.
3. Spread the ham so that it covers the flat surface of the butterflied roast.
4. Spread the truffle paste evenly over the ham.
5. Slice the fontina cheese thinly and place over the truffle paste.
6. Roll the roast and tie tightly with string. Be sure to enclose the ends so that the cheese will not ooze out when it melts.
7. Place the rosemary branches under the strings
8. Brown the meat at high temperature (425°F) for about ten minutes or until lightly browned.
9. Reduce temperature to 400°F for approximately one hour or until the internal temperature is 140°F.
10. Remove and let rest ten minutes before slicing.

Melanzane Parmigiana (Eggplant Parmesan)
Category: Verdure (Vegetables)
Origin: Anna Grazia and Mamma Cortellini
Serves 4–6

This is a recipe given to me by Anna Grazia Mosci while we were living in Milan. This recipe breaks tradition: instead of frying the eggplant, it is baked in the oven, which makes the dish lighter and less oily. Mom's version is more traditional than Anna's. Anna's makes a simple tomato sauce using tomato paste accented with oregano, which gives it a pizza flavor. Mom used a traditional marinara sauce made with onion, butter, and tomato sauce and some dried marjoram. Mom made a batter of eggs, milk, and flour and dipped the eggplant in the batter before frying in a skillet. In the recipe below, I use a basil and garlic marinara sauce with fresh Roma tomatoes and baked eggplant.

Ingredients:
Anna's Tomato Marinara Sauce:
  Small can tomato paste or equivalent in a tube
  Small glass white or red dry wine
  1 clove garlic smashed or pressed
  Dried oregano to taste
  Kosher salt and freshly ground black pepper to taste

Mom's Tomato Marinara Sauce:
  Small yellow onion, finely chopped
  2 Tbsp. unsalted butter
  2 Tbsp. extra-virgin olive oil
  Pinch of dried marjoram
  Kosher salt and freshly ground black pepper to taste

My Fresh Tomato Marinara Sauce:

10–12 plum or Roma tomatoes, finely chopped
¼ cup fresh basil leaves, julienned, not chopped
¼ cup extra-virgin olive oil
Pinch of chili pepper flakes
Kosher salt and freshly ground black pepper to taste

For the Eggplant:
2 medium-sized eggplants
2 eggs
Small amount of milk to thin the eggs
Breadcrumbs (homemade are better without spices)
Extra-virgin olive oil
Sliced fresh mozzarella cheese (bocconcini), enough to cover the eggplant
Grated *Parmigiano-Reggiano* cheese

Preparation:
1. Make the tomato sauce with the above ingredients or one of the tomato sauces in chapter #3 and chapter #17.
2. Slice the eggplant in half-inch slices and sprinkle with salt and pepper. Let drain for thirty minutes and pat dry.
3. Coat the slices in egg and milk, dredge in bread crumbs, and fry. Alternatively, cover a cookie sheet with tinfoil, coat the foil with olive oil, and place the slices on the cookie sheet. Bake at 425°F for fifteen minutes; no need to turn.
4. Put a thin layer of sauce on the bottom of a lasagna baking dish.
5. Place a layer of fried or baked eggplant in the dish, top with sauce and mozzarella, and sprinkle with *Parmigiano-Reggiano*.
6. Continue making layers in the same manner until all the eggplant and sauce is used.
7. Bake for another fifteen to twenty minutes or until browned.

Slicing and roasting the eggplant   Placing the eggplant in the lasagna dish

Topping with marinara sauce and baking

Bietole Soffritto (Sautéed Swiss Chard)
Category: Verdure (Vegetables)
Origin: Mamma Cortellini
Serves 4

This same process can be done with most green leafy vegetables such as spinach, beet greens, and dandelion greens. A variation of this would be to begin by sautéing the garlic and then adding the greens to wilt them in the garlic and oil; however, Roz finds that this technique tends to overcook the greens. The preparation technique below results in a more delicate taste.

Ingredients:
A large bunch of red or white Swiss chard (since the Swiss chard will shrink considerably
  when cooked, you need to purchase a sufficient quantity to render a reasonable serving)
2–3 cloves garlic, sliced thinly
¼ cup extra-virgin olive oil for frying the garlic
Kosher salt and freshly ground black pepper to taste

Preparation:
1. Clean the Swiss chard thoroughly.
2. Cut the stems in small pieces and the leaves crosswise in three- to four-inch widths.
3. Soak the Swiss chard in cold water to firm it up, rinse, and spin dry.
4. In a large skillet cook the Swiss chard without oil until it wilts, adding salt and pepper.
5. In a separate small skillet, add the oil and fry the garlic until golden, being careful
   not to burn the garlic.
6. While the oil and garlic are still hot, add to the skillet with the Swiss chard and simmer
   until the oil is infused into the vegetables.
7. Serve hot as a side dish to most meat and fish dishes.

Insalata Caprese (Caprese Salads)
Category: Antipasti (Appetizers)
Origin: Traditional Italian
Serves 4–6

Caprese salads are always a favorite as an appetizer. They are traditionally served layered with mozzarella slices covered by a slice of tomato and a basil leaf on top, drizzled with fine extra-virgin olive oil. As an appetizer, you might want to use the cherry-sized mozzarella called *ciliegine*, skewered with cherry tomatoes and basil leaves.

Ingredients:
Bocconcini of mozzarella di buffala (only use fresh if available; the size depends on the
  salad you are making)
Tomatoes
Small bunch of basil leaves
Fine extra-virgin olive oil, kosher salt, and freshly ground black pepper to taste

Preparation—Traditional Salad:
1. Place tomato slices on a serving platter.
2. Slice the bocconcini nor too thin and arrange the mozzarella slices over the tomatoes.
3. Sprinkle olive oil over the slices, and don't be stingy.
4. Salt and pepper to taste.
5. Place a leaf of basil on top of each.
6. Cover and store in the refrigerator until served.

Preparation—Caprese Skewers:

1. For this recipe you need to have miniature bocconcini, sometimes termed ciliegine.
2. Use small skewers that will hold one of the bocconcini and two cherry tomatoes.
3. Skewer the cherry tomatoes on each end, with the bocconcini in the middle and a small or half leaf of basil between the cheese and the tomato.
4. Arrange on a serving platter and sprinkle olive oil over the skewers.
5. Salt and pepper to taste and serve (again, can be covered and stored in the refrigerator until served).

Insalata di Carciofi (Fresh Artichoke Salad)
Category: Antipasti (Appetizers)
Origin: Traditional Milanese
Serves 4–6

The flavor of fresh artichokes provides a sweet aftertaste to this dish, which is delightful. Fresh artichokes are not commonly eaten due to their tough outer leaves and spiky middle choke. The solution is to use the very smallest of artichokes found in most Italian grocery stores. The outer leaves must be peeled away to reach the tender, light green inner leaves. The small artichokes should not have developed a choke. Coupled with the always delicious taste of *Parmigiano-Reggiano*, this dish is remarkable. However, to be successful, you must delay preparation until the last minute to avoid the discoloration seen when an artichoke is left uneaten for too long.

Ingredients:
10–12 baby artichokes
Juice of ½ large lemon
½ cup water
Extra-virgin olive oil to taste
Kosher salt and freshly ground black pepper to taste

Preparation:
1. Clean the artichokes by removing outer leaves until you reach the pale green leaves that are tender. Trim the base lightly and cut off the top third of the artichoke, which is still hard and prickly.
2. Slice the artichoke in half. As these should be very young artichokes, they should not have yet formed the choke. If there is a choke, you need to remove it.
3. Place the sliced artichokes one at a time into a mixing bowl with the squeezed lemon juice and one-fourth cup of water. Dip the cut artichokes into the lemon water to prevent them from turning brown.
4. Right before serving, slice the halves into quarters, slice the quarters in very thin slices, and place them on the dish to serve.
5. Sprinkle the olive oil over the artichoke slices.

6. Add salt and pepper to taste.

7. Shave the *Parmigiano-Reggiano* abundantly over the slices.

Tiramisu (Pick-Me-Up Dessert)

Category: Dolci (Desserts)
Origin: Milanese/Toscana
Serves 4–6

This is Nic's favorite Italian dessert. I remember having it for the first time in Milan when a manager from the bank took me to a Tuscan restaurant, which was appropriately called "Torre di Pisa."

To make this dessert, you need to have good ladyfingers that will not fall apart, good espresso, Italian mascarpone, and a fine cognac. I use Pavesini ladyfingers. They work the best as they absorb the coffee without falling apart and are light, not doughy. They can be found at most Italian grocery stores.

Best lady fingers

Ingredients:
1 package Pavesini ladyfingers
1 cup brewed espresso coffee, cooled
3 egg yolks
⅓ cup plus 1 Tbsp. confectioners' sugar
16 oz. tub of mascarpone (preferably Italian)
3 Tbsp. fine cognac
3 Tbsp. unsweetened dark cocoa

Preparation:

1. Dip one side of the ladyfingers in the coffee; quickly remove and place them, coffee side down, in the serving platter. Cover the bottom of the platter. As the Pavesini are packaged in halves, repeat another layer in the same manner.
2. In a small bowl, beat the eggs yolks with one-third cup confectioners' sugar until thick and lemon-colored.
3. Add the mascarpone cheese and cognac and mix thoroughly. It should be thick and creamy.
4. Pour half of the cheese mixture over the bottom layer of the ladyfingers, making sure that all the ladyfingers are covered. Sprinkle with half the cocoa.
5. Repeat the process for the top layer, cover with plastic wrap, and refrigerate overnight.
6. Before serving, sprinkle on a tablespoon of confectioners' sugar.

Pavesini and serving

Castagne al Carbone (Chestnuts Roasted over Open Flame)
Category: Dolci (Desserts)
Origin: Traditional Milanese
Serves 6

This is best done over charcoal. I recall walking the streets of Milan in late fall or early winter and relishing the aroma of the roasting chestnuts from the street vendors.

Ingredients:

2 lb. fresh chestnuts
Chestnut grilling pan
Stovetop, gas grill, or charcoal

Preparation:

1. Cut a slice on each chestnut, not cutting too deep, to slice the meat of the nut.
2. Roast over the fire, stirring continuously to cook evenly and not burn.
3.   When they begin to scorch, remove and serve immediately.

Zabaglione (Egg Custard)

Category: Dolci (Desserts)
Origin: Etta's Version of Traditional Italian Dessert
Serves 4

This is my cousin, Etta's version of the Milanese famous dessert that we devoured at the Trattoria Milanese. This recipe takes a half hour or so to prepare, plus time to refrigerate. The zabaglione is not cooked over direct fire but rather over boiling water. This is the reason that a zabaglione pan is rounded on the bottom; this way, it cannot be set on the stove or in a double boiler, so that the ingredients are cooked separately over boiling water.

Zabaglione pan

Ingredients:
4 egg yolks
⅓–½ cup granulated sugar
8 Tbsp. dry Marsala wine or vin santo
¼ pint heavy cream

Preparation:
1. In a stainless steel bowl or in a *Zabaglione* saucepan, whisk the egg yolks with the sugar (or use a double boiler).
2. When the mixture has risen and turned foamy, slowly add the Marsala wine or vin santo.
3. Cook the ingredients at a low heat while continuing whisking the mixture vigorously, avoiding boiling the mixture until the mixture is thick and foamy.
4. When the cream starts to thicken, remove it from the heat. You may need to remove it and put it back on the heat to avoid fully cooking the eggs.
5. Let it become completely cool; then add half of the whipping cream.
6. Put it in the fridge until it's completely cold; then add the remaining whipping cream.

Chapter 15

Paris Days

We arrived in Paris by train in early December 1983 with Mom. Roz and I had already selected an apartment in the seventeenth arrondissement during an earlier house-hunting visit. While we waited for our furniture to arrive, we stayed at La Tremoille Hotel near my office. The hotel was small but elegant, with great restaurants, brasseries, and bistros nearby. The hotel still exists today, and I recommend it to travelers whenever I can.

La Tremoille Hotel and 11 Rue Edouard Detaille

The apartment that we chose was just north of Parc Monceau in a turn-of-the-century neighborhood. It was a beautiful flat, with hardwood floors and fireplaces in most of the rooms. Our unit was on the third floor again, but this time we had an elevator. It was fortunate that Mom was with us as she helped decorate the apartment by making curtains.

The apartment was exceptionally large by Paris standards, with tall ceilings and decorated wall coverings.

The kitchen was not elaborate but the fireplaces were exceptional

The apartment was located at 11, Rue Edouard Detaille, near Avenue Villier, in the seventeenth arrondissement or the Batignolles-Monceau district. From there it was a short walk to Les Champs-Elysees and the Arc de Triomphe and easy access to places such as the Place de la Madeleine; the famous shopping street, rue du Faubourg Saint-Honore; and the Opera district.

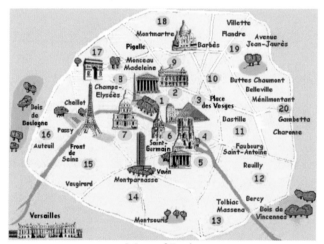

Map of Paris

The neighborhood was filled with beautiful apartment buildings, tree-lined avenues with flower shops, local cafés, fruit markets, *boulangeries*, and *patisseries* all conveniently located to destroy any chance of ever losing weight. Fresh oysters on the half shell (famous in Paris) were sold around the corner and made great appetizers.

Neighborhood tree-lined avenues

The local fruit market with neatly stacked
vegetables, which one does not touch, and
the local flower shop

Our local *patisserie, boulangerie ,*
(bakery and café) for café noire and
croissant on my way to work

The oysters sold by street vendors
were plentiful and exquisitely fresh

My daily commute to work consisted of a walk through Parc Monceau, one of the most manicured and beautiful parks in Paris, surrounded by elegant homes and embassies. This park has been the topic of many artist renderings, including Harold Altman, whose lithographs we have of Parc Monceau, Jardin du Luxembourg, Giverny, and Rue Mouffetard.

Altman's Parc Monceau

My daily walk to work took me through Parc Monceau, along Rue de Monceau to Rue de Courcelles, and then to Avenue Franklin Delano Roosevelt to Avenue Montaigne.

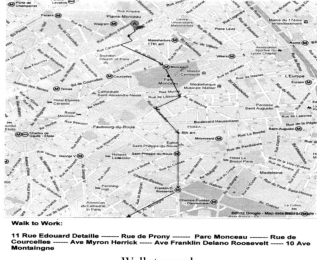

Walk to Work:

11 Rue Edouard Detaille ------- **Rue de Prony** ------- **Parc Monceau** ------- **Rue de Courcelles** ------- **Ave Myron Herrick** ------- **Ave Franklin Delano Roosevelt** ------ **10 Ave Montaingne**

Walk to work

My office was located at 10 Avenue Montaigne surrounded by fashion headquarters for Christian Dior, Chanel, Nina Ricci, and more. Our office was also near the Hôtel Plaza Athénée. My favorite lunch eatery was the Bar des Theatres. Many of the models from the fashion houses also ate lunch there. In the French custom, each meal began with a baguette and hot French mustard. With lunch we often consumed a bottle of slightly chilled Brouilly.

10 Avenue Montaigne and the Hotel Plaza Athenee

Bar des Theatre and a bottle of Brouilly on Avenue Montaigne

The Paris branch of Continental Bank had a similar customer base to that of its Milan branch. The principal customers were multinational US companies, and in addition, there were indigenous French customers. Most activities were related to trade financing and foreign exchange. The branch actually owned the premises it occupied on Avenue Montaigne. One of the branch's neighbors at the time was Marlena Dietrich. The appreciation of real-estate during this period in Paris was astronomical making owning this property one of the branch's best earning assets. The branch manager was initially Philippe Bouckaert, who was later replaced by Gael de Pontbriand. I brought Michel Kahn in from Milan to assist me, but the rest of the staff members were local French professionals. In Milan structural changes were required, but during my tenure at the Paris branch, the focus was on fine-tuning the existing operations and improving efficiencies. Unlike in Milan, in Paris, the language was more of a barrier for me in managing the staff. Although I took French lessons, I was never able to achieve the proficiency necessary to be effective in complex discussions. My Italian did help with the written French.

We did not travel throughout France as we did in Italy, although we did take the occasional excursion to places like Giverny, Rheims, and the Loir Valley. The language barrier was one of the reasons. Another reason was that traveling by car was more difficult—getting in and out of Paris was nightmarish. Also, we had a small BMW, and our parking garage was seven stories underground, with the elevator only reaching five stories, so that we had to walk the last two stories to reach our garage compartment, commonly called the box. The lights were on timers, so if we didn't reach the car and open the box, we would be left in pitch darkness. This was also true when leaving the car. Therefore, we got little use out of the car. However, the biggest reason of all for our lack of travel was that Paris was so filled with things to do and places to see that we did not have the urge to get away. In all the places we have lived, Paris was our favorite city.

Among the charms of Paris were the Palais-Bourbon district in the seventh arrondissement (where the Tour Eiffel [Eiffel Tower] is located), the Les Invalides (officially known as "L'Hotel National des Invalides"), and numerous museums, including the Musée d'Orsay, the Musée Rodin, and the Louvre.

The Luxembourg district in the sixth arrondissement has one of the world's greatest parks, the Jardin du Luxembourg, which makes this arrondissement popular with locals and visitors alike. We often visited this park, especially with guests from out of town. The sixth arrondissement also contains a number of landmarks like the Odéon Theatre, the Saint-Sulpice church, and the eleventh-century Saint-Germain-des-Prés, the oldest abbey church in Paris.

The Mollelo's and the Schantz's in the Jardin du Luxembourg and a painter

Relaxing in the Jardin with Roz's parents, aunt, and
uncle during their visit

The Louvre district, the first arrondissement, which is the least populated and the geographical center of Paris, contains historical sites such as the Louvre Museum, le Palais Royal (the Royal Palace), the Jardin des Tuileries, Forum des Halles, Bourse du Commerce, and the upscale Place Vendôme. Les Halles was one of our favorite places. It is the historical site of the Paris market and today features wonderful antique shopping. Also located there is Dehillerin, a fantastic cookware shop filled with every copper pot and pan imaginable. Walking through the Tuileries gardens in the autumn was spectacular.

Dehillerin, a favorite cookware store in Les Halles

Strolling through the Tuileries in autumn

The Butte-Montmartre district in the eighteenth arrondissement was another of the great districts of Paris; it is situated in an elevated portion of Paris, once a bohemian section of Paris and still today, a gypsy village-like setting catering to the arts. It boasts of spectacular views of the city and also contains the famous Basilique du Sacré-Coeur de Montmatre and the infamous Moulin Rouge cabaret.

Visiting Montmartre during and the Moulin Rouge,
and a traditional street singer playing the Musette Waltz

Tina and her husband visiting from their military base in Germany; Bob and Linda Thopy, visiting on a
cold day in Paris; and Mom with us at a Bohemian restaurant in Montmartre

The Hôtel-de-Ville district in the fourth arrondissement contains the southern part of the medieval Marais district as well as the Île St-Louis and the eastern part of Île de la Cité, the oldest part of Paris. The Cathedral of Notre-Dame and the beautiful Place des Vosges, which was the home of Victor Hugo, are located in this district.

Scenes of and from Notre Dame

Place des Vosges and apartments on Île de la Cité

Near our neighborhood was the Elysee district, or eighth arrondissement. This district includes the Champs-Élysées, probably the world's most famous boulevard, with the Arc de Triomphe and the Place de l'Étoile at one end and the Place de la Concorde at the other. Bordering the Champs-Élysées are the magnificent Grand Palais and Petit Palais, as well as the Élysée, the presidential palace. The arrondissement also features the temple-like Madeleine church and the romantic Parc Monceau.

The Arc de Triomphe, a view from on top of the Arc, and looking down the Champs-Élysées, which ends at the Place de la Concorde

Parc Monceau was one our favorite spots. Being so close to our residence, it was convenient for us to visit and enjoy the park's beauty in all seasons.

Parc Monceau in the winter

Paris, being a favorite tourist attraction, provided us with a number of visitors. The visit by Roz's parents was the only time they traveled outside the United States. They were accompanied by Roz's aunt and uncle, Joanne and Sam Owens. The six of us traveled to the north of France to visit the battlegrounds of Normandy, Mont Saint-Michel, and other attractions along the way. Roz's parents had the trip of a lifetime, and memories were re-lived by them for many years to come. We rented a Peugeot station wagon, which held all six of us (not easy to find in Paris), and we worked our way up and along the Normandy and Brittany coasts. We stayed overnight in a medieval chateau somewhere between Paris and Normandy and saw the Omaha and Utah beaches as well as Cherbourg, Avranches, Caen, and St. Malo in Brittany. We also spent a number of days showing them the beauty of Paris.

The overnight stay at a chateau

The spectacular l
Mont Saint-Michel

Atop the Notre Dame

Walking in the neighborhood and sadly leaving Paris

Other visitors from the United States included Tim and Patricia Shantz (who worked with me in Milan), Becky Fahy, Bob and Linda Thopy, Joe and Marilee Molello (also from Milan), and Roz's roommate at Stephens College, Jacquie Friend, with whom we traveled to Zermatt and Northern Italy.

Pat and Tim Schantz's visit from Milan; Becky Fahy (whom
we knew in the United States and Luxembourg), in Zermatt

Joe and Marilee Mollelo (visiting from Milan), in Giverny

Jacquie Friend traveling with us to Zermatt

Hiking the Zermatt foothills and Jacquie's dad's, Ted Drake;
portrait of Roz and me from a photo of the visit

We received visits from my Italian cousins, and took the opportunity to travel to Italy from Paris, adding to my collection of Italian recipes.

Mom returned to Paris. During her return trip, we traveled together to Ancona.

Touring Paris with Mom   In Chamonix en route to Ancona

Mom with her brother Raul and doing what we
do best in Ancona, eating

Mom and her sister Zia Marisa; Anna Maria and Paolo and their family in their home in Sirolo

On the food front, Paris cuisine seemed to me to be at the extremes—it was either very formal and expensive, and unquestionably very good, or rather common. The traditional brasserie dishes could be very well prepared and, more often than not, were to our liking. The three haute cuisine restaurants that I remember visiting were Taillevent, Lassere, and the Jules Verne at the top of the Eifel Tower. Actually I can't remember what I ate at these restaurants, but I do remember the view from the Jules Vern was more spectacular than its food.

Our preference was to frequent the many Parisian bistros and brasseries, and there were a number of good ones near our apartment and throughout Paris. Brasserie Lorraine was just a short walk from our apartment on Place des Ternes in the eighth arrondissement. The menu was that of a typical brasserie but in a more elegant setting. The waiters were aloof as normal, but the seafood was excellent, especially the sole meunière and amazing seafood platters, which contained a wide variety of crustaceans and mollusks, including langoustines, snails, fresh oysters, and more. Some of our favorite dishes were sole meunière, the crustacean, foie gras, entrecote avec pommes frites, and the profiterole.

Brasserie Lorraine entrance and seafood

A similar brasserie near my workplace in the eighth arrondissement was the Chez Francis at Place Alma. Zagat actually gives this restaurant a higher rating than Lorraine. The menu is almost identical, with an emphasis on seafood. The attraction there, however, was the setting and the spectacular, unobstructed view of the Tour Eifel. The best place to be seated is the terrace on a clear night or day.

Chez Francis with view of the Tour Eifel, both day and night

A famous brasserie that needs mentioning is La Coupole, noted for its interior dome and history dating back to 1927. It attracted famous artists such as Léger, Soutine, Man Ray, Brassai, Kisling, and Picasso. It is said that at this location, an unknown writer with tiny round glasses named Henry Miller took breakfast at the bar, Matisse sipped beer, and Joyce lined up his whiskeys. Although it is somewhat a tourist stop, with cranky waiters and rows of tables topped with linen or paper tablecloths, it is enchanting nonetheless. The food is actually quite good. Roz and I came here often to eat our favorite bistro foods like foie gras, steak aux poivre, and crème brulee.

Another well-known bistro we enjoyed, either alone or with friends, in Les Halle was Au Pied de Cochon, translated as "pigs' feet." This is a bustling, well-known tourist attraction in the old market district of Paris. The specialty, as you would guess, is pigs' feet prepared in a number of manners. It is a late-night eatery and always busy.

The lively atmosphere of the restaurant and waiters with their pig noses;
The specialty (not a vegetarian place) fried pigs' feet

Two of our favorite bistros in the eighth, again near where I worked, were Chez Andre and La Fermette Marbeuf. I never discerned the difference between a brasserie and a bistro except that, maybe, a brasserie is a bigger bistro. The New Casselle's French dictionary defines a bistro as a pub and a brasserie as a brewery or drinking saloon. Chez Andre was our favorite, with its traditional French cuisine and the best rice cake (gateau de riz).

Just like French restaurants are difficult to find in Italy, good Italian restaurants (not pizzerias) are likewise difficult to find in Paris. I can count on my hand the number of times when we ate Italian food (other than at home) in Paris. Most of these times were at an Italian restaurant near the Tremoille Hotel called Le Stresa. Actually, it was a good Italian eatery.

In addition to its restaurants, Paris is known for its high-class delicatessens, two of which are in the Place de la Madeleine. One is Fouchon and the other is Hediard. At each you can find the highest-quality foods, wines, candies, and prepared foods. I still have some Framboise and Kirch that I bought at Hediard.

Fouchon and Hediard

Our departure from Paris was much different than from Milan. It was devoid of fanfare. It was precipitated by the failure of Continental Illinois National Bank (CINB) on May 11, 1984. I remember that Friday vividly. We had just completed funding our treasury position for the day, and at 3:00 p.m. we received a call from head office, instructing us to reenter the money market and attempt to draw funds for the head office. The head office was in the middle of a run on the bank. We were unsuccessful in raising any funds for head office, and at the close of business this day, CINB borrowed from the Federal Reserve Bank's discount window to make up for the lost deposits, which reached a total of $3.6 billion.

There have been many articles written about the demise of CINB and why it failed; these articles are too long to discuss here. However, if you want to read more, follow this link on the Internet:

http://www.fdic.gov/bank/historical/history/235_258.pdf

In short summary, CINB amassed significant problem loans in executing its strategy to be the bank with the largest financing exposure in oil and gas energy financing. Due to a lack of internal controls, the Bank purchased bad loans related to oil and gas from the failed Penn Square Bank of Oklahoma. This failure, coupled with mounting problem loans, caused a lack of confidence in the bank. A run on the bank resulted in large depositors withdrawing over $10 billion in early May 1984. Unlike in California and other states, Illinois's regulatory scheme at that time prohibited the establishment of branches outside a short perimeter of the main office. This caused CINB not to have a diversified deposit base and made it dependent on large institutional customers and foreign banks for its deposit base. The lack of confidence due to CINB's growing loan problem quickly resulted in an acceleration of withdrawals of large deposits and a run of unexpected velocity. There was not much chance that fateful Friday that the Paris branch could turn the tide on the flight of deposits. Due to CINB's large size, regulators were not willing to let CINB fail—it was "too big to fail." To avert the financial disaster wrought by such a failure, the Federal Reserve Bank (Fed) and the FDIC infused over $4.5 billion to rescue the bank. The CINB board of directors and its top management were removed and replaced by two chairmen, one from the oil industry, John E. Swearingen from Standard Oil Indiana, and the other from banking, William Ogden, retired vice-chairman of Chase Manhattan Bank. What followed was a period of scaling down of CINB and a virtual gridlock caused by disagreements between the two chairmen on how to manage the bank.

The international division of the bank soon became the target of cost-cutting and liquidation. In the succeeding months, the head of the bank's European network, Jean Louis Reccousin, foreseeing the inevitable, put together a sell proposal for the acquisition of the entire European network, including branches and subsidiaries at a then-reasonable market price by Standard Chartered Bank of London. At that time the European network had a decent going concern value, as it was not affected by the gas and oil problems of the head office. The proposal was seen as self-preserving and disloyal by the two chairmen and was rejected by them. As it turned out, Standard Chartered Bank recruited talent from CINB's most profitable network units, including Philippe Boukaert, the Paris branch manager; Irv Knox from the Milan branch; and Peter McSloy from the Brussels subsidiary. The individual units in the European network were eventually sold or closed unit by unit mostly at substantial losses. I was offered a position with Standard Chartered Bank that would have required me to make an open-ended commitment to stay on in Europe for an indefinite period of time. Due to aging parents back home and an already long assignment in Europe, Roz and I decided to stay with CINB, which resulted in repatriation to Chicago. As in my choice to leave public accounting, once I made the decision, I never looked back.

In midspring of 1986, we packed our furniture once again for the Atlantic crossing and returned to Chicago to live in Lake Bluff. I was given a position in the controller's division of what was left of CINB with the title of international controller. The bank continued to flounder under the management of the two chairmen, so after several months, I accepted a position from the Continental Bank leasing subsidiary, which had been sold to Sanwa Bank as part of CINB's contraction. The leasing subsidiary was then operating under the name of Sanwa Business Credit. My position was assistant controller in charge of leasing operations. The transition was rather easy as most all the employees were ex-Continental people, some of whom I knew from CINB's international department. It was the right move for me as it allowed my reentry into the Chicago finance employment arena and a return to living in the north suburbs, this time in Lake Bluff. The home was in a neighborhood we knew and liked. Commuting to Chicago was easy, and entertaining at our home was enjoyable. My initial assignment at the leasing company was to convert the leasing system from the bank legacy system to ALAS, a packaged leasing system supported by software developers out of Georgia. Our three years in Lake Bluff were filled with good times and memories.

Sanwa Business Credit at 1 South Wacker Drive, Chicago, at the initiation of the Pride Program (a rather male-dominated group), and karaoke night at Sanwa, a favorite pastime

Lake Bluff home in summer and at Christmas

Roz and neighbor Martha playing a recital at Martha's home

Dave and Lorna Brown at Beth and Don's wedding and
New Year's Eve 1989 with Don and Beth and the Kubinski's in Chicago

I actually picked up very few French recipes during our stay in Paris, but thanks to Mom's visit and our travels to Ancona, I was able to add to my collection of recipes. Below are some recipes I recorded from those times.

- *Prosciutto con Fichi* (Figs and Prosciutto)
- Codfish Balls
- *Veluto do Cardi* (Soup of Cardoons)
- *Fusilli in Salsa di Noci* (Fusilli pasta in Walnut Sauce)
- *Spaghetti Marco Polo* (Spaghetti with Roasted Pepper, Garlic, and Herbs)
- *Gnocchi di Patate con Gorgonzola* (Potato Gnocchi in Gorgonzola Sauce)
- Boiled Beef and Peppers
- *Sole Meunière* (Sole in Butter Sauce)
- *Involtini di Spinaci* (Spinach Egg Crepes)
- *Verdure alla Griglia* (Grilled Vegetables)
- Viennese Green Beans (with Sour Cream and Dill)
- Rosemary Potatoes
- *Insalata di Fagiolini* (Green Bean Salad)

Prosciutto con Fichi (Figs and Prosciutto)
Category: Antipasti (Appetizers)
Origin: Traditional Italian
Serves 6–8

The salty taste of the prosciutto and the extreme sweetness of ripe figs make for an exciting appetizer taste and add a nice touch to a grouping of appetizers. It is important that the figs be mature (not dry) and extremely sweet. They can be peeled, but if mature, there is no need to do so.

Ingredients:
8–10 slices *prosciutto di Parma* sliced very thin
13–14 fresh figs, depending on size

Preparation:
1. Arrange the prosciutto slices on a serving platter.
2. If you prefer to peel the figs, use a sharp paring knife. Try to keep the fig intact. The riper the fig, the more difficult it is to keep the fig intact.
3. Slice the figs in half or in quarters and keep them in intact placing them on top of the

prosciutto slices.
4. Store, covered, in refrigerator; bring to room temperature before serving.
5. Alternatively, slice the figs in half and layer half a slice of prosciutto over the figs; store and serve in the same manner.

Codfish Balls
Category: Antipasti (Appetizers)
Origin: Unknown
Serves 4–6

Cod is a versatile fish, white in color, with mild flavor and robust texture. This is a great dish for an appetizer or can even be served as a main dish.

Ingredients:
2–3 medium russet potatoes, peeled and cut into large pieces
3 cups clam juice
1 medium yellow onion, quartered
1 bay leaf
1 lb. cod fillets, cut into large pieces
2 large eggs
3–4 Tbsp. fresh cilantro leaves, coarsely chopped; additional for garnish
1½ tsp. green Tabasco sauce
1 tsp. kosher salt
Zest of 1 lemon
Bread crumbs to coat the fish balls for frying—I use Panko crumbs

Preparation:
1. Place the potatoes in a pot with the clam juice.
2. Boil over medium heat for twenty minutes or until potatoes are tender.
3. Remove the potatoes and place in a bowl.
4. Add the onion and bay leaf to the clam juice liquid and simmer for three minutes.
5. While potatoes are still hot, mash them with a potato masher; do not use a ricer.
6. Add the cod filet pieces to the clam juice broth and cook about three minutes or until fish turns white and opaque.
7. Remove fish from the broth and add it to the bowl of potatoes, breaking up the large pieces.
8. In the bowl with the potatoes and fish, add the eggs, cilantro, Tabasco sauce, and lemon zest and mix until well combined. Cover with plastic wrap and refrigerate until completely

cooled and firm, at least four hours or overnight.
9. Preheat the oven to 400°F. Coat a baking dish with olive oil.
10. Place the bread crumbs in a dish.
11. Using an ice cream scoop, form a cod fish ball from the mixture and coat the fish balls with the bread crumbs.
12. Place each codfish ball on the coated baking dish and roll in the olive oil, which will make the crumbs crispy when baking.
13. Bake until codfish balls are nicely browned, twenty to twenty-five minutes.
14. Place the codfish balls on a serving platter and garnish with cilantro.

Vellutato di Cardi (Soup of Cardoons)
Category: Minestre (Soups)
Origin: Traditional Venetian
Serves 6

You can find cardoons at most grocery stores. The celery-like stalks would suggest that they are in the family of celery, but cardoons are actually related to the artichoke family and will turn dark when cut. The cardoons should not be too large; large ones tend to be stalky. Select the thinner stalks that are whitish in color. Avoid using store-bought croutons with seasoning. I prefer making my own croutons, as described below. Homemade croutons are generally tastier as they are free of excessive spices, which interfere with the taste of the cardoons. If you like the croutons with a garlic flavor, add garlic to the olive oil used to bake the croutons. Fry the garlic in the oil until golden and discard it before toasting the croutons. Also, you might want to add some flour to the boiling water to help the cardoons retain their natural light color.

Ingredients:
3 lb. cardoons, cut into small pieces
5 Tbsp. unsalted butter
1 small onion, finely chopped
2 qt. chicken stock (preferably homemade)
Kosher salt and freshly ground black pepper to taste
Fresh-squeezed juice and retain the flesh of 1 lemon
Croutons

Preparation:
1. Bring a large pot of water to a boil.
2. Clean the cardoons and remove the tough strings as you would from celery.
3. Cut cardoons crosswise into one-and-a-half-inch pieces.
4. Put into a bowl of cold water; and add some lemon juice and lemon pieces to maintain the color of the cardoons.
5. Melt the butter in a soup pot over medium heat and sauté the onion until soft and golden.

6. Add the cardoons, lightly browning them in the butter, and add the stock or use the chicken stock from the chicken broth recipe.
7. Bring to a boil and simmer the soup, partially covered, for thirty to forty minutes or until the cardoons are very tender. This will depend on the toughness of the cardoons.
8. Process the soup through a food mill or blender until it is pureed.
9. Strain the soup through a sieve. It should be very smooth (velvety) rather than thick. Season with salt and pepper and add some drops of the lemon juice to brighten the flavor.
10. Serve hot with croutons.
11. Instead of store-bought croutons, I prefer to make my own by using slices of Italian bread cut into one-inch cubes and placing them on a baking sheet with olive oil spread on the sheet. Bake the croutons at 375°F, turning them occasionally so that they become golden all over. Smaller amounts can also be prepared in a skillet at medium heat.

Fusilli in Salsa di Noci (Fusilli Pasta with Walnut Sauce)
Category: Paste (Pastas)
Origin: Etta DiSanto
Serves 4

This is a very simple sauce using walnut and cream and an excellent spur-of-the-moment recipe.

Ingredients:
½ lb. Fusilli pasta
20 (or more) whole walnuts
1 cup whipping cream
¼ tsp. dried marjoram
4 Tbsp. unsalted butter
Kosher salt and freshly ground black pepper to taste
Grated Parmigiano-Reggiano

Preparation:
1. Place the cleaned walnuts in a mortar dish and crush with a pestle to obtain a homogenous composition.
2. Place the nut composite in a bowl and slowly add the whipping cream until you obtain a creamy sauce.
3. Add salt, pepper, the marjoram to the sauce.
4. Blend the nut ingredients in a blender or food processor for several minutes.
5. In a skillet, melt the butter and add the Parmigiano-Reggiano; then add the nut sauce.

6. When the fusilli are cooked al dente, add them to the skillet; stir and serve.

7. Add additional Parmigiano-Reggiano at serving.

Gnocchi di Patate con Gorgonzola
(Potato Gnocchi with Gorgonzola Cheese Sauce)
Category: Paste (Pastas)
Origin: Mamma Cortellini
Serves 4–6

Potato gnocchi is a dish that you either love or don't. The objective is to make gnocchi that are light and digestible. However, making them with potatoes tends to leave them a bit heavy. Mom made her gnocchi sauce with a ragu of pork, which can be found in my recipe of Pasta con Cotolette di Maiale. However, I prefer to use a Milanese-inspired sauce with a foundation of Gorgonzola.

Ingredients:
2 large yellow potatoes per person
Kosher salt and a half tsp. of sugar
2½–3 cups "00" flour
2 eggs
¼ lb. gorgonzola cheese
1 Tbsp. unsalted butter
2 Tbsp. whipping cream
Kosher salt and freshly ground black pepper for the sauce
Parmigiano-Reggiano for the sauce

Preparation:
1. Boil the potatoes, skins intact, for thirty minutes or until a fork enters easily.
2. Peel and mash the potatoes while they are warm using a potato ricer.
3. On a pasta table, form a mound of the riced potatoes.
4. Make a volcano (or well) of the flour and add salt, sugar, and eggs in the center of the

volcano.

5. Knead the potatoes and flour, forming pasta dough.
6. Slice sections from the dough ball and roll out into long, cigarlike strands (one-half inch in diameter).
7. Cut each strand into three-quarter-inch pieces and sprinkle with flour.
8. Press a dimple in each piece.
9. Boil the gnocchi a few at a time; when they rise to the top, they are cooked.
10. Take them out of the water with a slotted spoon or a spider spoon and drain well before placing on a plate.
11. In the meantime, in a small saucepan, heat the butter, cream, and Gorgonzola, adding the salt and pepper and lots of *Parmigiano-Reggiano*.
12. When sauce begins to thicken, add it to the gnocchi and serve.

Spaghetti Marco Polo (Spaghetti with Roasted Red Bell Peppers, Garlic and Herbs)
Category: Paste (Pastas)
Origin: Italian Traditional
Serves 4

There are differing views as to whether Marco Polo actually brought spaghetti back from China. Whether he did or not, this recipe commemorates the seventeen years that Marco Polo, the famous Venetian merchant, spent in China dining with the likes of Kublai Khan.

A legend arose that the famed explorer must have introduced pasta to Italy. This recipe is known throughout Italy, and even Julia Child had her version. I received this version from Etta. It utilizes roasted red peppers, which I tend not to use in pasta—but with the Asian influence, the red peppers seem to work.

Ingredients:
⅔ cup chopped walnuts
1 cup black olives, coarsely chopped (Kalamata)
½ cup roasted red bell peppers, coarsely chopped
A large bunch of Italian parsley, chopped
Good-sized bunch of fresh basil leaves, julienned (½ cup)
2 garlic cloves, sliced
1 lb. thin spaghetti or fedelini
Pinch of hot pepper flakes to taste
¼ cup extra-virgin olive oil

Preparation:
1. Roast a red bell pepper (as you would on the stove top for the roasted pepper recipe). Peel and chop the red peppers into small cubes.
2. Roast the walnuts for two to three minutes.
3. Coarsely chop the walnuts, olives, and herbs and set aside.

4. Cook the spaghetti al dente.

5. In the meantime, heat the olive oil in a large skillet and add the garlic. Sauté the garlic until it becomes golden; do not let it turn brown. Add the pepper flakes to the oil.

6. Remove the spaghetti from the boiling water with tongs and add it to the skillet with the garlic. Retain some of the water in case the spaghetti gets dry.

7. Add the mixture of walnuts, olives, pepper, and herbs to the skillet and stir.

8. Serve immediately and top with *Parmigiano-Reggiano*.

Roast the walnuts and chop the olives

Chop the parsley and julienne the basil

Fry the garlic and toss the spaghetti

Serve with *Parmigiano-Reggiano*

Boiled Beef with Peppers
Category: Carni (Meats)
Origin: Ancona
Serves 4

In my recipe for *Brodo di Manzo* (Beef Broth and Boiled Beef), I use the beef broth for *Pastina in Brodo* (Little Pasta in Broth). As a complement to this broth, I suggest using the beef with peppers as a second course, or it can be used as a standalone dish in the following recipe.

Ingredients:
Boiled beef from the recipe of Brodo di Manzo (Beef Broth and Boiled Beef) in chapter #11
3 Tbsp. extra-virgin olive oil
1 medium onion, finely chopped
4 green or red peppers (red are sweeter), cleaned and thinly sliced lengthwise
2–3 fresh tomatoes, peeled and chopped
Kosher salt and freshly ground black pepper to taste
A pinch of hot pepper flakes (optional but recommended)

Preparation:
1. In a large skillet, sauté the onions in the olive oil until translucent and soft.
2. Add the pepper slices and sauté until tender.
3. Add the tomato pieces and hot pepper flakes.
4. Take the beef extracted from the beef broth and thinly slice it.
5. Mix the beef pieces (they may fall apart, which is OK) with the peppers.
6. Cook over low heat and stir gently to warm; it does not need further cooking.
7. Serve as a second dish after the soup or as a separate plate.

Boil the beef as a beef soup and extract it from the broth

Slice the beef and sauté with the peppers to serve

Sole Meunière (Sole in Butter Sauce)
Category: Pesci (Fish)
Origin: French Traditional
Serves 4–6

This was one our favorite bistro dishes. As Dover sole was readily available in Paris, we ordered it frequently when dining out. It is best prepared whole and cleaned at the table. In the States, however, you may need to settle for sole fillets. Dover sole is a remarkable fish, meaty and succulent but with a delicate flavor. When it comes to cooking it, the simplest way is the best, as in this classic French preparation where butter and lemon subtly enhance the taste and texture.

Ingredients:
6 (4–6 oz.) boneless, skinless sole fillets
Kosher salt and freshly ground black pepper, to taste
½ cup flour
10 Tbsp. unsalted butter
3 Tbsp. finely chopped parsley
½ lemon, thinly sliced crosswise

Preparation:
1. Season fillets on both sides with salt and pepper.
2. Place flour on a plate and set aside.
3. Heat four tablespoons butter in a twelve-inch skillet over medium-high heat.
4. Working in batches, dust fillets in flour, shaking off excess, and then place in skillet.
5. Cook, turning once, until browned on both sides and just cooked through, about six minutes.
6. Transfer fillets to warm serving platter or individual plates; sprinkle with parsley.
7. Wipe skillet clean and return to heat with remaining butter.
8. Cook, swirling pan, until butter begins to brown.
9. Add lemon slices, cook until heated through, and then pour evenly over fillets.
10. Serve immediately with lemon slices.

Involtini di Spinaci (Spinach-Stuffed Crepes)
Category: Verdure (Vegetables)
Origin: Mamma Cortellini
Serves 4–6

This is a dish Mom served as a vegetable. As it is made with a tomato sauce, Mom would serve it for her dinners where pasta with red tomato sauce was not served. She would always have it when my son Gino came to dinner as it was his absolute favorite. The key to success is to make the egg crepes as thin as possible.

Ingredients:
For the marinara sauce:
¼ stick of butter
½ small onion, chopped
Chopped Roma tomatoes
2–3 stems of thyme (optional)
Kosher salt and freshly ground black pepper to taste

For the crepes:
6 Grade A large eggs
2 boxes frozen chopped spinach
Grated *Parmigiano-Reggiano*
Kosher salt and freshly ground black pepper to taste

Preparation:
Marinara sauce:
1. Sauté the onion in butter in a saucepan.
2. Add the chopped tomatoes and thyme.
3. Cook until juices reduce and oil rises to the top.

For the crepes:
1. Place the chopped spinach in a small skillet. Add the rest of the butter.
2. Sauté the spinach until all the water evaporates.
3. Squeeze any excess water from the spinach and place in a bowl.
4. Salt and pepper to taste; add the *Parmigiano-Reggiano* and mix.
5. Beat the eggs as you would for an omelet.
6. In a crepe pan or small nonstick skillet, pour some egg on the hot skillet (a ladleful) and swirl in the skillet, making a very thin crepe. Turn to other side for ten to fifteen seconds.
7. Remove crepe from skillet and stack on a dish.

8. Place one crepe on a cutting board and lay a strip of spinach mixture on one side of the crepe.
9. Sprinkle with *Parmigiano-Reggiano*, salt, and pepper.
10, Roll the crepe into a tube, like cannelloni, and place it into a greased baking dish.
11. Continue making the crepes in this fashion until you fill the baking dish.
12. Cover the crepes with the marinara sauce, sprinkle with *Parmigiano-Reggiano*, and bake in the oven at 350°F for ten to fifteen minutes.

Fry the crepe on both sides

Flip the crepe and stack

Stuff the crepe with spinach and *Parmigiano-Reggiano* and prepare to cook

Cooking and serving

Verdure alla Griglia (Grilled Vegetables)
Category: Verdure (Vegetables)
Origin: Traditional Italian
Serves" As Needed

Grilled vegetables can be served as an appetizer or as a vegetable dish to accompany a main dish. This is best prepared in the summer when the vegetables are at their best and grilling is easier in the Midwest. When selecting eggplant to grill, they should not be too large and seedy. Tomatoes should also be firm and not overripe or contain too much liquid (i.e., not beefsteak tomatoes). Asparagus stalks should not be too thin as they will tend to burn. Zucchini should also be small and should be sliced thick enough so as to not fall apart. Red bell peppers should be cleaned, cored, seeded, and grilled, with skin side down initially. Vidalia or sweet onions should also be sliced thick to withstand the grilling and not fall apart.

Ingredients:
Quantities of vegetables depend on the servings needed and typical Vegetables Include:
Eggplant
Zucchini
Asparagus
Scallions
Red bell peppers
Sweet onions
The topping ingredients include:
    Chopped parsley
    Minced garlic
    Kosher salt and freshly ground black pepper
    Extra-virgin olive oil
    A touch of balsamic vinegar

Preparation:
1. The larger vegetables, such as eggplant, onions, and zucchini, need to be sliced in one-half to three-fourths-inch-thick slices. If sliced too thin, they may burn.
2. The thinner or smaller vegetables can be grilled whole.
3. Place vegetables in a bowl and coat with olive oil, salt, and pepper.
4. Grease the grill before using to prevent sticking.
5. Place the vegetables on the grill and turn once; grill marks will appear on the vegetables.
6. Remove from grill and let cool.
7. Prepare the topping by placing the ingredients in a small bowl and mixing them thoroughly infusing the herbs with the oil.
8. Arrange on serving dish and spread the topping over the vegetables. Sprinkle with extra olive oil if vegetables are dry.

Viennese Green Beans
Category: Verdure (Vegetables)
Origin: Mamma Cortellini
Serves 4–6

This dish was one of Mom's favorite ways of serving green beans. It was taught to her by her German friend and symphony patron Mrs. Beck. The dill seeds and sour cream provide it with a distinctive German flavor. It is a great accompaniment to meats and fish. I often pair it with Cotoletta Milanese (Breaded Veal Cutlet Milanese), Chapter #14.

Ingredients:
2 lb. green beans, fresh and not too big
3 Tbsp. extra-virgin olive oil
1 Tbsp. flour
1 medium onion, chopped
2 tsp. dill seeds
3 Tbsp. Italian parsley, minced
½ cup green bean water, retained from cooking
2 Tbsp. cider vinegar
½–1 cup sour cream
Kosher salt and freshly ground black pepper to taste

Preparation:
1. Cook green beans al dente (eight to nine minutes).
2. Drain beans, but retain one cup of the cooking water.
3. Sauté onion in olive oil until it becomes translucent.
4. Add flour and let brown.
5. Add the dill seeds and parsley.
6. Add the green bean water and boil for one to two minutes.
7. Add the green beans, vinegar, salt, and pepper.
8. Add the sour cream and simmer, but do not let the cream boil.
9. Serve warm as a side dish to meats and fish.

Patate al Rosmarino (Rosemary Potatoes)
Category: Verdure (Vegetables)
Origin: Mamma Cortellini
Serves 4

This is by far my favorite way of eating potatoes. They are excellent with grilled beef or lamb—or most grilled meats. I accuse Roz of never making enough and Nic of taking too large a helping. I can assure you that there are never any leftovers.

Ingredients:
15 small red potatoes, cut into small pieces
2 cloves garlic, cut into slices
3 stems fresh rosemary (or equivalent in dried rosemary)
¼ cup extra-virgin olive oil
Kosher salt and freshly ground black pepper to taste

Preparation:
1. Cut the potatoes in half; then cut the halves in half, and then cut into half-inch pieces.
2. Rinse the potatoes three times and pat them dry with paper towel.
   Be sure to thoroughly rinse the starch off the potatoes; otherwise they will stick.
3. Spread the olive oil on a baking or cookie sheet and add the potatoes, garlic, and rosemary and toss the potatoes so that the oil thoroughly covers the potatoes.
4. Salt and pepper to taste.
5. Roast the potatoes in the oven at 375°F.
6. Roast for at least one and a half hours or until the potatoes are golden brown and crispy. Don't rush them.
7. Remove the potatoes from the oven and serve hot.

 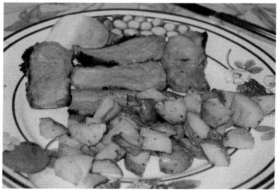

Insalata di Fagiolini (Green Bean Salad)
Category: Vari (Other)
Origin: Mamma Cortellini
Serves 4–6

This is the simplest of salads and good to accompany meats and fish. The key is to purchase very fresh green beans—the smaller, the better. Also you should use the best quality of extra-virgin olive oil as this is most important to the taste of the dish.

Ingredients:
1–1½ lb. fresh green beans
High quality extra-virgin olive oil
Kosher salt and freshly ground black pepper to taste
Freshly squeezed juice of ½ lemon

Preparation:
Boil the green beans until they reach al dente; they must not be overcooked.
Immediately after cooking, plunge into ice water to stop the cooking.
Drain and let cool.
Place in a salad bowl and add salt and freshly ground pepper.
Add olive oil and mix.
Just before serving, add the lemon and mix.
Serve as either a salad or as vegetable to meat, fish, or even pasta.

Chapter 16

London Days

Life in Lake Bluff after Paris was, to say the least, anticlimactic. However, it was a good reentry for us to American life. Our furniture took the hardest hit, making its second round-trip journey across the Atlantic.

Working for a Japanese company was a different experience. Unlike the CINB network of foreign branches, where we attempted to recruit local management who knew the lay of the land and were capable of making business decisions affecting the branches, in the Japanese company, top management was always Japanese. The Japanese worked long hours. They were not necessarily more productive than their American counterparts, but an employee or manager could not leave the office before his or her senior managers left. I also learned the concept of management by consensus where individual decision risk did not exist.

My job at Sanwa was challenging at first because we needed to create a breakaway organization from our previous parent (CINB) and create what amounted to a start-up leasing operation. This encompassed implementing a new lease accounting and administration system and converting the existing portfolio of leases to the new system. New policies and procedures needed to be written and internal controls created, which kept me well occupied for the first two years. However, as Sanwa was a foreign bank, there was no real opportunity to grow outside of the leasing company; and as my boss, Doug Shultz, was younger than I and not intending to make any moves, it seemed that my career growth was somewhat limited. Maybe as a consolation or as a reward, I did, however, have the opportunity to visit the Sanwa head office in Tokyo during my tenure, along with my Chicago colleague Dave Brown and other worldwide foreign employees. This was a ten-day visit that included a side trip to the ancient capital, Kyoto. This was my first trip to Asia, and it whetted my appetite for more travel in Asia.

Kimonos for formal tea and a visit to the local Disneyland

Cocktails at head office and drinks with the staff at night, "Kampai"

My career with Sanwa changed abruptly when Roy Okuto, SBCC executive vice president and COO, asked me to put together a feasibility study and projections for creating a de novo leasing subsidiary in London. Sanwa had a large presence in London as a bank, but it had a real need to provide vendor or equipment financing (product and asset based financing) for its key Japanese customers, such as Konica, Ricoh, Canon, and others, to enhance those customers' equipment sales in the United Kingdom. Because it lacked expertise in equipment leasing in the United Kingdom, the plan was to draw on the expertise of its US subsidiary in Chicago, Sanwa Business Credit Corporation. This prospect was extremely exciting and a perfect match for me, based on my previous overseas experience.

A team was created headed up by Roy Okuto. Don Nesta would be responsible for the business development, and I would be responsible for the operations and administration. The feasibility study and projections were approved, and we were given the go ahead. This new assignment would mean that Roz and I would once again need to relocate to Europe. This time it would be London, which thoroughly pleased Roz as there would be a minimal language barrier. Below is an article written in the *Sanwa Newsletter* concerning an interview with Don Nesta regarding the project.

In September 1989, Don and I met with Roy in London to execute our start-up plan. With the help of the legal department at the bank branch, we created a new entity named Sanwa Business Credit UK, Limited. We initially set up operations in an area with perhaps the most expensive real estate in London, near Leadenhall and Bishopsgate. The advantages of this location at first were that we were near the mother bank and in the heart of the financial district, and it facilitated needed contacts. However, the premises were old and too expensive for a start-up operation, and the location presented a difficult commute to and from the West End where we were staying. We soon moved the business to a more efficient building located at 36 Queen Street, not too far from the financial district, just before Southwark Bridge near the London Bridge (not to be confused with the fancy Tower Bridge).

My office in the new building (space at a premium)

Our first hire was Janet Rose, an administrative assistant who helped us set up interviews to staff the office. I hired a seasoned senior accountant, Godfrey Smith, whom I knew from my days at Continental Bank. Together we selected the accounting and lease administration system called GEAC out of Bristol, England, from several alternatives, including InfoLease, which was a system we used in the United States. InfoLease, although available in the United Kingdom, was not yet fully established for UK requirements. It would have been difficult enough to set up a new system without having to deal with an untried system. So our conclusion was to purchase a well-established UK-based system. Don hired John Bennett to head up the business development. He brought with him some experienced leasing professionals, and we began booking leases. With the balance sheet support of Sanwa Bank, we quickly built up a sizeable portfolio. We were able to manage our costs and were profitable within a short period. Believe it or not, the subsidiary we created survived the acquisition of SBCC by Fleet and was incorporated with the London activities of Bank of America in its acquisition of Fleet. Godfrey retired just recently, and I communicate with him occasionally.

While Don and I were consumed with the process of setting up the London operations, Roz remained back in Chicago, dealing with the selling of our home and the relocation issues. Godfrey helped Don and me look for temporary housing. He found for us a two-bedroom flat in the West End, adjoining the Dorchester Hotel on Park Lane across the street from Hyde Park in Mayfair. The apartment was more old than elegant, but the address was impressive. Thanks to a strong real estate market in the Lake Bluff area at the time, Roz was able to sell our home after it had been listed for only a few days. She soon joined me in London in the Mayfair apartment. Don moved to a permanent flat in the Regent's Park area on Devonshire Place.

The Mayfair apartment (brick building),
adjacent to the Dorchester Hotel

Roz and I later found an apartment very near Regent's Park through another colleague from Continental Bank who now worked for Schroder Bank in London. Wilson Snyder and his wife, Barbara, lived in a large, stately apartment building called Harley House on Marylebone Road. They informed us of a vacancy in the building, and we quickly grabbed it. The apartment was a three-bedroom flat with spacious rooms, fireplaces, and hardwood floors, very much in the style of our Paris apartment—and this time it was on the ground floor. As it turned out, Wilson worked in the London financial district, and his work provided him with a garage space, a rare commodity. This allowed me to commute with him to work and avoid a morning ride on the subway known as the tube.

While waiting for our furniture to arrive, we received a telephone call one morning around two o'clock from our friend and attorney, Bob Thopy. Roz answered the phone, and Bob explained that a doctor friend of his had a young patient nearing the delivery of her baby and that she wanted to consider a private adoption. Bob knew of our desire to have children, so he asked if we were interested in pursuing this adoption. Roz, startled and confused by the early morning call, told him that we would call back. After she roused me and explained why Bob called, I immediately called him back to confirm that we were most definitely interested in the adoption possibility.

In late November 1990, we were notified of Nic's impending birth, so Roz returned to Indiana to be with him after his birth. She received custody of Nic on December 3, 1990, the day after his birth. Roz and her parents drove with Nic to Bloomington that day during a driving snowstorm. Roz and Nic stayed with her parents in Bloomington while I remained at Harley House in London, boxes piled to the ceiling, unpacking our belongings. A couple of weeks later I joined Roz and Nic in Bloomington to spend our first Christmas together. And so began our life with Nicholas.

As you can imagine, the adoption was complicated by the different geographic locations involved —Nicholas's birth state was Indiana, and our home was then in London. We were fortunate that the sale of our Lake Bluff home had not yet closed, because that enabled the adoption to be processed as an interstate adoption, not an international one. The fact that we lived in the United Kingdom made the required home study difficult. This was facilitated by our Lake Bluff next-door neighbors, Donna and Don Dieball, who graciously provided the use of their living room for the interview. Until the adoption was completed, Bob acted as the court appointed temporary guardian while Nic was in Indiana.

Roz with Nic at the hospital   My first meeting with Nic

Life in London with a newborn dramatically changed our lifestyle. Our travel was curtailed while we dealt with baby formula, diapers, and sleepless nights. For the nursery we bought baby furniture, dehumidifiers, and prams (what strollers are called in the United Kingdom). We opened an account at Harrods, Selfridges, and John Lewis and spent most weekends shopping. Our mode of transportation now always included a stroller. London cabbies were great and quick to help load the stroller. Fortunately, our apartment was a stone's throw away from Regent's Park, one of London's most beautiful parks, and we took full advantage, using it like a backyard. Shopping for groceries and such was always a challenge. The stroller came in handy, as we would use its handles to hold the sacks of groceries. We destroyed two strollers during our stay. Harrods at Knightsbridge was our favorite weekend shopping destination. Nic had his first haircut at Harrods, and the toy department was unmatched, except maybe for Hamleys of London, Ltd., on Regent Street.

70 Harley House, 28–32 Marylebone Road, London NW1 5HN

Walking became our pastime as it kept Nic interested, provided us with exercise, and was perfect for getting to know London. As our apartment was centrally located, our favorite strolls were to places like Piccadilly Circus, Soho, Covent Gardens, Knightsbridge, Hyde Park, Oxford Street, and, of course, Regent's Park.

Nic in the stroller at Greenwich,
England, the site of 0° longitude
and the home of GMT

Nic's mode of travel at Regent's Park,
in Kensington, on Marylebone Road

Out of his stroller in the park

Nick's arrival at Harley House
and meeting Barbara Snyder

Learning to walk
at Regent's Park

Nic, boss of Harley House

Nic's first birthday and learning to eat pasta

Testing American food

Frequenting London's more exclusive restaurants was also somewhat curtailed, as most restaurants were not child-friendly. This allowed me to improve my recipes. We often had friends and colleagues over for dinner and occasionally hosted family visitors. Our restaurant choices were primarily Asian, Indian, and Italian, with the occasional Sunday pub lunch.

We did have access to some very good-quality food products as London was filled with Italian specialty food stores. One of our favorite places was the exotic food halls of Harrods, where we could find whatever we wished, and the quality was impeccable. Chinatown always provided a welcoming atmosphere and decent Chinese food anytime, day or night.

Harrods at Knightsbridge and its food halls

Any type of fish, vegetables, and cheese that you can imagine

In addition to our annual home leave, we managed to take two extended trips during our stay in London. One was a two-week vacation with Italo and Etta to a remote seaside resort in Sardinia on the Mediterranean called the Baia delle Mimose, not far from Sassari. It was a welcome break from the London weather and the city life. The other trip was an extended visit to Tuscany to meet Bob and Linda Thopy and visit with family in Lucca. Tuscany has no equal.

Nic raiding the fridge and making pasta in the kitchen (can you see Nic in this photo?)

Scenic Sardinia-   Nic's first swimming lessons

Roz in a peaceful moment and Nic never without his mode of transportation

My cousins Italo and Angela with their families in Florence

The incomparable San Gimignano and its towers with Bob and Linda Thopy

Assisi and a meal arranged by Gerry Masciello (Clelia's dad) in Florence, one of the best ever

Don Nesta and his son with my Alfa

Having a car in the city of London is more a nuisance than a necessity. I had a parking permit to park on the street in front of Harley House, but spaces were so scarce that once I found one, I would never want to leave it. I accumulated only about 1,200 miles on the car in the two and a half years we spent in London.

We continued our sojourn in London, building up the leasing operation for SBCC (UK) for another two years. Having structured an autonomous local organization, I was ready for my next assignment. This came in the form of a transfer to the Detroit suburb of Troy with Sanwa Leasing Corporation (SLC), a previously independent, small-ticket leasing operation acquired by SBCC. An audit at SLC had disclosed major deficiencies with its internal controls. I was tasked with stabilizing operations by invigorating the faltering effort to implement its new lease accounting system. We returned to the United States in the spring of 1993. After packing furniture for another transatlantic journey, transferring my Alfa Romeo to Godfrey, and saying good-bye to friends, we headed home.

Nic moving out of Harley House

After a short stay in temporary housing in Troy while waiting for our furniture to arrive, we purchased a newly constructed home in Rochester, Michigan, a north suburb not far from Troy. Despite the bad press it receives, Detroit has some of the more livable suburbs in the country, and Rochester was one of them. It so happened that my younger brother, Douglas, and his family lived in Plymouth, Michigan (a western suburb). It was good to have family near. Indianapolis and Bloomington were six and seven hours away, respectively, so we also had many occasions to visit Momma, Corrado, and Roz's parents. Nic began preschool in a Montessori school called the Brookfield Academy and we soon readjusted to an American lifestyle.

Pebble Pointe Drive, Rochester, Michigan; Meeting Doug and his family at the Detroit zoo and Nic's first car

Roz's parents and the Kubinskis in Rochester, Mom, Corrado, and Patty in Rochester

Nic begins his car love affair; Nic's first day of school at Brookfield Academy

I soon hired a sharp accountant for SLC and a talented IT manager. It took us less than a year to stabilize the operations and complete the system implementation. The small-ticket operation thrived as we added a number of Japanese vendor programs and added a highly successful vendor program with Dell Computers and Tandy.

After three years, I was ready to return to Chicago. However, Sanwa had no positions for me there and wanted me to remain in Detroit. Feeling pigeonholed, I began to look elsewhere. I accepted a senior operations position with LINC Anthem in downtown Chicago. This was a medical equipment leasing company that had been purchased by Anthem Blue Cross out of Indianapolis. As senior vice president of operations, I was responsible for accounting and lease administration. Roz, a little weary of moving by now, took it in stride. As the office was located in the center of Chicago, we needed to find a location commutable by train. We searched our old communities of Lake Forest and Lake Bluff but concluded that the housing we could afford was either too small or too old. We finally found a home in the fast-growing suburb of Naperville. Nic entered kindergarten and we met our neighbors, Tony and Dolorine Bartolotta, who remain good friends to this day.

Henning Court in Naperville   Nic at a soccer game

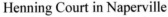

Nic's kindergarten class in Naperville

Unknown to me, when I was hired by LINC, it was an acquisition target. A Canadian financial venture company, Newcourt Credit Group, was in the process of performing its due diligence. After my initial acclimation, I was brought in to assist the prospective buyer with Newcourt's due diligence. Newcourt closed on its purchase of LINC, and the transformation began. Michel Beland was CFO, assigned to perform the integration, and I reported to him. After a period of eight months, a decision was made to move the North American headquarters of Newcourt Credit Group to Indianapolis. Newcourt had also purchased a small leasing operation in Indianapolis, which would form the nucleus of its headquarters, occupying three floors in the new Bank One Tower. I was asked to join Michel to help run the North American operations. Many of the Chicago staff refused to relocate to Indianapolis, but not me. Indianapolis was home to both Roz and me and afforded us more time to be with our parents Therefore, after only eight months in the Chicago area, we were once again moving.

We purchased a spacious home in Carmel, Indiana. Nic entered first grade at College Wood Elementary School in Carmel. We were happy to be able to spend time with our parents and family.

Mayfair Lane in Carmel and Mom

But this was also short-lived. Newcourt's appetite for growth was insatiable. Its top management continued to look for external growth opportunities, resulting in the acquisition of ATT Capital, a captive finance company of AT&T. This acquisition was the proverbial minnow swallowing the whale. To integrate this acquisition, Newcourt moved its US headquarters from Indianapolis to New Jersey, where ATT Capital was located. This had a devastating impact on the Indianapolis operations. Not knowing how this move would impact me personally, I began to look for a backup position and received an offer to return to Marty Zimmerman's new organization, which had survived the acquisition as a new LINC Capital. Upon informing Newcourt of this offer, I was offered a senior operations position in London, heading up the integration of the European branch operations of what had been an ATT Capital operation. ATT Capital had branches and subsidiaries in the European financial centers of London, Brussels, Paris, Frankfurt, Madrid, and Milan. Newcourt had also purchased a UK leasing company in Bristol, England. All of these operations needed to be integrated into Newcourt. Given the chance to return to Europe, I accepted the offer.

In the spring of 1997, less than a year after moving back to Indianapolis, we were once again headed across the Atlantic. This time we needed to find a location where Nic could attend an American school to lessen the impact of the cultural change. We found a small condo in a gated community known as Virginia Park in the village of Virginia Water in Surrey. As my next assignment would require significant travel, being close to Heathrow was also important. As it turned out, my traveling requirement was excessive. I had two offices, one in London at the old ATT headquarters on Buckingham Gate, near Buckingham Palace, and the other in Bristol at the office building that became Newcourt's headquarters. I would spend one day a week in London and one day in Bristol, taking the train from Virginia Water, and the rest of the week visiting European operations on the continent. As the coordinator for the integration of the operations group, I met with each of the European units to oversee its progress in the system conversion and in the development of policies and procedures.

Virginia Park at Virginia Water in Surrey

Nic on VW grounds

Nic's piano lessons

Our local Thai restaurant

Visiting Maurizio
in Milan

With Nic in Madrid

Visiting Venice in February while in Italy

At our old apartment in Paris and boarding the Metro and boarding the TGV

Obviously, my favorite unit to visit was Milan, where we had an office just off the Piazza Cairoli near Castello Forzesco. These visits afforded me the opportunity to reunite with my Italian family.

Nic attended second and third grade at the American Community School (ACS) in Egham and participated in sporting activities such as baseball and soccer. We met and befriended a number of American families through the school; some with whom we still maintain contact. We also did some traveling as Nic was now at an age to allow it. During this period we took a fabulous trip to the Amalfitana coast with Nick and Maryann Setteducato and their children, whom we knew through Nic's school. The recollections from this trip still live large in our memories. We also visited Ireland for the first time. Even in November, Ireland was spectacular. We drove from London to the coast of Wales for a ferry ride to the south of Ireland. We drove the Ring of Kerry, from there all the way up to the Cliffs of Mohair, and then back through Blarney to the coast. The trip was extraordinary, and Guinness is best in Ireland.

Nic at ACS and the class picture

Enjoying Sorrento in spring

Lunch in Positano

Nic and Michael in Sorrento

We also had a number of visitors from our past while in Surrey including the Kubinskis, Jack Sebesta, and Generoso Gallucio, as well as Italo and Etta.

Reunion with Gallucio and Jack Sebesta at VW

Italo and family

The excesses of Newcourt, including the purchase of a castle in Scotland as a training center, and its rapid expansion took a toll on its ability to raise capital. The minnow could not digest the whale. Unable to find a partner to come to its rescue, Newcourt eventually had to settle for a not-too-friendly acquisition by CIT.

Newcourt's castle

My catch from a lake at the castle (speckled trout) and the meal of the evening at the castle

Group picture of Newcourt's European management
at the castle (see the kilts), one of the last get-togethers

The acquisition by CIT turned hostile, and all the Newcourt management was fired, including me. In the spring of 2000, I found myself searching for a new position outside of the United Kingdom. Our return trip and furniture move to the United States was assured by contract with Newcourt. However, needing to stay in the United Kingdom to complete Nic's school year made searching for work in the States from London hopeless. Fortunately, a friend, David Kliefoth, whom I knew from Continental Bank, crossed paths with me in England. David then worked for Motorola at its Chicago headquarters. He was visiting Motorola's office in Basingstoke with his boss, Gary Tatje. Motorola Credit Corp, the financing captive subsidiary of Motorola, had an opening for a compliance and operations person back in Chicago. So one rainy night, I drove to Basingstoke to meet with Gary and Dave; and several weeks later, I received an offer, which I gladly accepted. I began work with Motorola in Schaumburg, IL, on May 8, 2000. Roz remained in Virginia Water until Nic completed third grade.

During this period of time in the United Kingdom, and because of more in-home dining with our expanded family, I had a chance to improve on my recipes. Included in this chapter are some of our favorite stay-at-home recipes.

- *Olive Sotto Olio* (Marinated Olives)
- *Pecorino Sotto Olio* (Romano Cheese Under Olive Oil)
- *Fagiolini con Tonno* (Canellini Beans with Tuna)
- *Crostini con Coppa e Rucola* (Canapés with Coppa and Arugula)
- *Frittata con Patate e Prosciutto* (Omelet with Potatoes and Ham)
- *Crema di Melanzane* (Eggplant Topping)
- *Pasta con Olive Marinate* (Marinated Olive Pasta)
- *Spaghetti al Pomodoro Fresco e Basilico* (Spaghetti with Fresh Tomatoes and Basil)
- *Riso in Cagnone* (Rice with Toma or Fontina Cheese and Sage)
- *Risotto alla Milanese* (Risotto with Saffron and Cheese)
- *Piccata di Vitello/Pollo* (Veal/Chicken Scallops with Lemon)
- Mom's Beef Stroganoff
- *Sformato di Carciofi* (Artichoke Casserole)
- *Carciofi in Umido* (Braised Artichokes)
- *Frito Misto all Italiana* (Italian Mixed Fried Plate)
- *Uova in Trippa* (Egg Strips in Tomato Sauce)
- *Torta di Nocciole* (Hazelnut Cake)
- *Limoncello del Gallo* (Lemon Liquor)

Olive Sotto Olio (Marinated Olives)
Category: Antipasti (Appetizers)
Origin: Traditional Italian
Serves 6–8

I first began marinating olives after buying some similar mixture from an Italian delicatessen in London. I guessed as to what the mix included, but my combination turned out to be pretty good. This is a great mixture and can be a big hit with guests as part of a combined appetizer serving. It can keep in the refrigerator for a week or so. I also use what is left to make Spaghetti con Olive (see separate recipe).

Ingredients:
4–6 oz. Kalamata black olives with pits
4–6 oz. green Cerignola olives with pits
4–6 oz. other green or black olives with pits, including oil-cured olives
6 green pepperoncini (hot)
6–12 whole small dried cayenne peppers
2 bay leaves
Whole black peppercorns
Dried marjoram and thyme
3–4 garlic cloves, peeled and cut in large pieces
Extra-virgin olive oil
Cracked black pepper to taste

Preparation:
Place the olives, drained of the brine, in a medium bowl large enough to hold the
    olives and then some.
Add the chili peppers and cayenne peppers, crushing several of the cayenne peppers
    over the mixture.
Add the bay leaves, peppercorns, dried marjoram, thyme, and garlic cloves.
Add freshly cracked ground pepper.
Add enough olive oil to coat the olives.
Stir the olives, cover, and refrigerate.
Stir occasionally.
Before serving, remove from refrigerator and bring to room temperature.

Pecorino Sotto Olio (Pecorino Cheese Under Olive Oil)

Category: Antipasti (Appetizers)
Origin: My Adaptation of Traditional Italian
Serves 6–8

Makes a great appetizer and is always totally consumed. The quality of the Pecorino is vital, and the hint of lemon with the salty cheese is refreshing.

Ingredients:
¼ lb. imported Pecorino (Romano) cheese, cut into ½-inch cubes
High-quality extra-virgin olive oil
Cracked black peppercorns
Hot chili pepper flakes (peperoncini)
Zest of ½ lemon

Preparation:
Place cheese cubes in a serving bowl.
Add enough olive oil to lightly coat the cheese cubes.
Add the ground pepper; peperoncini; grated lemon zest and stir to mix thoroughly.
Cover and refrigerate, stirring occasionally.
Before serving, remove from the refrigerator and bring to room temperature.

Fagioli Bianchi con Tonno (Cannellini Beans with Tuna)

Category: Antipasti (Appetizers)
Origin: My Adaptation of Traditional Piemontese
Serves 4–6

This is one of my favorite appetizers. It combines the delicate taste of the cannellini beans with the flavorable taste of good quality Italian tuna under olive oil. The key is finding the best tuna. The dish is also accented with parsley and red onion with a hint of lemon.

Ingredients:
15-oz. can cannellini white beans, drained and rinsed
6-oz. can good-quality tuna, packed in olive oil
½ medium red onion, thinly sliced
1 stalk celery, thinly sliced
Juice of ½ lemon

Zest of 1 lemon
¼ cup chopped parsley
Kosher salt and freshly ground black pepper to taste
Extra-virgin olive oil as a dressing

Preparation:
1. Dice the onion very thinly and place in cold water while you prepare the other ingredients. This will take some of the bite out of the onions.
2. Drain the tuna and empty it into a large bowl.
3. Add the beans to the tuna and gently stir to combine.
4. Add the onions, celery, parsley, black pepper, lemon zest, and lemon juice; gently mix to combine.
6. Add the olive oil to moisten the salad as needed.

Variations could include adding jalapeño or serrano chili peppers, arugula, and green olives, but I prefer it simpler.

Crostini con Coppa e Arugola (Crostini with Coppa and Arugula)
Category: Antipasti (Appetizers)
Origin: Traditional Italian
Serves 4–6

Crostini (made by oven-toasting pieces of Italian bread) is traditionally used to make appetizers in Italy and can be topped with a number of ingredients. I prepare crostini with cream cheese and black olive spread, change the *Coppa* for prosciutto or *Bresaola*, or add prosciutto with cream cheese and other toppings.

Ingredients:
1 loaf of ciabatta or baguette bread
¼ lb. *Coppa*, sliced thin
Arugula leaves large enough to cover the crostini
Extra-virgin olive oil

Preparation:
1. Slice the bread into thin slices (not so thin that they burn when toasted).
2. Lightly salt the slices and sprinkle with olive oil.
3. Toast the bread slices in the oven under a broiler as if you were making bruschetta (see separate recipe).

4. Let cool on a drying rack.

5. On a serving tray, place a slice of the *Coppa* on each bread slice.

6. Place a leaf of the arugula on top of the *Coppa.*

7. Serve as an appetizer. It is best not to store the crostini in the refrigerator; if you do, the bread may become moist.

An alternative way of serving the crostini is to make rolls of stuffed *Coppa* by placing cream cheese on the *Coppa* and rolling them on top of the crostini without arugula or you can use your imagination.

Frittata con Patate e Prosciutto Cotto (Eggs and Potato Frittata with Ham)
Category: Vari (Other)
Origin: Mamma Cortellini
Serves 4

This is a very versatile dish that can be served for breakfast, lunch, or dinner. You can vary the ingredients with most other vegetables or meats. Add or substitute green or red pepper, asparagus, artichokes, sausage, and so on. You can also add cheeses if you like. In Italy frittatas are often used to finish leftovers as the leftovers can be added as ingredients—even leftover pasta. This is a dish to prepare when you are in a hurry or when you can't think of anything else to prepare, reflecting the versatility and simplicity of Italian cooking.

Ingredients:
7 small potatoes (red potatoes with their skins), cut into ½-inch pieces
1 small yellow onion, chopped into small pieces
Leaves from a small branch of fresh rosemary, chopped
¼ tsp. fresh chopped or dried thyme
Extra-virgin olive oil to fry the potatoes
Chili pepper flakes (flakes of peperoncini) to taste
Kosher salt and freshly ground black pepper to taste
Small piece of smoked ham steak, chopped into small pieces (¾ cup)
7 eggs, beaten with a small amount of milk

Preparation:
1. Rinse the potatoes and cut into half-inch pieces, then place in a bowl of cold water to rinse off the starch.
2. In a large skillet, heat the olive oil and sauté the onions.
3. When the onion is soft and translucent, add the potatoes, rosemary, thyme, pepper

flakes, salt, and pepper.

4. Slowly fry over medium-low heat for at least forty-five minutes or until the potatoes are cooked, turning occasionally, as the potatoes must be browned all over.
5. Pour the beaten eggs and work the sides of the skillet, pushing the eggs toward the middle until they are set (not runny).
6. Only turn once by sliding cooked side of the frittata onto a large dish, then invert and slide back to the skillet to cook the other side.
7. Finish cooking the frittata (two to three minutes) and place on a serving plate.
8. Serve immediately by cutting wedges like a pie.

Pasta con Olive Marinate (Marinated Olive Pasta)
Category: Paste (Pastas)
Origin: My Imagination
Serves 6

This recipe was inspired from our visits to the many Italian delicatessens we found during our walks around London. There was one in particular in the West End that offered marinated olives, with a mixture of black and green olives. I first used the delicatessen's mixture but later developed my own. This is a simple dish with few ingredients, making the quality of the oil, olives, and cheese most important. I normally leave the garlic in the sauce, but it can be removed if someone doesn't want to eat fried garlic. My marinated olives include Kalamata olives and Cerignola (or other high-quality) green olives marinated in extra-virgin olive oil, sliced garlic, dried marjoram, thyme, and chili pepper flakes with abundant freshly ground black pepper and some whole peppercorns.

Ingredients:

If using pre-marinated olives, see my recipe for the marinade. If starting from scratch,
  use the following.

3–4 cloves of garlic sliced, but not too thin

16-oz. jar Greek Kalamata black olives, not pitted

8-oz. jar Italian Cerignola or similar green olives, not pitted

½ cup extra-virgin olive oil (I like oils from Puglia or Lucca)

Red chili pepper flakes to taste (at least ¼ tsp.); I also buy whole tiny cayenne
  peppers and crumble 3 or 4 instead of the pepper flakes

½ tsp. each dried marjoram and thyme, or more to taste

Kosher salt and freshly ground black pepper to taste

Grated Italian imported Pecorino or *Parmigiano-Reggiano*

1-lb. box Italian imported Fusilli or Orechietti pasta

Preparation:

1. An important step in the preparation of this sauce is the frying of the garlic. If you
   get it too brown, the oil will burn, and you will need to start over.
2. Pit the olives and chop finely. I use a mezzaluna (see picture) to chop the olives
   finely. Using a food processor would turn them into a paste and is not recommended
   as you want the consistency of olive pieces.
3. Put the oil in a skillet or saucepan and heat the oil. The skillet should be large enough
   to disperse the oil so you are not deep-frying the garlic but rather sautéing it. Don't skimp
   on the oil, as this is the main ingredient of the sauce.
4. Add the garlic and simmer over medium to medium-low heat.
5. When the garlic's color begins to change (golden), add the red pepper flakes, the chopped
   olives, salt, and pepper.
6. Add the marjoram and sauté for ten minutes. The olives don't need much cooking.
7. Stir well and remove from heat.
8. Cook the pasta al dente and remove it from the boiling water with a slotted spoon (retain
   a small portion of the boiling water to maintain some moisture in the pasta).
9. Return the skillet with the oil to low heat and stir in the pasta. Serve on individual plates
   or in a large pasta dish.
10. Serve at once. Sprinkle the grated cheese on each plate as you serve the pasta.

Spaghetti al Pomodoro Fresco e Basilico
(Spaghetti with Fresh Tomatoes and Basil)
Category: Paste (Pastas)
Origin: My Adaptation/Traditional Napoli
Serves 4

The quality of this dish depends upon the quality of the tomatoes. Roma or plum tomatoes are the best to use for this sauce; other tomatoes do not have the same consistency and may contain too much water, which will cause them to not reduce properly. Roz accuses me of using too much basil, but I believe you can't use too much basil. This is another dish that is easy and quick to prepare—and a default for when nothing else is in the cupboard.

Traditionally this sauce is served with spaghettini as it is intended as a light dish. I like to use fedelini. Nic likes it with penne or any other pasta. This is by far Nic's favorite spaghetti sauce. As I've said before, because of its simplicity, the quality of the ingredients is most important, so don't substitute. I normally leave the garlic in the sauce and eat it with the spaghetti. You can, of course, remove the garlic before mixing the sauce into the pasta, if you don't care to eat delectable fried garlic. I suspect that the origin of this sauce is Napoli. Our friends from London, Nick and Maryanne Setteducato and family (who traveled with us to Sorrento), termed this dish "Penne Pompodoro."

Ingredients:
1-lb. box of Italian imported spaghettini or fedelini (avoid using capellini or vermicelli)
4 good-sized cloves of garlic, sliced
Large bunch of fresh basil (at least 2 Tbsp.)
2 Tbsp. extra-virgin olive oil
12 Roma or Italian plum tomatoes
Red pepper flakes (peperoncini) to taste (at least ¼ tsp.; I also buy whole tiny cayenne
    peppers and crumble 3 or 4 instead of the pepper flakes)
Kosher salt and freshly ground black pepper to taste

The key to this sauce is the quality of the tomatoes. Normally I prepare this sauce in the summer, when the tomatoes are best. However, if you are lucky enough to find decent tomatoes in the winter, this dish is a refreshing reminder of summer.

Preparation:
1. Start by slicing the garlic. The slices need to be thick enough that they do not burn when frying them in the olive oil—and so that you can find them to remove them from the sauce before serving. If you get the garlic too brown, the oil is burned, and you will need to start over.
2. Cut the tomatoes in tiny cubes. This is done by first slicing the tomato in half lengthwise, then slicing the halves in thin slices, and finally slicing the pieces crosswise to make cubes. Most Italian cookbooks suggest parboiling tomatoes to remove their skins before cooking for sauces. I find that if I cut the tomatoes into small cubes, the skins aren't a problem, and the flavor is enhanced.
3. In a medium-sized, heavy saucepan, fry the garlic slices over medium-low heat. When the garlic turns golden around the edges, add the tomato cubes. It should fill most of the saucepan. Don't be concerned that there are too many tomatoes; they will cook down considerably.
4. The tomatoes will create their own juices for the sauce, so no added water is needed. You will need to reduce the juices by cooking the tomatoes for approximately thirty minutes or until the sauce thickens.
5. Chop the basil and add to the sauce along with the peperoncini flakes.
6. Add salt and freshly ground pepper and finished cooking the sauce, removing the garlic slices (optional) before mixing with the pasta.
7. While cooking the sauce, in a large pasta pan boil water adding salt to the water as it boils and cook the pasta according to the packaging instructions testing the pasta periodically to ensure it remains al dente. Adding salt to the pasta water adds flavor to the pasta as it otherwise is bland. Mario Batali says that the water should taste salty like the sea.
8. Drain the pasta in a colander or remove the pasta with thongs or a spider so as to retain

some of the pasta water to add to the pasta if it is too dry.
9. Place in a pasta bowl and add the sauce, and serve immediately. Do not add any cheese.

Typical sauce and great for kids

Riso in Cagnone (Rice with Cheese and Sage)
Category: Paste (Pastas)
Origin: Typical Lombard Dish
Serves 4

The name comes from the Lombard *cagnun* (meaning "insect larva") because of the appearance of the rice after cooking. This recipe is well-known in the rice-growing area of Italy known as the Po Valley in the province of Lombardy. The preparation is simple, but, precisely for this reason, some additional flavoring is suggested; garlic and sage are customary.

The sauce should be ready at the same time as the rice. The rice should be cooked al dente and drained to avoid overcooking. The butter should be heated almost to the point of smoking and have turned an intense hazelnut color. The dish is best enjoyed hot and can accompany such dishes as scallops, vegetables, or roasted chicken. You can pair it with a fragrant white dry wine, such as *Franciacorta Pinot Grigio* or Italian Riesling of *Oltrepò Pavese*.

Ingredients:
2½ cups white rice
4 Tbsp. unsalted butter
6 oz. aged Toma or Fontina cheese, sliced
Kosher salt and freshly ground black pepper to taste
8 sage leaves
2 garlic cloves, peeled and smashed *Parmigiano-Reggiano* for topping

Preparation:
1. Cut the cheese into thin slices (if using Fontina, remove its crust first) and set aside.
2. In a pot with about two quarts of salted water, boil the rice.
3. Place part of the cheese on the bottom of a serving bowl.
4. Cook the rice as you would pasta, for about fifteen to twenty minutes (al dente). Stir occasionally.
5. Drain the rice, leaving it a bit moist and pour over the cheese in the bowl.
6. In a small saucepan, melt the butter till very hot but not burning; add the smashed garlic and sage leaves and sauté to infuse flavors.
7. Add the remaining cheese on top of the rice.
8. Remove the garlic and pour the very hot butter over the rice.
9. Sprinkle on an abundant amount of *Parmigiano-Reggiano*, mix thoroughly, and serve hot.

Cook and mix the rice and serve hot

Risotto alla Milanese (Risotto with Saffron and Cheese)
Category: Paste (Pastas)
Origin: Traditional Milanese
Serves 4

This is a traditional Milanese dish. It can be served plain as a first course, or it can be combined with vegetables such as artichokes, asparagus, or zucchini by first sautéing the vegetables and then adding the rice. It is also served with white truffles when in season. Success in making this rice dish is best achieved by slow-cooking and adding slowly adding the stock a little at a time allowing the liquids to reduce and absorbing the flavors in the rice until it is cooked. Unlike pasta, the rice is not just boiled in water and removed when cooked.

Ingredients:
6 cups chicken stock, preferably homemade (see Chicken Soup recipe)
⅛ tsp. saffron threads
9 Tbsp. unsalted butter
1 cup *Parmigiano-Reggiano* or grana padano
1 small yellow onion, finely chopped
2 cups arborio rice
½ cup dry white wine
Salt and freshly ground black pepper to taste

Preparation:
1. Melt three tablespoons of butter in a heavy skillet or saucepan.
2. When it begins to bubble, add the onion and cook for two or three minutes, but do not let the onion turn brown.
3. Add the rice to the onion and stir well, coating the grain.

4. Add the wine and let most of it evaporate.
5. Start adding the stock a half cup at a time. Let each dose of stock cook down before adding more.
6. As the rice becomes tender, be sure to stir often to prevent it from sticking to the bottom.
7. Add salt, pepper, and saffron.
8. When rice is done, stir in the remaining butter and the cheese. Serve hot immediately and top with more cheese or truffles.

Piccata di Vitello/Pollo (Veal/Chicken Scallops with Lemon)
Category: Carni (Meats)
Origin: Mamma Cortellini
Serves 4–6

Traditional Italian meals are normally served in courses with pastas always served alone followed with the main course which could be a combination plate. The key is to serve pastas that compliment the main course. For example you Momma would not serve a tomato based second course if serving tomato pasta (too much tomato). She often served this dish on Sunday after having served pasta with a red sauce as it is rather neutral and lemony fresh. The key for this dish is to not overcook the meat, especially if you are using veal. Also, do not dredge the meat in the flour ahead of time, or the flour will get soggy and not fry crisply. Make sure that the oil is very hot when you place the scallops in the frying pan.

Ingredients:
1½–2 lb. chicken breast or boneless veal round, sliced ¼-inch thick and pounded thin
Flour for dredging
Kosher salt and fresh ground black pepper to taste
3–6 Tbsp. extra-virgin olive oil
½ cup chicken stock
¼ cup lemon juice
3 Tbsp. unsalted butter
1-2 tsp. capers under salt (use the small capers rather than large)
2 Tbsp. finely chopped Italian parsley

Preparation:
1. Warm the oven to 200°F to keep the scallops warm after frying.
2. Pound the meat thin, without tearing, so that the pieces are of consistent thickness.
3. Salt and pepper the scallops.
4. Spread the flour on a plate and dredge the meat through the flour.
5. Heat two to three tablespoons of the oil to sizzling in a large skillet.

6. Shake off the excess flour and fry as many of the scallops as will fit into the pan, not overcrowding.

7. Cook as rapidly as possible (not more than two minutes on each side) and, when cooked, transfer to a warm plate in the oven and continue cooking the rest of the scallops.

8. Repeat until all the scallops are done; add more oil to the pan if needed.

9. Pour off the oil from the skillet, raise the heat, and add the chicken stock. As the chicken stock comes to a boil, scrape up and stir in all the brown bits from the bottom of the skillet.

10. Add the lemon juice; season with salt, pepper, and capers and cook for another minute or so.

11. Add the butter and parsley and stir to blend. Return the scallops to the skillet, warm, and serve immediately.

Frying the scallops and adding stock

Serving

Mom's Beef Stroganoff
Category: Carni (Meats)
Origin: Mamma Cortellini
Serves 4–6

Obviously, this is not an Italian recipe. Mom received this recipe from the Bishoffs, who were symphony friends. Its place of origin is likely Russia. Only occasionally would Mom deviate from the traditional Italian cuisine. However, this stroganoff dish was one of her non-Italian successes. Served over fettuccini, it could almost be considered an Italian dish. It is one of those comfort foods to be served in cold weather with a good Italian red wine such as an Amarone.

Ingredients:
1½–2 lb. beef sirloin or tenderloin
1 whole clove garlic, peeled and used to rub on the meat
Kosher salt and freshly ground black pepper to taste
1 Tbsp. unsalted butter
2 Tbsp. extra-virgin olive oil
1 medium onion, finely chopped

1 can (10¾-oz.) mushroom soup
1 lb. sliced mushrooms
Small bunches Italian parsley, chives, and dill
1–1½ cups sour cream

Preparation:
1. Rub both sides of the meat with garlic clove.
2. Tenderize the meat by pounding (spread some flour over the meat before pounding it).
3. Cut meat into one-inch by one-and-a-half-inch slices.
4. Sauté the mushrooms in a skillet with the oil until cooked and then remove from the skillet.
5. Place the meat in the skillet with oil and butter; sauté until browned but still rare.
6. Add the onions and continue to cook until the onions turn golden and soft.
7. Add the mushroom soup and the sautéed mushrooms. Add a little milk to thin the soup and simmer slowly for thirty minutes, or until meat is tender.
8. If serving later, add sour cream just before serving; heat but do not boil. If serving right away, turn off the heat, stir in the sour cream, and serve.

Sformato di Carciofi (Artichoke Casserole)
Category: Verdure (Vegetables)
Origin: Mamma Cortellini
Serves 4–6

Ingredients:
½ lb. potatoes (about 2 medium-sized potatoes)
1 can artichoke hearts in water, combined with some marinated artichoke hearts for added flavor cut into slices
1–2 stalks celery, finely chopped
1 large carrot, finely chopped
1–2 garlic cloves, minced
Medium-sized onion, finely chopped
2 Tbsp. extra-virgin olive oil
Kosher salt and freshly ground black pepper to taste
1 tsp. freshly ground nutmeg
4 large eggs
½ cup grated *Parmigiano-Reggiano*
½ cup milk
Homemade bread crumbs

Preparation:
1. Boil and rice the potatoes while still warm.
2. In a large skillet, add the finely chopped vegetables and garlic; sauté in olive oil.

3. Add the artichoke slices and continue cooking for 10 to 15 minutes.
4. Stir in the riced potatoes and blend.
5. In a separate bowl, beat the eggs; add salt, pepper, and nutmeg. Remove vegetables from heat, add the egg mixture to the vegetables, and blend thoroughly.
6. Butter a baking dish and cover the bottom with bread crumbs.
7. Add the vegetable and egg mixture to the baking dish and cover with more bread crumbs.
8. Bake in the oven at 350°F for forty-five minutes to one hour, or until cooked and brown.

Ricing the potatoes and cooking to blend

Baked and served

Carciofi in Umido (Braised Artichokes)
Category: Verdure (Vegetables)
Origin: Zia Marisa
Serves 4–6

The artichoke, termed by ancient Linnaeus "the plant that stings," was later catalogued in the family of composite under the name "Cynara Carduncul." Its name derives from the Arabic "korshef." In Sicily artichokes were introduced from North Africa or Ethiopia, where they grew in nature.

Artichokes are a lovely gift of spring. They can be cooked in many different ways or eaten raw in a salad. This simple dish makes a great side, or it can be served as an antipasto. It is desirable to prevent the artichoke from turning dark when it is cut and exposed to air and to allow it to retain its natural green color. To achieve this, the artichoke must be dipped in lemon water after peeling.

Braised artichokes make a great vegetarian dish. Cooked in a pan, they make a great second or side dish. The stems should not be cut or thrown away as they are as delectable as the core.

Ingredients:
12–18 small fresh artichokes
Fresh homemade bread crumbs
Large bunch Italian parsley, finely chopped
2 large garlic cloves, minced
Kosher salt and freshly ground black pepper to taste
Extra-virgin olive oil to fry the artichokes
Glass of dry white wine
2 medium Roma tomatoes, diced
1 lemon

Preparation:
1. Peel and clean the artichokes, removing the hard outer leaves; cut off the spiny tops, cut in half, and remove any choke.

2. To prevent them from turning dark, place artichoke halves in a bowl with the juice of a lemon and a small amount of water.

3. In another bowl, mix the bread crumbs, minced garlic, parsley, and olive oil to make the stuffing.

4. Fill the artichoke cavity and in between the leaves, spreading them and inserting the stuffing mixture.

5. Place the stuffed artichokes in a frying pan or a heavy saucepan with the olive oil and sauté for a few minutes.

6. Add the wine and tomato dices and let simmer over low heat until the artichokes are tender. Cover the pot and cook for thirty to forty-five minutes, depending on the size of the artichokes. You may need to add some water if the pan becomes too dry.

Baby Artichokes

Cooking the artichokes

The serving

Fritto Misto al Italiana (Italian Mixed Fried Plate)
Category: Vari (Other)
Origin: Paolo Rismondo in Ancona
Serves 6–8

This is a recipe given to me by my cousin's husband, Paolo Rismondo. It is a typical Italian mixed fried plate combining fish, meat, and vegetables.

Ingredients:
4 artichokes
1 small cauliflower
1 large white onion
1 firm-fleshed apple
2 green zucchini
10 sage leaves
6 lamb chops, fried, or 6–10 shelled shrimp

Batter:
   5 oz. flour
   3 oz. rice flour
   2 Tbsp. brandy or whiskey
   Water (enough to make a thick batter)
   Kosher salt and freshly ground black pepper to taste

Preparation:
1. Remove the artichoke leaves, leaving only the central lighter green potion of the artichoke.
2. Cut each artichoke into four wedges and place in a bowl with water and lemon.
3. Parboil (al dente) the cauliflower and onion (do not overcook).
4. Divide the cauliflower into bite-size pieces and cut the onion into rings.
5. Peel the apples, remove the core, and cut into slices of about a half inch.
6. Cut the zucchini into sticks (like French-fried potatoes).
7. Wash and dry the sage leaves.
8. Dry all the ingredients, dip them in batter, and fry in plenty of peanut oil.
9. Lastly, fry the lamb chops or scampi (shrimp) with the same batter.
10. Salt lightly and serve hot with lemon wedges.

Uova in Trippa (Egg Strips in Tomato Sauce)
Category: Vari (Other)
Origin: Mamma Cortellini
Serves 4

   Contrary to its title, this recipe is not a tripe recipe. It is so called because the egg strips resemble tripe, and the sauce is similar to how tripe is cooked. However, one should rest assured that it contains no meat or animal parts. The eggs are made from a simple frittata and cut into strips, resembling how tripe is cut.

Ingredients:
1 onion, finely chopped
1 carrot, finely chopped
1 celery stalk, finely chopped
¼ cup extra-virgin olive oil
Fresh Roma tomatoes chopped (if ripe) or one box chopped Pomi tomatoes or
   San Marzano tomatoes
Spices: either fresh basil, oregano, or marjoram, as you prefer
4–6 large Grade A large eggs

Preparation:

1. Make a frittata in a large skillet, spreading the eggs in the skillet so they are not too thick. This is similar to the Involtini di Spinaci recipe in a previous chapter.
2. When cool, roll the frittata and slice it crosswise to make thin strips.
3. Prepare a simple marinara sauce by sautéing the onion, carrot, and celery in the olive oil; when vegetables are cooked, add the tomatoes and cook until juices are reduced and oil rises to the top.
4. When the sauce is ready, add the egg strips and simmer for another ten minutes.
5. Serve hot or at room temperature; can also be served on Italian bread.

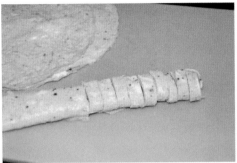
Rolling the egg crepe and slicing it

Unfolding the egg slices and combining with sauce

Serving-

Limoncello del Gallo (Lemon Liquor)

Category: Dolci (Desserts)
Origin: Generoso Gallucio from Napoli
Makes Two Bottles

This is a recipe for the well-known after-dinner drink called Limoncello from the Naples area—more specifically, Sorrento. My crazy colleague and very good friend from Continental Bank Milan, Generoso Gallucio (Gallo), sent me this recipe, which I found to be one of the best among the many I have made.

Limoncello is traditionally associated with the wonderful lemons grown in Naples and surrounding area, specifically, Sorrento. As Gallo's roots are in Naples, I can only conclude that this recipe is genuine.

Ingredients:
1 liter (quart) pure drinkable grain alcohol (approximately 75% pure), also known as rectified spirits (do not use vodka)
1 liter (quart) purified water
1 lb. granulated sugar
15–20 lemons with thick, colorful peelings (the quality of the lemon peelings is the most important aspect)

Preparation:
1. Thoroughly wash and dry the lemons.
2. Peel the lemons with a sharp knife or potato peeler, being careful to only extract the yellow zest portion of the peeling and not the white pulp portion.
3. Pour the alcohol into a container or jar with a large opening and place the lemon peels in the container.
4. Seal the jar, leaving the peels to soak for ten days in a cool place without direct sunlight. Stir the content of the jar daily.
5. After ten days, prepare a syrup by bringing water to a boil and dissolving the sugar into it. Allow the syrup to cool completely.
6. Remove the lemon peelings from the alcohol. Filter both the alcohol and syrup before mixing them together.
7. Pour the alcohol mixture into serving bottles and seal them tightly.
8. Let stand for forty to forty-five days before serving.

Below is an image of Gallo's original recipe. I include this to assure his authenticity as truly Neapolitan.

LIMONCELLO DEL GALLO

Head of Limoncello

Lemons originating from the Neapolitan region produce an exquisite liquor called LIMONCELLO (here a picture) made with water, alcohol, sugar and lemon peel. If you don't have lemons from Neapolitan areas, I am sorry but "these are your cases" (sono cazzi tuoi). The colour varies from yellow to light green depending upon the ripeness of the lemons and their moment of picking.

RECIPE INGREDIENTS: 1 litre of pure alcohol; 1 litre of water; 500 g. of sugar; 15/20 lemons.

INSTRUCTUCTIONS: wash the lemons well and dry them, thinly slice the peel (without the white) and leave it to soak in the alcohol for approximately 10 days in a bottle with a large opening and sealed closure. Store in a cool dry place out of direct sunlight (honestly, I put it at the direct sunlight) and shake the bottle almost every day. After 10 days prepare a syrup with the litre of warm water and the sugar and allow to cool completely. Remove the peel from the alcohol, filter both the syrup and the alcohol before mixing together. Pour into a bottle and close firmly. Wait at least 40/45 days before serving. I do not resist, so I taste just the day after and, tasting by tasting, I finish the bottle .... in 40/45 minutes.

Chapter 17

La Vita e Breve

The years after London brought stability to Nic's life. We did not uproot him every three years. But it was a period filled with change and sadness in the loss of loved ones. During this period I advanced the idea of writing a family cookbook. The inspiration for the book was Mom's talent for combining food and laughter at the dinner table. It allowed me to channel deep feelings of love and gratitude for the journey Mom and Dad started for me. Unlike the Italian expression "*al tavolo non s'invecchia mai,*" in reality, life does play its dirty trick, and sooner or later we all realize that we are mortal. So I hastened to gather what I could of the thing my mother did so well and began to put together her recipes, and those of others, in a tribute to my Italian heritage. This final chapter includes some of the more recent recipes from Mom and from friends.

After I obtained an employment commitment from Motorola, I began work in Schaumburg on May 8, 2000. Roz and Nic remained in London into June to allow Nic to finish third grade at the American School in Egham. Having lifted the heavy load of finding work, and before taking my new position in Schaumburg, I was able to enjoy our remaining time in the United Kingdom and Europe. We took the opportunity to make one last visit to our favorite places in Europe and to say farewell to our Italian family. We didn't know if or when we might see each other again. My final visit to Europe was a return to Virginia Water in June, to help Roz pack, and we all flew back together.

Once Roz and Nic arrived back in the States, we began a long search for housing. We eventually decided to purchase a house under construction in North Barrington, Illinois, in a residential community called Wynstone. We were assured it would be completed in time for Nic to begin his school year in August 2000. As it turned out, we moved in just before Christmas, requiring that Nic commute to school from Schaumburg to North Barrington.

After a week of orientation at Motorola, I began my assignment, which was to strengthen internal controls of the worldwide customer financing operations. Due in part to an earlier failed attempt by the previous Compliance Director at Motorola Credit Corporation to implement internal control policies, it was clear to me that success in this task would be dependent upon my ability to be seen as the owner of the policies by those who would be governed by the policies. Therefore, I created a task force made up of key managers to whom I assigned the tasks of writing policy for each manager's area of responsibility. I created A policy committee to review completed policies and to obtain senior management support for implementation. Due to significant exposure at Motorola Credit to risks associated with long-term customer financing, tighter internal controls were needed to be implemented by the credit company. In addition to creating policies, I was charged with the responsibility of strengthening controls over contract compliance to ensure that Motorola Credit's conditions for credit approval were satisfied. This required hiring competent personnel, including an attorney and an accountant, and the establishment of what we called "exception management" for those situations, hopefully limited in number, when the preestablished conditions for credit approval were not satisfied.

I was also charged with the responsibility of managing the lease and loan administration and accounting system called InfoLease. I knew this system firsthand, as it was the same system I helped implement for Newcourt in Europe. The year before I arrived, Motorola management had decided to implement InfoLease. The accounting manager then charged with implementing the system was the only Motorola person familiar with the system. Internal staff members at Motorola responsible for the day-to-day operations of the system lacked user understanding, and internal controls were absent. I hired a former colleague from Link Anthem to stabilize the operations and to write operating procedures to standardize controls in its use.

When I first arrived at Motorola, it had a worldwide employee base totaling over 160,000 with a wide range of product initiatives. It achieved high profitability with its popular flip phone model known as the "Razr," but that part of its business declined when it failed to keep abreast with the rapidly changing world of the smartphone. As a result, Motorola became a company with a narrow product range and limited growth potential.

During this period Mom's health deteriorated significantly. She contracted Parkinson's disease, with complications that required she enter an assisted living facility. Corrado remained at her house on Sherman Avenue and was able to visit her often. He married Patricia Scott in 2002, and shortly afterward, we sold Mom's home to support her living expenses. Mom's death in February 2005 ended the life of a courageous woman whose whole life was dedicated to family. She made many personal sacrifices to keep the family together—and close. Corrado, Douglas, and I maintain a close relationship full of the laughter and love inspired by our mother, Anna Maria.

Mom's eighty-first birthday

Celebrating her birthday at her home on Sherman Avenue, just before entering assisted living.

Corrado's wedding was quite an event. The ceremony was at Christ the King church on Kessler Avenue, the church and school he and I first attended in 1952 when we lived on Indianola Avenue. Mom was able to attend, and we had the chance to reunite with her old friends and symphony members Irving and Bea Finkand Joe and Joan Bellissimo.

Corrado's and Patty's wedding with Tony and Sandra playing flutes

Corrado with Irv and Bea Fink and Joan Bellissimo and Tony and Sandra with Joe Bellissimo

During this same period, we enjoyed spending time in Bloomington, Indiana, with Roz's parents, whose health was also deteriorating. Her father, Louis C. Mundy, died in his sleep of a heart attack in 2002. Shortly after Dad's death, Roz's mother, Norma, moved in with us in North Barrington. Norma died in November 2005 following complications from open heart surgery. In a matter of three years, we lost all three of our remaining parents.

Nic's favorite pastime in Bloomington

The loss of our parents forever changed our lives

Dunhill under construction

One of the advantages of living in Wynstone was having a beautiful community swimming pool available. This allowed Nic to develop his swimming skills, which he had first learned in Sardinia. The Wynstone club team competed with other clubs in the area. Nic won a number of awards between 2004 and 2007 in his age bracket. The club won two championships during this period, and Nic still holds the club record for freestyle.

Nic's swim team

With Nic being in school, our family trips had to be coordinated with the school vacation calendar. As Nic was an avid Cubs fan, we made a few trips to the Cubs' spring training camp in Arizona. We did a road trip to the Grand Canyon with stops in Sedona, Arizona, and Santa Fe, New Mexico. We highly recommend both as vacation destinations. We also did a trip to Portland, Oregon, and Seattle, Washington, where we visited friends from the United Kingdom, Elaine and Sam Purcell. We were finally able to explore America after seeing so much of Europe. We also made our annual visits to Florida. We managed to squeeze in some fishing during these trips. On one charter we caught several massive grouper, and Nic reeled in a barracuda bigger than himself.

Cubs spring training in Arizona; Road trip west, trail ride in Sedona, and the Grand Canyon

Crossing the Puget Sound
to Seattle

Pike Place Fish market

Nic reuniting with classmate
Sam from the UK

Our big catch of grouper and the huge barracuda caught by Nic

In 2003 Roz's brother Lou returned to Bloomington from Florida. Within a year he met Elise; and after a short engagement, they married. The outdoor wedding occurred on a typical hot August day in Indianapolis. In attendance was Lou's son, Lou Jon (LJ), who married my cousin Clelia (granddaughter of my dad's sister) from Torino. LJ is now practicing law in Chicago, and Clelia recently graduated from the University of Chicago with a PhD in Italian studies. They have two lovely children, Eliot and Emily.

At Lou's wedding, Lou, LJ, Clelia, and Nic

Clelia's graduation with Betta, Angela, and Roz

In August 2003, on our return from a vacation trip to Door County, Wisconsin, Nic and I made a detour to the middle of Wisconsin to pick up our first dog. She is a black Cockapoo, and when we first got her, I could hold her in the palm of my hand. Roz, not previously an animal lover, has fallen in love with this dog, which she named Chloe. Our friends, the Kubinskis, bought her half-sister from the same kennel.

Chloe

After his retirement from public accounting, our friend Jim Kubinski and his wife Cindy moved from Milwaukee to a golf community near Atlanta known as Reynolds Plantation. We missed not being closer to them, but we met often, either in the Vail area, where they had a condo, or in Georgia. We spent most New Year's holidays together in Vail and most Thanksgivings in Georgia. Vail was always a great time, with its many fantastic restaurants. One New Year's Eve, as a surprise, Jim Kubinski (Kub) hired a Hummer (then a big craze when they were still a novelty) with a driver as a birthday present for Nic to haul us to and from the restaurant. The driver was ticketed for speeding on the return trip, providing many laughs after the officer finished his paperwork. We also began a tradition of celebrating Thanksgiving with the Kubinskis at their home in the Reynolds Plantation. One year we accidentally cooked the turkey upside down. It turned out well, as the breast meat was surprisingly tender. Another time the grill caught fire. We discovered that charred turkey is not bad. Jim and Cindy have two beautiful daughters, Ashley and Lauren, who both now work and live in Atlanta.

Another notable wedding during this period was the marriage of Joseph, my brother Douglas's middle son, to a lovely girl named Allison, his college sweetheart. The marriage took place at a country club in the Detroit area on a very hot September day in 2011. Attending the wedding from Ancona were Francesco and Valeria Rismondo, my cousin Anna Maria's youngest son and wife.

Corrado and Patty, Francesco and Valeria, and the wedding couple

I couldn't resist joining in the singing
of Malefemena with the Italian
ensemble at the reception-

The wedding party

In 2011 we attended the wedding of the son of good friends in our community, Renee and Chuck Seccombe. We became acquainted with the Seccombe family through Teri Ekman, Roz's friend from Virginia Water. The wedding took place in the Washington University area of St. Louis. This was the first time I visited the gateway to the west. The wedding was quite an event. We also made a side trip to the "Hill" district of St. Louis, which is the old Italian section. We paid a visit to the Volpi outlet headquartered in St. Louis. Volpi is a salami brand that I use for appetizers. It is the best salami available in the Chicago area, as salamis made in Italy are still not imported to the United States.

Chuck and Renee Seccombe
at the wedding

At Visiting Volpion the "Hill"

One of the most interesting aspects of working for Motorola was the need to travel abroad. The international nature of its worldwide credit business necessitated compliance reviews in areas of high credit risk and concentration. I led a team made up of Teresa Dixon, Doris Toher, and members of the credit insurance group out of London. During my tenure with Motorola, we made repetitive visits to London, Milan, Madrid, Krakow, Sao Paulo, Bahrain, Hong Kong, Beijing, and Shanghai. We also implemented the InfoLease loan and lease management system in Beijing and Hangzhou near Shanghai. We had annual "global meetings" at off-site locations in the United States and Europe.

Motorola global meetings in the UK and in Arizona

The MCC management group at Gary's house and compliance testing in the UK and Milan

With the Madrid staff

Shopping in Beijing with Angela and at dinner
with colleagues William Liu and Angus Cho

With William and staff in Hangzhou and with Walter in Hong Kong

Hong Kong skyline and eating scorpion in Beijing

Implementing InfoLease in Beijing and visiting the Great Wall and the Forbidden City

Eating Italian food in Krakow and singing with the staff at the anniversary dinner-

We have enjoyed visits at Dunhill Lane from friends and family, including Vera, Italo DiSanto's daughter; Maurizio and Anna Grazia; Francesco and Valeria; and Jim and Becky Fahy. In addition, our relative proximity has allowed the renewal of relationships with Bob and Linda Thopy and with Jim and Cindy Kubinski. As Clelia's parents visited her often, this afforded us the opportunity to get together with Angela and Gerry. Angela is the eldest daughter of Dad's sister.

Vera's visit with Clelia, Angela, and Gerry from Lucca

Maurizio, Anna Grazia, Marino and Anna visiting Chicago

Kubinskis in Georgia and Bob and Linda at Nic's school where Linda taught

Bob and Linda in Flordia, Making Pasta in Georgia, and Nic and Ashley

Christmas time was a magical period at Dunhill. We could never take photos on Christmas morning as Nic would wake at 4:00 a.m. to open presents, and we were not ready for the camera. Christmases were joyful at Dunhill but were never really the same after the passing of our parents. Since then we have often enjoyed the Christmas holiday with LJ, Clelia, and kids.

On the occasions of my business trips to Italy, I was able to touch base with my friends and cousins in both Milan and Ancona. I was also able to pick up some new recipes for the cookbook project. In November 2004, while working in Milan, I introduced my colleagues Teresa Dickson and Doris Toher to my cousins and my good friend and colleague from Continental Bank, Generoso Gallucio. With Generoso (Gallo) and significant other, Nicoletta DeVercelli, we returned to some of our favorite restaurants, such as the great Tuscan restaurant known as Terza Carbonaia and a fantastic fish restaurant called Cuocco d'Abordo (Cook on Board). My cousin Maurizio also hosted my colleagues and me for a fantastic Italian meal at his apartment. I believe that my Motorola colleagues still remember those dinners today. Unfortunately, my good friend Gallo was stricken with cancer several years ago and just recently passed away, ending an era that will live forever in my memories. He was one of a kind, and I know I dearly miss his smile and his humor.

Introducing Milan restaurants to colleagues and at Maurizio's home

Gallo's office in Milan and visiting our old apartment from 1980. This was the last time I saw Gallo

In August 2004 I had a follow-up trip to Milan; I was able to fly from Milan to Ancona to meet once again with the family of Mom's sister in Ancona. I had a chance to also meet with Viviana Miserocchi and Paola Frisoli, the daughters of Mom's brother; their husbands, Franco and Lino; and Paola's daughter, Raffaella. I also spent some time with Zia Marisa, Mom's sister, who was then nearing ninety years of age.

Anna Maria with me in Sirolo; Anna Maria with her son Francesco and my Aunt Zia Marisa, still looking good

We dined together at a farm near Ancona. Restaurants at farm locations are becoming popular, replacing the traditional urban restaurant. In many parts of Italy, there are now numerous cooperatives calling themselves "Agriturismo," which offer locally made wines and locally grown vegetables and meats, some with overnight accommodations.

At the Agriturismo is Paola with Massimo's wife, Doriana, and Raffaela, Paola's daughter

In a follow-up business visit to Milan in August 2006, I did not visit with Gallo, as he, like most Italians in the month of August, was away on vacation. However, I was able to meet up with Maurizio and Anna Grazia in Milan. They hosted a birthday dinner for Anna Grazia in the restaurant of one of their closest friends near the Corso Buenos Aires. I was pleased to learn that the restaurant's owner had a brother in Chicago who also owned a restaurant. It is called Riccardo Ristorante and is located in the Lincoln Park area. When Maurizio visited us, we took him to this restaurant, and he brought Riccardo up to date on news from Milan.

Anna Grazia, Maurizio, Marino, and Teresa at Riccardo's brother's restaurant in Milan

Upon leaving Milan, I took a train to Senigallia, just north of Ancona. This is a place where Mom took us swimming when we were children. I went there to meet my father's half-brother, Italo Cortellini, and his wife Edy and daughter Laura. I had not seen them since 1972, when Roz and I were on our honeymoon. Italo and Etta DiSanto met me there with their daughter, Vera. Also staying there were Vittoria (Italo DiSanto's second sister); her husband, Alberto Calvani; and their son Marco and his wife, Luisa, vacationing from Rome. The weather was hot, the wine was flowing, and the seafood was outstanding.

Group shot at the restaurant; the two Italos

From Senigallia I traveled to Sirolo with Italo and Etta to meet my cousins from my mom's side of the family. This was an unforgettable trip as it was the last time that I saw my Mom's sister, Zia Marisa. She died in 2012 at the age of ninety-nine.

The master cook, Paolo, Anna Maria, me, and Zia Marisa at age ninety-one

Franco Rismondo and Gabriella (Franco happens to be Paolo's brother), Gabriella's daughter Christina, and her daughter

Our lunch on Anna Maria's porch began with my favorite shellfish, Canocchia al Limone and followed by pasta, Paolo and Anna (see chapter 17 recipes). The food kept coming: Scampi con Sugo di Pomodoro (see recipe in chapter 15), Pomodori Ripieni al Forno (see recipe in chapter 12), followed by a long walk at Fortino Napoleonico in Portonovo on the Riviera del Conero (a Napoleonic fort) at the base of Monte Conero. I'd love to stay there the next time I visit.

Fortino Napoleonico in Portonovo

After Mom's death it was difficult to find occasions to hold the family together. To prevent drifting apart, Corrado, Douglas, and I began an annual event we call the Annual Cortellini Reunion. We meet at various locations. To date we have held them at: Cadillac, Michigan (Allison's parents own a cabin on the lake there); the Outer Banks in North Carolina; New Buffalo, Michigan; and Plymouth, Michigan.

The Cortellini reunions began in 2007 with a long weekend stay at Allison's parents' cottage in Cadillac, Michigan. Meals were pitch-ins but generally great, with each fixing one of Mom's recipes. This was the beginning of a continuing tradition.

In 2007 we met in Cadillac Michigan at the cottage of Allison's parents

In 2008 it was a repeat of Cadillac—only this time, we had a pontoon boat.

Doug and his boys; Corrado on the guitar; and Nic fishing with Doug's dog, Abby

In 2009 we all met at the Outer Banks in North Carolina in a town called Duck, about two blocks from the ocean and a large pool in the backyard. There were about eight bedrooms, all with baths, and a great room with a table to seat everyone. It was perfect for Italian dining.

The Cortellini brothers
at the Outer Banks

We're having fish tonight!

Fresh pasta and the ideal dining table, sunset in front of the house

In 2010 we all reunited for Joe's wedding in Plymouth, Michigan.

In 2012 we all met in New Buffalo, Michigan, which is along the southeastern banks of Lake Michigan. It was a short but hilly walk to the beach, but we had a great pool and good food and drink.

The pool was better than the walk to the lake

Great portraits

Departing shot: the T-shirts donated by Corrado
from his campaign for the Indianapolis city council

In 2013 we met at Doug's home in Plymouth and inaugurated his new pool. One night Doug fixed pizza on the grill, Corrado prepared flank steak and mixed seafood on the grill, and I fixed Olive al

Ascolane, Bucatini al Amatriciana, Tacchino Tonnato, and Verdure Grigliate from my cookbook. There was an excessive amount of a super Verdichio di Metallica. That party will be hard to beat next year.

Doug's new pool, the group eating Bucatini al Amatriciana,
and the waiters serving verdure and Tacchino Tonnato

Group shot

My daughter Tina continues to live and work in Indianapolis. Her older daughters are now living separate lives. Tina's youngest daughter, Sabrina, is now in high school and lives with Tina just north of Indianapolis in the town of Cicero. Roz's parents once ran a diner in Cicero called the Char-Burg. In 2012 Tina and Sabrina visited us at Dunhill Lane. We enjoyed the time together and the chance to get to know Sabrina better. In 2007 my son Gino passed away, at the age of forty-two, after a protracted battle with cancer. As he was in the military, he received a full military funeral.

Tina visiting with Sabrina

Rendering of the Char-Burg in Cicero, Indiana

Gino's military funeral

After retiring from Motorola, I was able to devote considerable time to the completion of my family cookbook. I have created a sizable circle of friends through networking, and I share my recipes with them through a blog I have created. I have also tested my recipes with friends and family. One blog follower invited me to her home for dinner—she prepared two of my recipes for Roz and me. Every chance I get, I test my recipes and make modifications as needed.

Testing recipes with Ed and Vickie Wike

Chuck and Diane McDonald

Test kitchen with colleagues Gary Tatje and Dave Kliefoth and their wives, Joan and Donna

Test subject, Stuffed Fresh Anchovies   and Risotto with Oysters and
                                                              Asparagus

(see Chapter 17 both recipes)

Now that Nic has graduated from Northern Illinois University, we are considering a move to a place with warmer winters. Bloomington, Indiana, is high on our list.

Nic on Graduation Day

My blog has allowed me to reunite with many relatives and friends. Recently my second cousin Irene Cioffi Whitfield contacted me after becoming aware of my blog. Irene is the granddaughter of my great-uncle Antonio Cortellini who so graciously hosted my father and assisted him in his entry into the United States (see Chapter 4). Irene grew up in New York City. She and her husband, Clovis, each achieved a PhD at NYU's Institute of Fine Arts. Irene specialization is eighteenth-century Italian painting, and Clovis's is seventeenth-century Italian painting. They have both lived in Rome for extended periods and ultimately decided to live in London, where Clovis sells old master paintings (www.whitfieldfineart.com) and Irene later trained as a Jungian analytical psychologist (www.igap.co.uk).

As a coincidence, Irene and Clovis live in the West End of London, just a short distance from where Roz and I lived on Marylebone Road. We lived there during the same time period but unfortunately didn't know it until Roz and I were living back in the States. Irene filled me in on the interesting background of the branch of Cortellini that settled in the Bronx.

Great-Uncle Antonio and his first wife settled in Philadelphia and had six children, including Filomena, Ornella, and Eneo. Antonio lost his wife and three of his children, whose names were never given to me, as the result of the Philadelphia flu epidemic of 1918. After that tragedy, Antonio returned to Pescara, Italy, with his remaining children, Filomena, Ornella, and Eneo. While there, he met Leonia Sestini, a woman in her late thirties who lived with her sister. She helped Antonio raise his remaining children. Antonio and Leonia eventually married and returned to New York City, where Erina was born in 1922. After Antonio established residency in the USA, the three remaining children in Pescara followed Antonio to New York City and settled in the Bronx. The three children by Antonio's first marriage remained close to Leonia throughout her long life until she died in 1996. Erina, the only child born of Leonia, never knew that Leonia was not the natural mother of her half-brother and sisters until she was in her twenties. The descendants of Antonio's three children by his first wife now live on the east coast. Irene the daughter of Erina lives in London and has a home near Orvieto, Italy. We hope that someday soon we can visit her there and meet her family.

Erina Cioffi   Clovis and Irene

Roz's and my travels have afforded us the opportunity to experience some of Western Europe's finest restaurants. For that we are grateful. However, none matched the delight of a meal prepared and enjoyed in Mamma Cortellini's home. I think Martin Scorsese summed it up best when he said, "If your mother cooks Italian food, why should you go to a restaurant?"

- Artichoke Quiche
- *Fave con Tartufo e Pecorino* (Fava Beans with Truffle Oil and Pecorino Cheese)
- *Olive all'Ascolane* (Fried Stuffed Green Olives)
- *Pasta con Asparagi* (Pasta with Asparagus)
- *Fusilli con Cavolfiore* (Fusilli [or other pasta] with Cauliflower Sauce)
- *Pasta con Pomodori* Arrostiti (Pasta with Roasted Tomato Sauce)
- *Risotto con Ostriche e Asparagi* (Risotto with Oysters and Asparagus)
- *Spaghetti al Paolo e Anna* (Spaghetti with Seafood and Zucchini)
- *Pollo al Parmigiano* (Parmesan Chicken)
- *Petto di Tacchino Stuffato* (Stuffed Turkey Breast)
- *Lombo di Manzo con Aloro al Forno* (Seared Beef Tenderloin with Bay Leaves, Juniper Berries, and Olive Oil)
- Grilled Marinated Flank Steak
- *Vongole ai Porri e Vino Bianco* (Clams with Leeks and White Wine)

- *Alice Ripiene* (Stuffed Fresh Anchovies)
- Roasted/Marinated Spicy Jumbo Shrimp
- *Filleti di Zucchine Friti Marinate* (Fried Filets of Zucchini, Marinated)
- Mom-Mom's Persimmon Pudding
- *Arancino (*Orange Liquor)
- Frozen Oranges Filled with Orange Sherbet
- Watermelon Cake

Artichoke Quiche
Category: Antipasti (Appetizers)
Origin: Teri Eckman-London Friend
Serves 6–8

This recipe was provided by our London neighbors at Virginia Water, Teri and Chuck Eckman. Roz would make this for me to take to the Motorola Christmas pitch-in lunch, and it would be consumed within minutes. It makes a very good appetizer.

Ingredients:
Pie crust for a 9-inch pastry pan, partially cooked before filling
Two 6-oz. jars marinated artichoke hearts
1 small onion, finely chopped
1 garlic clove, minced
4 large eggs
¼ cup homemade bread crumbs
2 cups grated cheddar cheese
2 Tbsp. finely chopped parsley
⅛ tsp. black ground pepper
⅛ tsp. dry oregano
⅛ tsp. Tabasco sauce

Preparation:
1. Drain the artichokes hearts, retaining some of the marinade, and slice the artichokes into smaller pieces.
2. In a skillet, sauté the onion and garlic in the retained marinade for about five minutes.
3. Beat the eggs in a large bowl.
4. Add to this the bread crumbs, salt, pepper, oregano, and Tabasco sauce.
5. Stir in the cheese, parsley, artichokes, and the onion mixture.
6. Pour this mixture into the partially baked pastry shell and bake at 325°F for forty-five minutes.
7. Let cool slightly; it is best served warm.

Fave con Pecorino e Tartufi (Fava Beans with Truffle oil and Pecorino Cheese)
Category: Antipasti (Appetizers)
Origin: Traditional Italian
Serves 4–6

There is no flavor as unique as the flavor of truffles. The saltiness of the Pecorino combined with the unique taste of the truffles makes this appetizer extraordinary.

Ingredients:
1½ lb. fresh fava beans in their pods (larger ones are preferred)
White truffle oil or cream of truffles
Kosher salt and freshly ground black pepper to taste
Italian Pecorino cheese to shave

Preparation:
1. Clean the fava beans by removing them from their pods.
2. Boil the beans until tender (it will take longer for larger beans).
3. Remove the light green outer membrane to extract the tender darker green center.
4. Place the beans in a serving dish.
5. Add salt and pepper to taste.
6. Add the truffle oil or paste, stir well, and taste for sufficiency. The truffle taste should be subtle and not dominate.
7. Shave very thin shavings of the Pecorino over the beans. Use a truffle shaver or a vegetable peeler to shave the cheese.
8. Cover and store in the refrigerator until ready to serve. Let stand to room temperature before serving.

Olive Ascolane (Fried Stuffed Green Olives)
Category: Antipasti (Appetizers)
Origin: Michele Rismondo
For: 60–90 Olives

This recipe was given to me by Michele Rismondo, who is Anna Maria's eldest son. His wife, Regina Nardinocchi, is from Ascoli Piceno, where this recipe originates. She is an expert at preparing this dish. These olives are so good but take so much effort to prepare. The olives from Ascoli Piceno are green, tender, and very large. The large size is necessary as you must peel them from the pit in a circular manner (as you would an apple), preferably in one strand, retaining as much of the flesh as possible. The peeled strand is formed back into the shape of the olive, with the stuffing replacing the pit, before frying. The most time-consuming step in the preparation of this dish is peeling the olives. A batch of sixty to ninety could take you the better part of half a day. Michele uses green olives in brine. He has access to the Ascolana Tenera variety of green olives, but large green Cerignola olives would probably work as well. They should be taken out of the brine and soaked in water overnight. To fry the olives, use peanut oil; olive oil is too heavy for frying and has a lower smoking temperature. Place the oil in a smaller frying pan so that the olives are totally submerged when cooking. Fry a small bunch at a time. The most difficult part of preparing these olives is cutting the flesh of the olive off of the pit. You must get as much of the flesh as you can so you need to slice close to the pit. Below is a YouTube video link that is very helpful in preparing these olives. Unfortunately (or fortunately), it is in Italian.

When preparing the olives, keep in mind that you can freeze them after they are prepared to the point of being ready to fry. It is important to keep them separated on a tray before putting them in the freezer. When removing them from the freezer to fry them, you need to do so a few at a time in order not to cool the oil and to prevent them from sticking together.

http://www.facebook.com/l/1AQHK3OGHAQFX4guny338X_u-jVKhOSmwFGiqVGMls7tl2w/www.youtube.com/watch?v=utcn8mqZwm0

Ingredients:
1 lb. olives, Ascolana Tenera variety or green Cerignola
⅓ lb. lean beef or veal, cut in small pieces
⅓ lb. pork, cut in small pieces
¼ lb. chicken meat or turkey, cut in small pieces
¼ lb. grated *Parmigiano-Reggiano*
½ onion, chopped
1 small carrot and 1 small stalk of celery
2 small garlic cloves, minced
½ glass white wine
Flour for dredging
Breadcrumbs for dredging
Extra-virgin olive oil to taste,
Pinch of nutmeg
Kosher salt
3 eggs, separated (one for the stuffing and the other two for the dredging)
Zest of one lemon with cloves inserted in the lemon

Preparation:
1. Chop the celery, onion, and carrots and sauté in a small skillet with olive oil.
2. Cut the beef, pork, and poultry into small pieces for ease of cooking and seasoning; place in skillet with the vegetables and cook over low heat.
3. When the mixture begins to stick and the onion is translucent, deglaze the mixture with the white wine.
4. When meat is fully cooked and tender, pour mixture into food processor and finely grind it until a smooth stuffing mix results.
5. To the mixture add one egg, *Parmigiano-Reggiano*, and a pinch of nutmeg; grate the zest of a lemon with cloves inserted in the peel and add this to the mixture.
6. Mix thoroughly until a smooth mixture is achieved.
7. Cut the flesh of the olive in the form of a spiral, trying to stay close to the pit.
8. Recompose the olive by wrapping the strand of olive flesh around a clump of stuffing.
9. Dredge the olive first in the flour, then dip in the beaten egg, and then dip in the bread crumbs.
10. At this point you can freeze the olives to fry at a later date. If you choose to freeze, be sure to lay the stuffed olives on a flat surface in the freezer, not touching other olives until they are fully frozen.
11. In a smaller skillet or a small deep fryer with sufficient depth so that the oil covers the olives, heat the oil until hot (350/375°F or before smoking point for the oil) and fry the olives until the breading becomes golden.

12. Remove the olives with a spider and place them on a paper towel to remove the excess oil.
13. Serve them hot.

Olives and stuffing

Stuffed olives

Freezing the olives

Frying the olives

Serving the olives

Pasta con Asparagi (Pasta with Asparagus)
Category: Paste (Pastas)
Origin: Roz Adaptation of Traditional Italian
Serves 4

This is a recipe created by Roz combining a risotto and pasta recipe using asparagus and utilizing some of her homemade bread crumbs.

Ingredients:
2 lb. fresh asparagus
½ cup homemade fluffy bread crumbs
⅓ cup extra-virgin olive oil

3 cloves garlic (2 sliced, 1 minced)
Grated *Parmigiano-Reggiano* for topping
Pinch of red pepper flakes
¼ cup Italian parsley, finely chopped
Zest from ½ lemon
1 lb. dried pasta like fusilli, gnocchi, or linguini

Preparation:
1. Place the bread crumbs and one tablespoon olive oil in a small frying pan over moderate heat, stirring until crisp and golden; then set aside.
2. Clean the asparagus and snap off the woody bottoms.
3. Cut asparagus on the diagonal into two-inch pieces, slicing the pieces in half lengthwise.
4. In a large skillet, warm the oil and sauté the asparagus with the garlic.
5. Add the parsley, lemon zest, and red pepper flakes and continue to cook until asparagus is tender.
6. Cook pasta al dente; remove with a spider and transfer to the skillet.
7. Serve, adding bread crumbs and *Parmigiano-Reggiano*.

Asparagus cleaned and sautéed with garlic,
parsley, pepper flakes, and lemon zest in olive oil

Toasted bread crumbs; served with
bread crumbs and *Parmigiano-Reggiano*

Fusilli con Cavolfiore (Fusilli Pasta with Cauliflower Sauce)
Category: Paste (Pastas)
Origin: Mama Cortellini
Serves 4

I'm not sure of the origin of this dish, but I suspect it is from southern Italy. It is similar to the

Pugliese pasta made with orecchiette and broccoli. In fact Mom would combine both broccoli and cauliflower to make this dish. However, I prefer just using cauliflower. Don't be concerned about leaving the garlic in the sauce since it practically dissolves with the cooking of the cauliflower. Also make sure to fully cook the cauliflower to the point of almost burning it. Use plenty of chili pepper flakes to give it a bite.

Ingredients:
1 whole head cauliflower, chopped in small pieces (cut the flowerets, and then cut into slices)
4 cloves garlic, sliced
Extra-virgin olive oil to fry the cauliflower
1 tsp. red pepper flakes (peperoncini flakes) or to taste
Small bunch fresh Italian flat-leaf parsley, finely chopped
Parmigiano-Reggiano cheese or Pecorino for a stronger taste
Kosher salt and freshly ground black pepper to taste
1 lb. dried fusilli or other pasta

Preparation:
1. In a large skillet, cover the bottom with olive oil.
2. Add the garlic and fry in the olive oil until it begins to turn golden. As always, be careful not to burn the garlic.
3. Add the cauliflower (it reduces, so don't be concerned that you have too much cauliflower).
4. Add salt and pepper flakes to taste.
5. Cook the cauliflower until it becomes brown (just before it starts to burn). Don't undercook it. The cauliflower needs to be very soft. so you need to cook it slowly (at least half an hour).
6. Cook the pasta al dente (we like fusilli). Drain it quickly, leaving some of the pasta water.
7. Add the pasta to the cauliflower in the skillet and stir in the parsley; then sprinkle on some additional olive oil to moisten.
8. Serve immediately and add the *Parmigiano-Reggiano* and freshly ground pepper at the table.

Serve the pasta with a hearty white wine such as a Verdichio, Corvo, or a Spanish white wine like a Malvasia.

Sautéing the cauliflower and adding *Parmigiano-Reggiano* cheese before serving

A derivation of this dish is to add broccoli with the cauliflower; the flavors are complimentary. As the origin of this dish appears to be Puglia, the more correct serving of this dish is with orecchiette (little ears). Serve in the same manner and use Pecorino (Romano) instead of *Parmigiano-Reggiano*.

Orecchiette with cauliflower and broccoli

Pasta con Pomodori Arrostite (Pasta with Roasted Tomato Sauce)
Category: Paste (Pastas)
Origin: Adaptation from Lidia
Serves 4–6

The roasting of the cherry tomatoes releases and intensifies the sweetness of the tomatoes for an exceptional taste. Adding the pasta water to the garlic softens the sharpness of the garlic for a delicate flavor, making an excellent pasta dish.

Ingredients:
1 lb. dried pasta (spaghettini, fedelini, penne, or gemelli)
6 cups cherry tomatoes, sliced in half
½ cup (or more) extra-virgin olive oil
⅓ cup bread crumbs (preferably freshly made)
¼ tsp. pepperoncini flakes or to taste
10 good-sized garlic cloves, peeled and sliced
3 Tbsp. Italian flat-leaf parsley, chopped
1 cup fresh basil leaves, julienned
½ cup grated *Parmigiano-Reggiano* plus more for plate servings

Preparation:
1. Preheat oven to 400°F.
2. Place the tomato halves in a large bowl with three tablespoons of the olive oil.
3. Season with salt and pepper, add the pepperoncini flakes and bread crumbs over the tomatoes, and toss well.
4. Pour the tomatoes and other ingredients onto a parchment-lined baking sheet and spread in a single layer.
5. Roast the tomatoes until they are lightly caramelized (about twenty-five to thirty minutes).
6. While the pasta is cooking, pour the remaining olive oil into a large skillet over high heat and add the slices of garlic; cook until the garlic begins to lightly color.
7. Ladle two cups of the pasta water into the skillet and bring to a hard boil; let boil until half of the water evaporates.
8. Lower the heat, add the chopped parsley, and reduce the heat to barely simmering.
9. When the pasta is al dente, remove the pasta from the water and add it to the skillet, still over low heat.
10. Toss the pasta quickly with the garlic and parsley and add the roasted tomato halves

over the pasta.

11. Sprinkle the shredded basil over the pasta until it is evenly coated by the sauce.

12. Add the *Parmigiano-Reggiano* and stir once again. Serve right away.

Cooking the garlic and herbs   Final serving

Risotto con Ostriche e Asparagi (Rice with Oysters and Asparagus)

Category: Paste (Pastas)
Origin: Paolo Rismondo in Ancona
Serves 6

This is another Adriatic dish given to me by my cousin Paolo Rismondo. We tested this recipe with our good friends and colleagues from Motorola, Gary and Joan Tatje and Dave and Donna Kliefoth. In the land of the "BIG," finding small oysters is not easy to do, but Gary and I found the perfect oysters (Pacific oysters) in a fish market in downtown Chicago. The subtlety of making this recipe requires slowly, gently cooking *small* oysters just enough to make them open. Overcooking will make them tough. The recipe was given a four-thumbs-up by the participants at our test run.

Ingredients:
24 small oysters, store the oysters in the refrigerator, dry, do not soak them in water
12 asparagus tips and tender stalks
5–6 Tbsp. extra-virgin olive oil
1 lb. (Arborio or Carnaroli) rice
1 small onion and 1 leek, chopped very fine
1 water glass of champagne or dry sparkling wine
Kosher salt and freshly ground black pepper to taste
1 Tbsp. butter
1 Tbsp. (or more) chopped parsley

Preparation:
1. Scrub and wash the oysters very well.
2. Poach asparagus for five minutes in a little water.
3. Place the oysters in a pot with a pint of water and bring to a boil with pot covered, turning occasionally until oysters have opened.
4. After oysters open, remove them from the pot and leave to cool.
5. Strain the water used to boil the oysters into a large pitcher through a very fine sieve or coffee filter, removing all the sediment.
6. Remove the oysters from the shells and cut the asparagus tips into small pieces.
7. In a large pot, sauté the onion and leek (don't let brown) in olive oil.
8. Put the rice into the pot and turn continuously until it becomes slightly translucent.
9. Pour the champagne and let it evaporate for a few minutes.
10. In a separate pot, heat the water set aside from the oysters to a boil.

11. Slowly add ladles of this water set aside from boiling the oysters to the rice. If water is not sufficient to cook the rice, add some vegetable or chicken stock.
12. Salt and pepper to taste; add the oysters and asparagus and continue cooking, stirring constantly.
13. When the rice is cooked (twenty to twenty-five minutes, taste for readiness), stir in the butter, a sprinkling of freshly ground pepper, and a tablespoon of chopped parsley.
14. Serve immediately.

Small oysters, scrubbed

Making the risotto and serving immediately

Spaghetti al Paolo e Anna (Spaghetti with Seafood and Zucchini)
Category: Paste (Pastas)
Origin: Paolo and Anna Rismondo
Serves 6–8

This is a recipe I learned when traveling to my cousin's home in Sirolo (just south of my hometown of Ancona). It is a wonderful combination of the fruits of the Adriatic Sea. The delicate sauce accentuates the sea flavors. Making this in the United States will be difficult as you will have to find a substitute for the canocchia. The zucchini provides a smooth consistency to the sauce as it practically dissolves and blends in with the seafood.

Ingredients:
½ cup extra-virgin olive oil to fry garlic
½ yellow onion, finely chopped
3 garlic cloves, smashed
1 lb. small clams, in shell
½ lb. whole calamari, cut in strips
3 lb. small mussels, cleaned
½–¾ lb. small to medium shrimp
4–5 canocchia (also called *cicale del mare*, or sea crickets) or equivalent

2 zucchini, cut in rounds, not too fine
Kosher salt and freshly ground black pepper to taste
Fresh Italian parsley, chopped
1 lb. Spaghetti fini or Fedelini

Preparation:

1. Lay the mussels and clams in a large pan, setting aside ten or twelve mussels and twenty or so clams for later. Cover the pan and cook over high heat until they open. They should release the water contained in the shells as they open.
2. After they open, separate the meat from the shells; discard the shells.
3. Retain the water from the clams and mussels; either filter the water or let it decant and set aside.
4. In a large pan (large enough to contain the shellfish, sauce, and pasta), place the oil, garlic, onion, and half of a glass of the clam water. Cook over medium heat.
5. Add the sliced zucchini and simmer until the zucchini is almost cooked.
6. After the onion softens, add the sliced calamari and canocchia and cook for five minutes.
7. Add the ten or so mussels and twenty or so clams previously set aside and cook over high heat for five minutes, or until they open.
8. If the sauce is too thin, add a small amount of whole milk to thicken it.
9. Cook the spaghetti in a separate pan until al dente and then add it to the sauce.
10. Sprinkle parsley over the pasta, and serve immediately.

The finished pasta

The pasta served

Pollo al Parmigiana (Parmesan Chicken)

Category: Carni (Meats)
Origin: Marianne Setteducato-Friends from London
Serves 6–8

One of our friends from London gave this recipe to Roz. It is an alternative to frying the chicken breasts and uses less fat as it is baked rather than fried. Serve with vegetables or fresh arugula.

Ingredients:

½ cup melted butter
2 tsp. Dijon mustard
1 tsp. Worcestershire sauce
1 cup dried bread crumbs
½ cup grated *Parmigiano-Reggiano*
6–8 boneless, skinless chicken breast halves

Kosher salt and ground pepper

Preparation:
1. In a shallow bowl, combine butter, mustard, and Worcestershire sauce.
2. On a plate, combine bread crumbs and cheese.
3. If the chicken breasts are thick (greater than ¼ inch), pound them with a meat tenderizer to make them uniformly thin.
4. Dip chicken pieces in the butter mix, and then coat with the mixture of bread crumbs and cheese.
5. Salt and pepper to taste.
6. Place the coated chicken breasts in an ungreased baking dish (13x9x2 inches).
7. Drizzle lightly with the remaining butter mix or olive oil.
8. Bake at 350°F for thirty minutes.
9. Serve hot with lemon wedges.

Petto di Tacchino Ripieno (Stuffed Turkey Breast)
Category: Carni (Meats)
Origin: Italian—Variations on Capalbo
Serves 6–8

This is a good alternative to cooking a whole turkey, considering that many Americans like only the white meat. The key, however, is keeping the breast moist and adding flavors to enhance the meat. Slicing the turkey roll makes an excellent presentation with the meat surrounding the vegetable and ham stuffing. This is not pressed turkey meat. You need to use a fresh whole or half turkey breast. The ham can either be cut into matchsticks or layered on top of the butterflied turkey breast. I have done both. You can also serve it cold and slice it before serving, but if you do so, I recommend you omit the sauce.

Ingredients:
1 whole turkey breast, deboned about (2–3 lb.)
1 large carrot, cut into matchsticks
1 medium zucchini, cut into matchsticks
Thinly sliced ham to layer over the breast
2 pieces of bread, soaked in milk and drained
10 green olives, pitted and finely chopped (I like Cerignola olives)
1 clove garlic, finely chopped
4 Tbsp. flat-leaf parsley, finely chopped
4 Tbsp. fresh basil, finely chopped
1 egg
Zest of ½ lemon

2 Tbsp. grated *Parmigiano-Reggiano*
Kosher salt and freshly ground black pepper to taste
4 Tbsp. extra-virgin olive oil
1 cup fresh or canned chicken stock
½ lemon, cut into thin wedges
2 Tbsp. butter

Preparation:
1. Butterfly the turkey breast by slicing the thickest sections part way through, opening up the breast so it lies flat.
2. Pound the thick portions with a mallet to further widen and thin the meat so it is evenly thin.
3. Blanch the carrots and zucchini in a small saucepan of boiling water for no more than two minutes, being careful not to overcook the zucchini.
4. Drain the vegetables and set aside.
5. Squeeze off the excess milk from the bread and shred it into a mixing bowl. Stir in the olives, garlic, herbs, and egg. Add the lemon zest and *Parmigiano-Reggiano* and season with salt and pepper.
6. Spread the ham over the turkey breast. Then spread the bread and herb mixture over the ham in one thin layer, leaving a small border of meat to seal the loaf.
7. Cover the mixture with the matchsticks of carrots and zucchini.
8. Roll the turkey, keeping the stuffing from falling out of the roll.
9. Tie the roll in several places.
10. Heat the oil in an ovenproof casserole dish large enough to hold the turkey roll.
11. Sear the roll on all sides.
12. Remove from heat; add the chicken stock and arrange the lemon wedges around the meat.
13. Salt and pepper to taste, cover, and place in the oven at 400°F.
14. After fifteen minutes, remove the cover, discard the lemon wedges, and baste the meat. Continue cooking uncovered for twenty-five to thirty minutes, basting occasionally. When done, allow to stand ten minutes before slicing.
15. Strain the sauce, stir in the butter, and taste for seasoning.
16. Slice the loaf for serving and top the sliced loaf with the sauce.

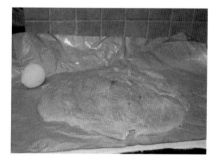 

Butterflying the turkey breast and spreading the filling

Cooking and slicing the turkey

Lombo di Manzo con Aloro al Forno
(Seared Beef Tenderloin with Bay Leaves, Juniper Berries, and Olive Oil)
Category: Carni (Meats)
Origin: My Own Creation
Serves 6–8

The rich taste of bay leaves is infused in the cooking oil that tops the servings. Key to success is buying a quality beef tenderloin and cooking it at high heat to sear it and seal in the flavors being careful to not overcook it. It is best served rare or medium rare.

Ingredients:
4–5 lb. beef tenderloin, trimmed of all fat
10-15 fresh bay leaves
2 Tbsp. whole black peppercorns
1 Tbsp. whole juniper berries
Extra-virgin olive oil
Kosher salt and freshly ground black pepper to taste

Preparation:
1. Trim the silverside and fat from the tenderloin.
2. Tie string around the tenderloin, widthwise, with one string every three to four inches. Do not tie the string too tight as the bay leaves need to be slipped under the strings.
3. Slip the individual bay leaves under the string so that they form an even line of leaves lengthwise, secured by the strings. There should be four lines of bay leaves, one on each side of the tenderloin.
4. Place the tenderloin in a shallow pan or in an oval baking dish.
5. Pour the olive oil over the meat and turn the tenderloin so that it is coated on all sides with the olive oil, and so there is a small amount of oil resting in the baking dish.
6. Sprinkle juniper berries over the meat and in the baking dish.
7. Sprinkle the meat with whole peppercorns.
8. Up to this point, the preparation of the dish can be done the day before, and the meat can be covered and placed in the refrigerator overnight.
9. Take the tenderloin out of the refrigerator at least two hours before cooking to allow it to reach room temperature.
10. Before placing in the oven, salt and pepper the meat.
11. Sear the meat in the oven at 450°F for twenty-three minutes for rare and twenty-six minutes for medium rare. Use a meat thermometer to ensure correct cooking temperature. The olive oil may cause some smoking, so be sure there is plenty of ventilation.
12. Remove from oven; cover with tinfoil and let rest for twenty minutes before carving.
13. Slice one- or two-inch slices to serve and top with some of the excess olive oil from the cooking pan.

Grilled Marinated Flank Steak
Category: Carni (Meats)
Origin: Unknown
Serves 4–6

This is a very tasty grilled meat with some heat to it due to the chili oil and pepper flakes. We often prepare this dish for backyard barbecues in summertime. The thinness of the flank steak allows the marinade to penetrate the entire steak and assures that the spicy flavor does not just burn off. This makes for a great summer steak, especially when served after Spaghetti al Cecco and a light Italian red wine or rosé.

Ingredients:
1½ lb. flank steak
For the marinade:
2 Tbsp. freshly squeezed lime juice
Zest of one whole lime
2 cloves garlic, minced
1 tsp. Asian sesame oil
½ tsp. hot chili oil
2 Tbsp. olive oil
1 tsp. (or more) hot pepper flakes
½ cup dry red wine
2 Tbsp. golden brown sugar, packed
½ cup soy sauce
1 Tbsp. fresh ginger, grated
Kosher salt and freshly ground black pepper to taste

Preparation:
1. In a small bowl, mix all the ingredients for the marinade and stir well.
2. If needed, tenderize the flank steak by pounding it with a meat mallet.
3. Place the steak in a large zip lock freezer bag.
4. Pour the marinade into the freezer bag with the steak and mix thoroughly, coating the entire steak.
5. Refrigerate at least two hours (preferably overnight), turning occasionally.
6. Before grilling, remove the steak from the freezer bag and pat it dry with some paper towels reserve the marinade. Salt and pepper the stake to taste.
7. Place the meat on a grilling rack (four to six inches above the flame).
8. Grill for ten to twelve minutes, turning it only once and brushing it occasionally with the marinade. The meat should be cooked on the rare side.
9. Carve the meat across the grain on a diagonal to make the slices larger.

Vongole ai Porri e Vino Bianco (Clams and Leeks in White Wine)
Category: Pesci (Fish)
Origin: Unknown
Serves 4–6

Clams are my favorite shellfish. The clams found in the United States are much larger than the vongole veraci found in Italy and sometimes have a tougher quality. Nevertheless, I love them in pasta, fish soup, and even raw. However, my favorite ways to enjoy clams is to simply sauté them in butter and olive oil and serve them in their own broth to bring out the taste of the sea, with a sprinkle of parsley. Set on a bed of bruschetta, they are irresistible.

Ingredients:
1½ lb. tiny manila or little neck clams, washed and scrubbed
4 tsp. extra-virgin olive oil
2 cups leeks (white and light green portions), diced
2 Tbsp. Butter
Pinch of red pepper flakes to taste
Small bunch Italian parsley, chopped
1 cup dry white wine
Kosher salt and freshly ground black pepper to taste
Bruschetta (toasted Italian bread rubbed with garlic)

Preparation:
1. Clean the clams by scrubbing the shells and eliminating all the sand; remove any clams with broken shells. Let the clams soak in ice-cold water for a couple of hours. Soaking the clams allows them to purge themselves of impurities before cooking.
2. In a large pot, sauté the leeks in oil and butter until soft.
3. Add the clams, white wine, and pepper flakes.
4. Cover and let the clams steam, releasing their water (seven to nine minutes), until the clams open. Remove any clams that do not open.
5. Add the parsley, salt, and pepper; drizzle with olive oil.
6. Serve over toasted Italian bread that has been rubbed with garlic (bruschetta).

Sautéing the sauce and preparing the toast

Steaming the clams and serving

Alice Ripiene (Stuffed Fresh Anchovies)
Category: Pesci (Fish)
Origin: Paolo Rismondo in Ancona
Serves 6–8

This is a recipe given to me by Paolo Rismondo and is typical of the Adriatic region. Paolo's version bakes the anchovies, which is probably lighter than the fried version, which I have also included for those who like fried fish. Trying to find fresh anchovies in the Chicago area is harder than trying to find a needle in a haystack. We tested the baked version with some friends and colleagues, the Tatjes and the Kliefoths, and it was a big success. Even Dave, who tends to be squeamish about fish, enjoyed this dish. I was able to find frozen whole anchovies at a local Italian Market. After cleaning, they were a relatively good substitute for the fresh anchovies. I bought a few fresh smelt (small freshwater fish like anchovies) to cook along with the anchovies as a comparison. The smelt was an OK substitute but did not have the saltwater taste of the anchovies. I recommend using the anchovies even if they are frozen.

Ingredients:
1 lb. fresh anchovies
1 clove garlic, minced very fine
1 Tbsp. parsley, finely chopped
1 Tbsp. chopped basil
2 Tbsp. grated Parmigiano-Reggiano
2–3 Tbsp. bread crumbs, preferably homemade
10–15 pinoli (pine nuts), chopped fine
Extra-virgin olive oil, kosher salt, and freshly ground black pepper to taste.
Drops from a freshly squeezed lemon

Preparation:
To clean the anchovies:
1. Remove the head and guts of the fish and thoroughly wash the cavity, removing all membranes and skin.
2. Open the fish by cutting the underside so it can be laid flat.
3. Place your index finger under the dorsal bone and gently slide your finger underneath it to remove it from the fish; cut the dorsal bone at the tail and remove it. Leave the tail on the fish.
4. Wash the fish under cold water and lay it on a plate; cover with a wet paper towel.
5. Repeat for all the fish so that you have a plate of clean fish, as shown below. You will need two fish for each packet.

Whole anchovies and cleaned

6. Preheat oven to 360°F.
7. Mix the garlic, parsley, basil, Parmigiano-Reggiano, pine nuts, and bread crumbs to form a stuffing, moistening it with the olive oil to form a fairly solid mixture.
8. Place a teaspoon of stuffing between two anchovies of similar size, making a sandwich like packet; place on a baking sheet. See below:

9. Sprinkle the fish with some homemade bread crumbs, a little oil, a few drops of lemon juice, and a little salt and pepper.
10. Place them in the preheated oven for about fifteen to twenty minutes.

Frying Alternative (Not Tested)
Frying Ingredients:
2 eggs
All-purpose flour for dredging
Bread crumbs or panko for frying
Oil for frying

1. Prepare the anchovy packets as indicated on the baking version.
2. In a bowl, beat the egg, adding a pinch of salt. Before creating the packets indicated in point3 above, dredge the anchovies through a thin layer of flour, then through the lightly beaten egg, and finally through the bread crumbs.
3. Place the frying oil in a large heavy skillet; when it reaches the right temperature, fry the stuffed anchovies on both sides until they are well browned.
4. Place them on a plate covered with a paper towel to absorb the excess oil. Serve hot with lemon slices.

Roasted Marinated Spicy Shrimp
Category: Pesci (Fish)
Origin: Adaptation by Roz
Serves 6–8

This is a spicy way of fixing shrimp. The shrimp are prepared in the oven under the broiler but can also be placed on the grill. You can vary the spices for different tastes. I prefer this way of roasting/grilling shrimp without having to use skewers.

Ingredients:
3–4 lb. jumbo shrimp with shells and tails
3 Tbsp. extra-virgin olive oil
Juice of ½ lemon and zest of 1 lemon
½ cup white wine
3 cloves garlic, minced
½ cup chopped Italian parsley
¼ tsp. crushed red pepper flakes
Kosher salt and fresh ground black pepper to taste
¾ cup clarified butter
1 cup fresh bread crumbs
Lemon wedges for serving

Preparation:
1. Peel and clean shrimp and place in a large bowl. Mix with olive oil, lemon juice and zest, wine, garlic, parsley, and pepper flakes to form the marinade.
2. Season shrimp with salt and pepper.
3. In a large freezer bag, add the marinade and shrimp and mix well to coat the shrimp.
4. Refrigerate for thirty to forty-five minutes.
5. Remove shrimp from refrigerator and place them on a shallow baking sheet, retaining the remaining marinade.
6. Transfer the marinade to a medium saucepan and bring to a boil over medium-high heat.
7. Remove from heat, let cool slightly, and then drizzle over shrimp, being careful not to add too much liquid for roasting.
8. Preheat the broiler or grill.
9. Spoon a half teaspoon of the clarified butter over each shrimp; sprinkle the shrimp with bread crumbs. Bake at 400 to 425°F until they are opaque (four to six minutes). In the last few minutes, broil them to toast the bread crumbs.
10. Serve immediately with lemon wedges.

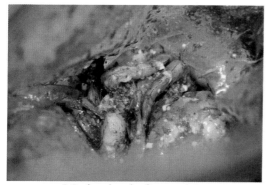
Marinating in freezer bag

Laying out the shrimp on baking dish

Adding marinade, clarified butter, and the bread crumbs and roasting

Filleti di Zucchine Friti Marinate (Fried Filets of Zucchini, Marinated)
Category: Verdure (Vegetables)
Origin: Mamma Cortellini
Serves 4–6

This is an appetizer Mom made on special occasions only, as the filets are a pain to fry. However, the result is delicious. When we prepare this recipe, it is not unusual if only half of what we fry reaches the dinner table.

Ingredients:
3–4 zucchini, firm and very green
All-purpose flour for dredging
Seed oil or peanut oil for frying
1 garlic clove, minced
Bunch of Italian parsley, finely chopped
Red wine or cider vinegar
Kosher salt and freshly ground black pepper to taste

Preparation:
1. Cut the zucchini in half or in thirds, depending on the length of the zucchini.
2. Slice the zucchini pieces lengthwise into thin filets.
3. Put the filets in a colander, salt the pieces, and let stand for one hour to drain the water from them.
4. Dry the filets with a paper towel.
5. In a small bowl, place the flour, salt, and pepper; mix well.
6. Dredge the zucchini filets through the flour a few at a time.
7. Place them back in the colander to shake off excess flour.
8. In a nonstick frying pan, heat enough oil to submerge the zucchini.
9. Fry the zucchini a few at a time until they become golden, but do not burn them.
10. Place the fried zucchini on a paper towel to absorb the excess oil; then arrange them on a serving plate, layering them flat, with a little overlap.
11. Mince the garlic and parsley together.
12. Sprinkle the vinegar over the zucchini.
13. Sprinkle the parsley and garlic mixture lightly over the zucchini.
14. Serve at room temperature.

Slicing and frying the zucchini

Serving

Mom-Mom's Persimmon Pudding
Category: Dolci (Desserts)
Origin: Norma Mundy
Serves 4–6

This is a recipe handed down to us from Roz's mother and is one of the best desserts that we make. The sweetness and density of the persimmon pulp creates a moist, delicious pudding (in the English meaning). We always have this dessert at Christmas, but it can be enjoyed year round. The key is finding persimmon pulp that is rich in flavor. We have made this by pulping fresh persimmons, and although good, it was not as good as when we used pulp obtained from Dillman Farms in Bloomington, Indiana. Therefore, this is truly a Hoosier dessert.

Ingredients:
1 cup persimmon pulp
1 cup granulated sugar
1 cup sifted all-purpose flour
1 cup buttermilk
½ cup sweet cream
1 tsp. baking soda dissolved in buttermilk
1 tsp. cinnamon
Pinch of salt
2 eggs, beaten
¼ cup melted butter

Preparation:
1. Blend the ingredients in a large mixing bowl.

2. Pour into a greased baking dish.
3. Bake for one hour at 275°F (one and a half hours for double recipe).
4. Serve with whipped cream.

Arancino (Orange Liquor)
Category: Dolci (Desserts)
Origin: Italo DiSanto
Makes One Quart

This is a recipe given to me by my cousin Italo. It is the orange equivalent to Limoncello.

Ingredients:
Peelings of 6 oranges and 4 lemons, preferably organic (the peeling must be very thin and
    have as little of the white pulp as possible)
½ qt. pure grain alcohol
½ qt. water
1 lb. granulated sugar

Preparation:
1. Wash and dry the oranges and lemons. With a paring knife, remove the ends. With a
    vegetable peeler, remove only the rind, leaving the pith intact.
2. Place the lemon peel in a glass jar with a rubber-seal lid. Add the grain alcohol, making sure
    the lemon peel is completely covered. Seal the jar with the lid. Store in a cool, dark place,
    shaking the jar once each day to agitate the lemon peel.
3. On the thirteenth day, bring the water to a boil in a large saucepan. Add the sugar and remove
    from the heat, stirring until it is dissolved. Cover and let cool to room temperature.
4. Place a colander on top of the saucepan and strain in the contents of the glass jar.
5. Stir to combine the liquids (about one minute).
6. Seal in a glass container and store for the remainder of the forty days in a cool, dark place,
    shaking to agitate the liquid twice a day.
7. After forty days, transfer the Arancino to a smaller bottle that can be sealed with a rubber
    stopper and store bottle in freezer. Serve directly from the freezer.

Frozen Oranges Filled with Sherbet
Category: Dolci (Desserts)
Origin: Roz and Paul
Serves As needed

This is a simple dessert and is very refreshing, especially in the summertime. I carve out the oranges, and Roz stuffs them with the sherbet. This is always a good way to end a meal.

Ingredients:
Thick-skinned navel oranges (the more colorful the better), one for each guest
Sherbet (we tend to use orange sherbet, but other flavors also work)

Preparation:
1. Thoroughly wash the oranges before starting.
2. Slice the top of the orange, exposing a good-sized circle of the pulp.
3. With a grapefruit knife, carve out the majority of the pulp.
4. Using a spoon, carve underneath the orange skin, between it and the white pith of the orange, and remove the remaining pulp, being careful not to puncture the skin.
5. Fill the orange cavity with sherbet up to the top of the orange but not too full, as the sherbet may rise when refrozen and push open the top.
6. Replace the top (previously sliced off) and place the orange in the freezer upright so that the top does not fall off. Once refrozen, they will hold together.
7. When serving, remove from the freezer and place the orange on a small plate with biscotti.

Recipe Index by Category: by Chapter

Meats (*Carni*)

Grilled, Sliced Sirloin Steak with Rosemary and Garlic (*Tagliata di Manzo*) - Chapter #14
Veal or Pork Roast Stuffed with White Truffle Paste (*Arrosto/Codone al Tartufo*) - Chapter #14
Boiled Beef and Peppers - Chapter #15
Veal/Chicken Scallops with Lemon (*Piccata di Vitello/Pollo*) - Chapter #16
Mom's Beef Stroganoff - Chapter #16
Parmesan Chicken (*Pollo al Parmigiana*) - Chapter #17
Stuffed Turkey Breast (*Petto di Tacchino Stuffato*) - Chapter #17
Seared Beef Tenderloin with Bay Leaves, Juniper Berries, and Olive Oil (*Lombo di Manzo con Aloro al Forno*) - Chapter #17
Grilled Marinated Flank Steak - Chapter #17

Fish (*Pesci*)

Stuffed Calamari in Pea Sauce (*Calamari Ripieni con Piselli*) - Chapter #3
Baked Fish with Rosemary Topping (*Pesce al Forno con Rosmarino*) - Chapter #10
Fish Soup Anconetana (*Brodetto or Zuppa di Pesce*) - Chapter #12
Mussels Luxembourg Style or Mariniere (*Moules a la Luxembourgeoise*) - Chapter #13
Trout in Riesling Sauce (*F'rell am Reisleck*) - Chapter #13
Sole in Butter Sauce (*Sole Meunière*) - Chapter #15
Clams with Leeks in White Wine (*Vongole ai Porri e Vino Bianco*) - Chapter #17
Stuffed Fresh Anchovies (*Alice Ripiene*) - Chapter #17
Roasted/Marinated Spicy Jumbo Shrimp - Chapter #17

Vegetables (*Verdure*)

Braised Lentils (*Lenticchie Brasate*) - Chapter #8
Sweet and Sour Cabbage (*Cavolo Agro Dolce*) - Chapter #8
Ratatouille - Mom's Version (*Ciabotto*) - Chapter #11
Sautéed Fennel with Parmesan (*Finocchi alla Parmigiana*) - Chapter #11
Green Beans with Potatoes and Tomatoes (*Fagiolini, Patate, e Pomodoro*) - Chapter #11
Stuffed Roasted Tomatoes (*Pomodori Ripieni al Forno*) - Chapter #12
Sautéed Artichokes with Parsley and Garlic (*Carciofi alla Giudia*) - Chapter #12
Grilled Polenta with Mushroom Ragu (*Polenta all Griglia con Ragu di Funghi*) - Chapter #14
Eggplant Parmesan (*Melanzane Parmigiana*) - Chapter #14
Sautéed Swiss Chard (*Bietole Soffritto*) - Chapter #14
Spinach-Stuffed Crepes (*Involtini di Spinaci*) - Chapter #15
Grilled Vegetables (*Verdure alla Griglia*) - Chapter #15
Viennese Green Beans - Chapter #15
Rosemary Potatoes (*Patate al Rosmarino*) - Chapter #15
Artichoke Casserole (*Sformato di Carciofi*) - Chapter #16
Braised Artichokes (*Carciofi in Umido*) - Chapter #16
Fried Filets of Zucchini Marinated (*Filleti di Zucchine Friti Marinate*) - Chapter #17

Desserts (*Dolci*)

Mom's Apple Pie and Coffee - Chapter #10
Anise Cookies (*Pizzelle*) - Chapter #11
Italian Tart with Preserves (*Crostata di Marmelatta*) - Chapter #13
After Ski Drink (*Grolla di Buon Amici*) - Chapter #13

Pick-Me-Up Dessert (*Tiramisu*) - Chapter #14
Chestnuts Roasted over Open Flame (*Castagne al Carbone*) - Chapter #14
Egg Custard (*Zabaglione*) - Chapter #14
Lemon Liquor (*Limoncello del Gallo*) - Chapter #16
Mom-Mom's Persimmon Pudding - Chapter #17
Orange Liquor (*Arancino*) - Chapter #17
Frozen Oranges Filled with Orange Sherbet - Chapter #17

Other (*Vari*)

Eggs with Tomatoes and Onion (*Uova con Pomodoro e Cipolla*) - Chapter #11
Green Bean Salad (*Insalata di Fagiolini*) - Chapter #15
Eggs and Potato Frittata with Ham (*Frittata con Patate e Prosciutto Cotto*) - Chapter #16
Italian Mixed Fried Plate (*Frito Misto all' Italiana*) - Chapter #16
Egg Strips in Tomato Sauce (*Uova in Trippa*) - Chapter #16

End